Houses of Noir

ALSO BY RONALD SCHWARTZ

Latin American Films, 1932–1994: A Critical Filmography
(McFarland, 1997; paperback 2005)

Houses of Noir
*Dark Visions from
Thirteen Film Studios*

RONALD SCHWARTZ

McFarland & Company, Inc., Publishers
Jefferson, North Carolina, and London

LIBRARY OF CONGRESS CATALOGUING-IN-PUBLICATION DATA

Schwartz, Ronald, 1937–
    Houses of noir : dark visions from thirteen film studios / Ronald Schwartz.
      p.   cm.
    Includes bibliographical references and index.

    ISBN 978-0-7864-7593-3
    softcover : acid free paper ∞

    1. Film noir—United States—History and criticism. I. Title.
PN1995.9.F54S37 2014
791.43'655—dc23   2013039329

BRITISH LIBRARY CATALOGUING DATA ARE AVAILABLE

© 2014 Ronald Schwartz. All rights reserved

No part of this book may be reproduced or transmitted in any form or by any means, electronic or mechanical, including photocopying or recording, or by any information storage and retrieval system, without permission in writing from the publisher.

On the cover: Claudia Drake and Tom Neal in *Detour*, 1945 (Producers Releasing Corporation/Photofest)

Manufactured in the United States of America

McFarland & Company, Inc., Publishers
  Box 611, Jefferson, North Carolina 28640
    www.mcfarlandpub.com

For my wonderful wife Amelia,
our son Jonathan and
Charles Mitchell, who also loved to sit
in the dark and watch films noirs...

Acknowledgments

I must thank my circle of friends who are enamored of the crime film, especially "film noir." If it was not for their inspiration, I would never have embarked on writing a third volume on the subject. Friends like Ray Meola, Jeff Leibowitz and the Mandelbaum brothers, Howard and Ronald of Photofest, have been particularly encouraging.

Also, I thank my editors at McFarland — a very professional staff who had faith that I could bring this original work to fruition.

Special thanks go to Christianne and Jazz van de Lima in our co-op as well as to Ken Eisner. I am grateful for the encouragement of my childhood friend Dr. Allen Richman of Stephen F. Austin State University and his wife Joan. And on a personal note, I would like to thank Dr. Benjamin Zaremski and Dr. Gary Giangola of Lenox Hill Hospital in Manhattan, who saved my life.

Contents

Acknowledgments vi
Preface 1
Introduction 3
  1. Allied Artists and *The Gangster* (1947) 9
  2. Columbia Pictures and *Gilda* (1946) 22
  3. Eagle-Lion Studios and *Hollow Triumph* aka *The Scar* (1948) 32
  4. Metro-Goldwyn-Mayer and *The Asphalt Jungle* (1950) 42
  5. Monogram Pictures and *I Wouldn't Be in Your Shoes* (1948) 55
  6. Paramount Pictures and *Double Indemnity* (1944) 64
  7. Producers Releasing Corporation and *Detour* (1945) 80
  8. Republic Pictures and *House by the River* (1950) 90
  9. RKO Radio Pictures and *Out of the Past* (1947) 100
10. 20th Century–Fox and *Laura* (1944) 116
11. United Artists and *Too Late for Tears* (1949) 130
12. Universal Pictures and *The Killers* (1946) 142
13. Warner Bros. and *Possessed* (1947) 157
14. Independent Production Units 172
15. The Runners-Up 175
Conclusion 185
Selected Bibliography 187
Index 189

Preface

The crime film always interested me for as long as I can remember. I used to escape to the movies as early as five years old and even played truant from school just so I could see a double feature at the local Surf Theatre in Coney Island in 1942. But the Technicolor pirate and adventure and musical films didn't interest me as much as the black and white crime dramas with those intricate plots. I remember watching *Double Indemnity* for the first time in 1944 or 1945 and was so impressed by its actors, plot, music and photography that I went to see it twice!

The same thing happened when I watched Lana Turner and John Garfield in *The Postman Always Rings Twice*. The actors absolutely sizzled on the screen. I was a bit too young to know about sex and murder, but I knew that crime never paid and no one got away with his or her chicanery. That was back in 1946, when a French writer called these films "noir" — black, or dark.

I became such a film addict that my parents had to drag me home from the local theater to have supper on time and prepare for school the next day. But my real education took place in the local cinemas, watching those wonderful crime films by Alfred Hitchcock, Billy Wilder, Robert Siodmak and Jules Dassin. I was hooked on noir and, decades later, decided to write a few books about it.

Now it is 2013 and I am still as excited as that five-year-old child back in the forties, always anxious to see revivals of the great old films. It is still the films of the forties and fifties I find the most fascinating. In my introduction I will concisely identify what "film noir" is and discuss why each major, minor and independent studio during the period from 1940 to 1958 chose to produce this type of film.

Introduction

What is film noir?

Film noir is a style that predates the 1940s and continues into the twenty-first century. *Noir* is a French word meaning "black," and although "film noir" literally means "black film," it refers to the mood of many black-and-white American films made between 1940 and 1960 in which a male protagonist is usually led to his destruction by a femme fatale and winds up getting neither the money nor the dame.

It is a gloomy style of American film identified by the French film critics. Nino Frank coined the term "film noir" in 1946 and the French authors Raymond Borde and Etiènne Chaumenton, in their seminal critical work *Panorama du film noir américain (1941–1953)*, used "noir" to define a particular sort of American cinema just before World War II until the late 1950s even though the roots of film noir can be seen as early as silent days.

It has its silent stylistic predecessors in films by D.W. Griffith (*Musketeers of Pig Alley*) and Raoul Walsh (*Regeneration*), its pre-noir tendencies in the '20s and '30s films of Josef von Sternberg (*Underworld*) and Fritz Lang (*M*), before it finally emerged as a style in Boris Ingster's *Stranger on the Third Floor* (1940), Orson Welles' *Citizen Kane* (1941) and John Huston's *The Maltese Falcon* (1941).

The popularity of film noir reached its zenith during World War II with films such as Billy Wilder's *Double Indemnity*, Howard Hawks' *The Big Sleep* and Tay Garnett's *The Postman Always Rings Twice*. If one could imagine oneself in Paris in 1945, watching these and *The Maltese Falcon* and *Murder, My Sweet*, and other noir films of that era, one would get a very negative view of America, a sexually debased, perverse and amoral society.

The French saw this type of movie as part of American cinema's New Wave. These crime films had their antecedents in the French Poetic Realism of the '30s (the films of Jean Gabin, for example) and in German Expressionism of the '20s and '30s. The European influences of cinema impressed many Hollywood directors.

The French public was no longer interested in the artful but predictable Hollywood musicals but the gutsy mysterious film noirs where a femme fatale (fatal woman) can seduce a dull or dumb lover into killing her husband or other lovers, his first step on the road to ruin.

There were also hommes fatales (fatal men) who seduced women into labyrinthine schemes but they usually met their end in lethal shoot-outs or unpredictable events like car accidents.

Film noir uses low-key lighting, highly angled camera set-ups and dark music to tell its stories. Shot mostly in black and white, the cycle of noir films ends in 1958 with either *Odds Against Tomorrow* or *Touch of Evil*. It must be said that no American director during that period ever used the word "noir," nor did he or she set out to create a style or genre. It was the French critics who applied the word "noir" to this group of films that shared a similar photographic, artistic and thematic style. Therefore, noir is *not* a genre, but an unconscious stylistic movement shared by many directors in 1940s and 1950s Hollywood.

It is also certain that societal influences contributed to the design of these particular films. Their thematic pessimism can be attributed to the post–World War II disillusionment of returning servicemen on a variety of issues, such as their replacement by women in the workforce and the difficulty they had adjusting to postwar values. Coincidentally, there was a rise in acceptance of the "hard-boiled" school of writers, whose escapist, masculine themes provided entertainment during the war years. The novels of James M. Cain, Raymond Chandler, David Goodis, Dashiell Hammett and Cornell Woolrich were widely read and provided the raw material for film noirs. Also, because of the use of new high-speed film stock and the ease of photographing outside of the studio (on location), real people and streets were used in a great number of films of the period. And, finally, many émigrés from France and Germany, who filmed in Hollywood and on location, brought with them a style of "expressionist" cinema that developed in Europe in the early 1930s and reached its fulfillment in the film noirs of the 1940s and 1950s.

There are many qualities and characteristics of film noir: chiaroscuro lighting; screenplays set in urban milieus filmed mostly at night; frequent images of water and reflections of street lights; inverted frames (cameras

Introduction

held diagonally and vertically), reflecting the inner thoughts of the protagonist; and very complex and convoluted plots, usually described in voiceover by a central character or a detective or a femme fatale who flashes back to the past. There is much violence and crime; eroticism and hetero- and homosexuality abound. Characters share obsessive behavior; males are generally untrusting and misogynistic, and become victims of their own paranoia. All of the aforementioned characteristics are framed in a pervasive darkness; photographers combine low-key lighting with deep focus shots that provide a claustrophobic ambience. The viewer is constantly jarred by the editing, always surprised by the asymmetrical compositions within the frame of the camera, the mystery of the plot, and the xenophobia of the characters as they move through the darkness toward an unknown conclusion.

Why the emergence of film noir? The reasons for the eruption of the film noir style during the forties and fifties also reflect the socio-political developments of World War II plus the post-war problems such as McCarthyism, the Communist or "Red Scare," as well as the development and use of nuclear weapons. The blacklists of the McCarthy era altered or aborted careers in all phases of film production, especially those actors, writers, directors and producers associated primarily with film noir — John Garfield, Abraham Polonsky, Joseph Losey and Edward Dmytryk, for example.

Other forces within the film industry of the forties helped to perpetuate and enlarge the film noir cycle after World War II: the "B" program picture (the second half of the double feature), the development of more sensitive, fine grain negatives, high-speed lenses, smaller camera dollies, portable power supplies and the extensive use of location shooting that insured greater verisimilitude in the depiction of realistic events in film production. Also, because of greater post-war economies, the use of existing sets, the greater use and exploitation of stock film libraries combined with the style of chiaroscuro lighting and newer technological innovations available since the aftermath of World War II, post-war film noirs became a cheaper, more visually homogeneous and popular group of films with American audiences because of one cohesive, visual style.

So film noir, as a cycle, seemed to end informally in the late fifties because of a multiplicity of reasons: There were severe changes in the patterns of exhibition of films as well as a huge cut in the number of films produced. Films that were non-color, non-widescreen and shot in low-key lighting simply lost their popularity. But most important was a post–World War II malaise that set in, with America's special preoccupation with economic recession and foreign entanglements.

Thus noir films diminished gradually in their production, practically vanishing in the late fifties. However, the resurrection of the noir sensibility, or "neo-noir," began in the early sixties, as actors, producers, directors, composers and writers shared a common ethos — to revive the dark side of the American persona.

The reasons film noir and neo-noir are so popular are because the central figures in these films (whether the 1940s–50s peak noir characters reflecting existential bitterness or the 1960s–2007 neo-noir figures) still find themselves drowning or doomed outside the social mainstream, thus representing a true cultural reflection of the mental aberration and dysfunction of an America that is still a nation in uncertain transition. So neo-noir, then, is the revival of '40s and '50s noir style in American films from the '60s into the new millennium, capitalizing on those doom-laden themes and characters of that earlier era.

This book, however, will restrict itself to film noir only, defining the particular studio style that made each film a distinct Hollywood product of its era. It will delve into art direction, set design, music, cinematography, acting, writing and other aspects of production that make each film noir unique to a certain studio. Thirteen major (and some minor) studios contributed most heavily in the production of film noir.

My aim is to comment upon the distinctive visual and aural characteristics of film noir of the '40s — about the specific camera and lighting techniques, especially exploring the visual aspect of this uniquely American stylistic phenomenon.

The following parameters for each chapter will be followed: First, the history of each studio will be presented, then one of their noir films will be critically scrutinized: a complete, detailed plot outline, short biographies of the principal actors as they pertain to film noir, and profiles of the producer(s), director(s), screenplay writers, cameramen, composers, art and set directors, also as they pertain to film noir. Then there will be a critical examination of two stills from each film and finally a critique of the film's importance as a reflection of the studio and its role in the film noir cycle. The order of studios is alphabetical and their best effort to express film noir style is represented by the chosen film with accompanying stills. The last chapter also includes the second choice of film from each major or minor studio in the noir style so as to give a perspective of the path the studio took making film noir–styled films. I will also list after each chapter a group of film noir made by each studio that are also worthwhile reviewing with a brief description of their content. A comprehensive, detailed view may be found for each film discussed by consulting the Internet Movie Database (imdb.com) or Alain Silver and James Ursini's fourth edition of their classic work *Film Noir* (2010). Unlike Silver and Ursini, whose work is coded thematically, my book explores all studio representations of film noir style including some "independents" during the same period with many of the same films discussed but many others not even touched upon, whether by a major or minor studio.

CHAPTER ONE

Allied Artists and *The Gangster* (1947)

Allied Artists was founded in 1946 as a subsidiary of Monogram Pictures, a very small studio, to handle exclusively the production and distribution of higher-budget motion pictures. However, by 1953, Monogram was releasing its "B" pictures through Allied Artists and so the former studio ceased to exist as a "B" studio. Allied Artists competed with the big studios and its policy was to put out second-rate material through its subsidiary Monogram, although it is difficult to tell the difference between the quality of the two companies. Some of their 1950s releases included the film noirs *Cry Vengeance, Loophole, The Big Combo* and *The Phenix City Story*. But the production and artistic lines became blurred. Budgets were minimal and production values poor, but the studio provided a home for talent on the way up or down or talent that was too individualistic to survive the big studios.

The Gangster (1947) was the first in a series of film noirs made by Allied Artists. It was produced by the King Brothers, who had hoped to recapture the success of their earlier B film noir *Dillinger* which made a star of Lawrence Tierney in 1945. The King Brothers, Frank and Maurice, were the dominant independent producers of low-budget films before the fifties and usually released their films through Poverty Row studios. Among them were Monogram, as well as the more respectable United Artists and Allied Artists companies. I chose this film as the most representative of Allied Artists' first attempt at making a film noir. Its star Barry Sullivan was ascending in the Hollywood universe from B to A films. The script and outdoor scenes also reminded me of my youth in Brighton Beach, Coney Island and Sea Gate. In fact, in one outdoor shot reminded me of the Coney Island boardwalk where one could make out the famous Steeplechase Parachute Jump tower as well as the Half-Moon Hotel. So Brooklyn of the forties is featured and was the real scene of many murders of famous criminals of that era.

The Gangster is based upon a novel by Daniel Fuchs entitled *Low Company*. Sullivan as Shubunka (no first name) narrates the entire film, except for a few words at the conclusion.

The title cards are viewed against a darkening sky which turns into a thunderstorm, full of lightning and heavy rain. Louis Gruenberg's music score captures the pounding rhythms of the rain soaking the streets of Neptune City, which looks very much like the skyline of Coney Island, complete with parachute jump at Steeplechase Amusement Park and the no-longer-existent Half-Moon Hotel along the boardwalk where the real-life murder of Jewish gangster Abe Rellis took place a few years earlier.

We first see Shubunka in an apartment he shares with his mistress Nancy Starr (played by Belita). He is looking at a marvelously dark reproduction of an unidentified Goya painting and then moves over to a mirror, stroking a vertical scar on his right cheek as he watches his own hand trace the line on his face. The apartment is elegant, one of the three set pieces in the film that convince us of the "luxuriousness" of crime. It has huge mirrors, closets of men's suits and other accoutrements that make you believe these people were never deprived or that the United States had just gone through a world war. Amidst all this luxury, Shubunka reveals in an interior monologue how he despises people who despise him, how he has pulled himself out of the gutter on the backs of the "little people" from whom he profits through gambling, protection, numbers games and other rackets detailed on a "real estate" list, giving locations. Shubunka is nattily dressed in a double-breasted suit and maintains a serious, threatening pose as if he always had a gun in his right hand. He wears a dark hat and dark shoes that contrast with a three-pointed handkerchief in his left jacket upper pocket — proper dress for an upcoming gangster.

Another wonderful set piece is the boardwalk's Sweet Shoppe with a modern glass front (which we only see from the inside). Owner Nick Jammy (Akim Tamiroff) deals in "real estate" and is Shubunka's partner. Henry Morgan plays Shorty, the soda jerk (dressed in whites complete with hat), who is interested in seducing the Russian widowed next-door neighbor. Finally, there is Dorothy (Joan Lorring in an early role), the cashier who represents symbolically the "innocence" of the little people and is also the moral porte-parole of the author, Daniel Fuchs.

One — Allied Artists and *The Gangster* (1947)

The Sweet Shoppe has a wonderful black and white squared linoleum floor, which can sometimes be reflected on the ceiling. There are red-leather booths on one side and stools at a bar with a long counter on the other. Most the film's problem personages enter through the main glass doors and take seats on either side. One patron, accountant Karty (John Ireland), is a compulsive gambler, trying to recoup $1300 he stole from his wife's brothers' garage business. Virginia Christine plays Karty's wife, wearing the same disheveled evening dress in every scene, searching for her shameless thief of a husband who never has a kind word for her.

Jammy leaves during a rainstorm and is approached by two hoods in the middle of the street. He is given a card with a telephone number on it and the name "Cornell." As the rain lets up, Shubunka is seen entering the Henrik Hudson Hotel (like the original Half-Moon Hotel complete with a frigate on top of it much like the one Henry Hudson used to sail into New York) and going to the suite he shares with Nancy. The hotel's façade and lobby comprise the film's third most fascinating set.

We see Nancy (Belita) for the first time, her head entering the frame from below, pinning back her blonde hair. She swoops into the frame much like Rita Hayworth's opening shot in *Gilda*, when George Macready asks his new bride, "Gilda, are you decent?" Hayworth's hair enters the frame from below and with bowed head looking up, she answers, "Me, decent?" Obviously cameraman Paul Ivano appropriated the same technique, literally copying it to very fine effect in *The Gangster*. Nancy is beautiful. Shubunka is her antithesis. He feels he is ugly, and with that scar on his right cheek, he does look ugly. Although they do live together, you feel he never takes his clothes off. There is something very asexual about their relationship even though he pays all of her bills.

Nancy says she must visit her sick sister in Queens and cannot spend the afternoon with Shubunka. The latter trails her on the subway and finds she has a date with a Broadway agent in Manhattan, Mr. Beaumont (Leif Erickson). Shubunka reveals himself and Nancy heads off a possible storm. "I never know what goes on in your mind," she tells him as he asks her why she lied to him.

Shubunka returns to the Sweet Shoppe. The film spends some time on the subplot of Shorty and Mrs. Ostrovich, the soda jerk and the Russian proprietor of a corset shop next door to the Sweet Shoppe (Shorty loses out in his effort to seduce the Russian lady). But when Shubunka arrives, he inspires fear in everyone! Dorothy the cashier visibly flinches when she sees Shubunka and his scarred face. Wearing a Peter Pan collar and a revealing wool sweater, she wants nothing to do with him and his "dead" looks. Shubunka corners Jammy in a booth and they discuss the trouble "the syndicate" is making for them through Cornell. Shubunka will handle the problems as he had for the last six years. In fact, everyone in the Sweet Shoppe has some sort of problem. When Karty's wife finally catches up to him, he says of her, "I never had a good day with you from the beginning." The film is full of these two-shots, where intimate details are revealed about each character's life.

Jammy and Shubunka keep on talking in the booth as night falls. The sun sets, the shadows darken, become longer, and Jammy confides to Shubunka: "You only need one person near and dear to you!" The camera then cuts to Nancy's apartment and Shubunka enters their bedroom and watches her sleeping. She awakens to the news that he went uptown and brought her something—a new mink coat! Confiding to her maid Essie how beautiful it is, Nancy tells Shubunka, "I hate you, I could kill you. I really don't want a Broadway show." He answers, "I really can't believe I have you."

The scene shifts to an elegant Neptune City restaurant (reminiscent of Gargiulo's in Coney Island) where Jammy has been invited by Cornell (played by Sheldon Leonard) and sits between two thugs as the former mixes a salad dressing and is told to hand over his list of "real estate" locations to the syndicate. "Don't worry about Shubunka. He's being taken care of at this very moment," says Cornell.

The scene switches to the beach. Shubunka refuses to get into a bathing suit, wearing a jacket, trousers, hat and tie on the sand. We see the sea gulls, the sky, a beautiful day as the music by Louis Grunenberg indicates—although the entire setting is studio-bound. Nancy is on a blanket, knitting, as Shubunka, with jacket and hat removed, lies on the sand. Suddenly, two shadows obliterate their view of the sun and shore: Cornell has sent two thugs, Elisha Cook, Jr., in an outrageous blue pinstripe suit and Ted Hecht to give Shubunka a message. The latter offers them $3000 each to do Cornell in but thinks better of it and calls them "small-timers." Shubunka is pistol-whipped by the thugs, delivering "Cornell's message" but he believes now that Nancy sicced the gunsels on him, distrusting everyone around him. (How did they know where he was and with whom?) Because of Shubunka's paranoia, Nancy collapses into a crying fit.

One — Allied Artists and *The Gangster* (1947)

Shubunka tries to rally support from his former pals and politicos, but everyone has been threatened by Cornell. The camera follows him into bars, pool halls, hotel rooms. Every scene is low-lit — shadows are everywhere. We hear the elevated train rolling along the tracks outside of the windows of every place Shubunka visits in Neptune City, which could easily double for Brighton Beach. Shubunka finally winds up at the ice cream parlor, brightly lit. Meeting Jammy and telling him not to panic, Shubunka is told by Dorothy that her boss took the "real-estate list" and sold Shubunka out. In a panic, he calls and tells Nancy to begin packing and to get out of town.

Back at their apartment at night, Nancy tells Shubunka she'll pawn everything he's given to her — "I'm true, I'm yours!" Shubunka returns to the ice cream parlor looking for Jammy. Karty tries to borrow money from him and Shubunka refuses. Dorothy, watching Shubunka reducing Karty to tears and representing the "morally right vision" of the novelist, says to Shubunka, "You're sick, twisted." The latter runs out and visits Cornell's office.

As he goes up the dimly lit staircase, we see black and white linoleum squares on the steps leading to Cornell's darkened office. Shubunka and Cornell discuss the "ethics" of what the latter is doing. Shubunka built up the business for six years and he's being offered an $80 per week job as a collector. And Jammy is just a racketeer caught in the middle. Cornell declares, "If anything happens to Jammy, you'll be a dead man twenty minutes later." Facing off against Cornell, Shubunka declares, "You can't stop me!"

Fate seems to be the motif that governs the rest of the action of the film. As the camera swoops into the darkened garage of Karty's brothers-in-law, who are beating him because he stole their hard-earned money, the latter promises them he'll get some money somehow and goes to Jammy's back room where the latter usually prepares his bank deposit of the daily receipts. As Jammy greets his new cashier Hazel (played by a youthful Shelley Winters), a loud jazz score is heard on the juke box. Jammy enters the darkened room and sees Karty, who hits him with a frying pan on the head, not even taking the money. Karty runs hysterically out the back door, leaving it open, with Jammy lying on the floor, bleeding to death. Right next door, Shorty has just been thrown out of Mrs. Ostrovich's house — she wanted "platonic" love; Shorty wanted a sexual affair. As Shorty leaves, the camera moves past the fence of the Sweet Shoppe to focus on to Jammy's dead body through the open door.

The scene shifts to Nancy's apartment. Beaumont arrives with gun in hand (he apparently was Cornell's agent) and we discover Nancy did really have a part in Shubunka's demise. "You made me hate you," she says twice. "You tortured me, you're ugly." Rattled by this disclosure, Shubunka leaves his wallet and his hat. He is all alone sitting in the dark and even hears Cornell saying he will not keep his promise to Nancy about putting her in a Broadway show. As Shubunka sits in the apartment all alone, the only light is coming from the seascape glimpsed by the camera through the window. Shubunka finally gets up to leave.

There is much agitation in the hotel lobby over the death of Jammy. Shubunka overhears conversations as he walks through the lobby out into the rain. He looks straight into the camera and shouts, "I didn't do it!" He begins to run on the boardwalk, past many concession stands with voiceovers, faces, past dialogue and memories swirling all about him, ending with "You'll be a dead man twenty minutes later" as a rainstorm breaks suddenly, sending people scurrying for cover. All alone in the rain, he remembers Dorothy's address: 12 Beach 33rd Street.

Shubunka arrives at Dorothy's darkly lit, poorly furnished apartment which she shares with her sick father. She tells Shubunka that Karty killed Jammy and admitted it to the police. Everyone must have heard the news on the radio. Shubunka believes he is safe now, but Dorothy's father feels they should let him stay a while longer. Dorothy says, "Let him pay for his sins — he's rotten, no good. Get out!" Shubunka answers: "I should have been meaner, more rotten, should never have loved a woman, should have gotten Cornell first. What do *you* know!"

Shubunka walks out in the rain. A car drives up. We hear the screeching of brakes. The mob is still after him. Looking directly at the camera in the pouring rain, he talks to the audience: "You can have it all — watch the ugliness creep into your heart, your face — take it all, yes, take it all!" We hear many shots as the camera surges towards Shubunka's face and we watch him fall into the street, next to a storm drain by a curb as water swirls all around him, face down in that pouring rain.

A new narrator greets us on the next sunny day. The camera pans across the boardwalk along the coast as we note the wonderful weather and the narrator says nothing of Shubunka. Too bad Jammy isn't around to enjoy it. The end title card shows clear skies as clouds are swept away by the wind.

One — Allied Artists and *The Gangster* (1947)

Some of the scenes that inform the noir style were used as publicity for the film. It was not too hard to look at Barry Sullivan as a gangster, fully dressed in a suit in a scene with a single source of light, emphasizing the scar on his right cheek, standing in a hallway of an anonymous nightclub waiting for his lover, Belita. His dark hat and shoes are contrasted with that three-pointed handkerchief in his jacket upper pocket, proper dress for an up-and-coming gangster.

In another scene, the tranquility of the Sweet Shoppe is interrupted by two gangsters, noir actors Charles McGraw and Ted Hecht, dressed exactly as Shubunka. That the latter should use the Sweet Shoppe as a meeting place where innocent teenagers are customers and others also work for their boss Jammy is also astounding. On the counter, where the owner usually reads the paper, we find Jammy has left in a hurry, rumpling his discarded newspaper and leaving by the back door. Joan Lorring as the cashier Dorothy seems a bit frightened when the gangster duo asks for Jammy, her boss. Dorothy knows there is something underhanded going on between Jammy and Shubunka but projects a smile of innocence, wearing a long wool skirt, a cotton blouse and a "heart" dangling from a chain around her neck, typical teenage dress for the era.

Another notable scene takes place in the Sweet Shoppe when Jammy appears outside of his office talking to the new cashier Hazel (played by an uncredited blonde Shelley Winters); he has just collected the daily receipts from her in a paper bag while he shows her a picture of his wife. She feigns interest in the photo while also looking at a travel folder in her other hand. She is probably looking for another job already suspecting the fate of the owner since Jammy is affected by the violence and paranoia as pressure is brought to bear by Cornell, the new real estate magnate (gangster); both are now willing to sell out Shubunka.

The Gangster represents Barry Sullivan's third starring role in a noir film. He worked with Belita before in Monogram Pictures' *Suspense* (also produced by the King Brothers) in 1946, then for Columbia Pictures opposite femme fatale Janis Carter in *Framed* (1947) before making *The Gangster*. The role of Shubunka propelled him to stardom, making the transition from B studio productions to the A pictures of Metro-Goldwyn-Mayer. Continuing his ascension into noir roles, his most riveting performance was as Loretta Young's duplicitous husband in MGM's *Cause for Alarm* (1951) and after as Doris Day's best friend in the noir thriller *Julie* (1956) where he is pursued and nearly killed by Day's psychotic husband (Louis Jourdan).

Belita began her career as an ice-skater and, much like Sonia Henie, tried to make films using this talent. Except for *Suspense*, *The Gangster* and *The Hunted* (1948) with Preston Foster, her three noir films, Belita made little impact on American cinema.

The cast of "character actors" in *The Gangster* is certainly loaded with talent: Joan Lorring, of English-Russian descent, graduated from teen roles into hateful noir women as seen in Jean Negulesco's *The Verdict* (1946), Walter Wanger's *The Lost Moment* (1947) and the Paul Muni film *Stranger on the Prowl* (1953).

Akim Tamiroff was best known for his character roles in *The General Died at Dawn* (1936) and *For Whom the Bell Tolls* (1943). In *The Gangster*, he played his first of three noir roles; there were two more for Orson Welles, *Mr. Arkadin* (1955) and, most notably, *Touch of Evil* (1958), one of the last of the black and white film noirs to officially close the cycle of this style of film.

Harry Morgan was no stranger to noir as a character actor. He worked for several studios, notably Fox (*Somewhere in the Night*, 1946), Paramount (*The Big Clock*, 1948, *Dark City*, 1950, *Appointment with Danger*, 1951), RKO (*Race Street*, 1948), Republic (*Moonrise*, 1948) and Columbia's *Scandal Sheet*, 1952). His greatest noir fame came on national television collaborating with Jack Webb as in NBC's famed *Dragnet* series.

John Ireland began his career as a noir actor for the B studios. He worked for PRC in Anthony Mann's *Railroaded* and *Raw Deal* (1947). After making *All the King's Men* (1949) with Broderick Crawford for Columbia, his career rolled downhill after some disastrous marriages. A latter-day noir role was as a detective in the 1975 version of Raymond Chandler's *Farewell, My Lovely*, produced in London by Dick Richards.

Charles McGraw is perhaps the most popular noir character actor to have worked in the forties and fifties for a multiplicity of studios, even playing a starring role opposite Marie Windsor in RKO's *The Narrow Margin* (1952). He will be remembered as one of the title characters in *The Killers* (1946) alongside of William Conrad and in some A-noirs like John Farrow's *His Kind of Woman* (1951) with Robert Mitchum and Jane Russell. He died abruptly in 1980 in a household accident.

Sheldon Leonard was no stranger to noir roles. His earliest was in Paramount's *Street of Chance* (1942) with Burgess Meredith, taken from a

One — Allied Artists and *The Gangster* (1947)

Cornell Woolrich novel. Despite appearing in some other notable B-noirs, such as *Decoy* and *Somewhere in the Night* (both 1946), he is mostly remembered today as a television producer.

Elisha Cook, Jr., had a great deal of success in noir films beginning as the "gunsel" Elmer in John Huston's *The Maltese Falcon* (1941), the film which many critics agree opened the "noir cycle." But most memorable are his roles as the jazz drummer trying to seduce Ella Raines in Robert Siodmak's *Phantom Lady* (1944), the bellboy murderer of Carole Landis in Fox's *I Wake Up Screaming* (1941), the innocent cab driver accused of murder in RKO's pre-noir *Stranger on the Third Floor* (1940) Agnes' dupe Harry Jones, who would rather swallow poison than reveal her whereabouts in Howard Hawks' great noir based on Raymond Chandler's *The Big Sleep* (1946) and finally, as the weak-willed husband of Marie Windsor in Stanley Kubrick's intense racetrack heist film, *The Killing* (1956).

Jeff Corey worked in films since the early forties and appeared in many film noirs, most notably *The Killers* (1946) and *Brute Force* (1947). He is barely seen in *The Gangster* as a pal of Shubunka's. He continued playing character roles even into the mid–nineties as well as maintaining an acting school in California.

Turning to the production of *The Gangster,* Frank and Maurice King were very well known in the forties and fifties, producing a variety of films for the smaller studios such as Monogram and Allied Artists. They were among the first independents who had control of scripts, budgets and stars. They zealously guarded their terrain to produce films dealing with crime, violence and sexual perversity. One of their greatest hits was Monogram's *When Strangers Marry* (1944), a mystery about a disappearing husband starring Robert Mitchum, Kim Hunter (in her first starring role) and Dean Jagger as the murderer; also, there was *Suspense* (1946), the ice-skating noir thriller that united Belita and Barry Sullivan for the first time, both caught in a revenge plot initiated by Albert Dekker, also for Monogram. For Allied Artists, the King Brothers produced *Gun Crazy* (1950), Joseph Lewis' film about guns and sexuality, an earlier version of *Bonnie and Clyde*. Finally there was *Southside 1-1000* (1950), an FBI noir thriller about trapping counterfeiters with Don Defore and Andrea King. Although the King Brothers' reign as independent producers was brief, their canon of work in film noir was inventive and entertaining.

The Gangster was director Gordon Wiles' only noir contribution. He

The Gangster **(1947): Barry Sullivan (left) listens intently to John Ireland pleading desperately for a loan.**

was an art director for Fox in the thirties; his directing accomplishments are unrecognized by most critics. On the other hand, screenwriter Daniel Fuchs is very well-known in Hollywood for his work on hard-boiled gangster subjects as early as 1942: Humphrey Bogart's *The Big Shot*, Paul Henreid's *Hollow Triumph* aka *The Scar* (1948), and Burt Lancaster's *Criss Cross* (1949), which was made as the neo-noir *The Underneath* (1995).

Cameraman Paul Ivano worked in Hollywood with some wonderful directors, among them Josef von Sternberg for United Artists' *The Shanghai Gesture* (1941) and Robert Siodmak for Universal's *Uncle Harry* (1945) and *Black Angel* (1946). His work for Wiles in 1947 does not appear terribly distinctive although there are some inventive noir techniques. But *The Gangster* is, after all, a conventionally filmed noir with a rather flat style. It is in the performances that Ivano captures on film with his conventional camera that give the film most of its real style.

But the true star of *The Gangster* is art director F. Paul Sylos. His

One — Allied Artists and *The Gangster* (1947)

designs of its three major set pieces are very inventive, making effective use of spaces and angles. Sylos worked for both big and small studios and was an expert in noir designs for the films he made for Monogram, Allied Artists, United Artists, Enterprise Studios and Columbia. The originality of his art direction can be seen as early as 1944 in *When Strangers Marry,* totally filmed on a studio set looking like Manhattan. In Paramount's *Fear in the Night* (1947), based on a Cornell Woolrich story and set in Los Angeles and environs, he makes use of actual locations. And in the Phil Karlson 1953 film *99 River Street,* he employs outdoor New Jersey locales as John Payne, playing an ex-boxer taxi driver, searches for the murderer of his two-timing strangled wife (Peggie Castle), aided by his newfound love, Evelyn Keyes.

There are two important stills that inform the noir style used in Allied Artists' *The Gangster*: The first shows Barry Sullivan (left) and John

The Gangster (1947): This noir-angled shot shows Barry Sullivan (center) surrounded by five gangsters.

Ireland (right) conversing about a loan in the Sweet Shoppe owned by Akim Tamiroff. Note the black and white squares on the linoleum-tiled floor and the ice cream bar to the left, full of glassware and fountain machinery to make sodas and frappes. As Shubunka calmly sits at his table with his back to the main entrance (glass doors in a wooden frame), Karty makes his pitch for a loan. Both men are wearing jackets, ties and hats inside the somewhat brightly lit Sweet Shoppe. There are some people sitting at a booth behind Karty but out of their listening range. Note the fluorescent light in the windows and one over the ice cream bar. The shop is also an "innocent" location in which to conduct underworld activities, similar to Jerry's Supermarket, where Barbara Stanwyck and Fred MacMurray discuss a murder scheme to rid Stanwyck of her penny-pinching husband in Billy Wilder's brilliant noir *Double Indemnity* (1944).

The second still has a noirish point of view with the camera pointing down the staircase of an anonymous "club." There are dark shadows on the top man at the head of the stairs while Shubunka is being frisked for a gun as three other gangsters stand around him in the cheap lobby, again with black and white tiled floors.

The Gangster is a highly stylized mood piece. It is also about control: how a gangster uses money to obsessively control his girlfriend by getting her into show business, a familiar theme. The director has created on his limited budget a story of social decay where the protagonist is decidedly almost alone in the minimalist décor created by the art director. The three basic set pieces of the film are the Sweet Shop, Nancy's apartment which she shares with Shubunka and the nightclub where Shubunka waits for Nancy. The stills and the their framing capture the minimalist style of the décor which reinforces the acting of the principals. At the end, we feel very little for the gangster, lying riddled with bullets on the curb of a wet street. He lost his grip on life and the society he tried in vain to perpetuate.

Allied Artists produced a minimal number of film noirs, the first of which was *The Gangster*. I will now list the company's best noir films, adding the year of release, the director, the important stars and a line or two about the plot. Allied Artists released a total of nine film noirs and the best are the following:

Cry Vengeance (1954), Mark Stevens, director. Cast: Mark Stevens,

Martha Hyer & Skip Homeier. Innocent man jailed seeks vengeance against gangster for killing his family; filmed in Alaska.

The Phenix City Story (1955), Phil Karlson, director. Cast: Richard Kiley, Edward Andrews, John McIntire. A lawyer and a newspaperman fight corruption in a small Southern town following the Kefauver hearings.

The Big Combo (1955), Joseph Lewis, director. Cast: Cornel Wilde, Richard Conte, Jean Wallace. A policeman and a mobster are in love with a society femme fatale. There's extraordinary photography by John Alton and much sexual innuendo.

Murder Is My Beat (1955), Edgar G. Ulmer, director. Cast: Paul Langton, Barbara Payton, Robert Shayne. This convoluted murder plot involves a femme fatale and two detectives.

The Naked Kiss (1964), Samuel Fuller, director. Cast: Constance Towers, Anthony Eisley, Michael Dante. An ex-prostitute becomes a nurse and falls in love with a child molester but is redeemed by the love of a local cop. Surprising conclusion.

Although *Southside 1-1000* (1950), *Loophole* (1954) and *World for Ransom* (1954) may contain the classic elements of film noir, they are less interesting movie fare. *Loophole* stars Barry Sullivan as a bank teller who is accused of robbery but is exonerated at the film's end.

If I were to choose an Allied Artists runner-up to *The Gangster*, it would be *The Big Combo*.

CHAPTER TWO

Columbia Pictures and *Gilda* (1946)

Columbia Pictures, founded in 1924 by Harry Cohn, was the biggest of the "Poverty Row" studios created during the early 1920s. It was originally called C.B.C. (Cohen-Brandt-Cohen aka Corned Beef and Cabbage) and survived mainly due to low-budget westerns and action pictures. In the 1930s, director Frank Capra was largely responsible for the studio's survival, making the hits *It Happened One Night* (1934) and *Mr. Smith Goes to Washington* (1939). In the 1940s, there were a series of low-budget film noirs and a young musical star named Rita Hayworth that propelled the studio into the major leagues. Among its most famous film noirs were *Johnny O'Clock* (1947), *Dead Reckoning* (1947), *The Lady from Shanghai* (1948), *In a Lonely Place* (1950), *The Big Heat* (1953), and *The Brothers Rico* (1957). But it was largely one film made in 1946, *Gilda*, starring Rita Hayworth, that was the undisputable masterpiece of noir, demonstrating the height of studio filmmaking. It featured one of the most unforgettable femme fatales and was one of *the* biggest post–World War II moneymakers, along with Columbia's musical *The Jolson Story*.

Gilda is set in Buenos Aires shortly before the end of the Second World War. After watching the main titles (set to one of the romantic songs which Rita Hayworth sings and dances to late in the film, "Amado, mío"), the camera swoops up from below a sidewalk where a huge pair of dice (probably "loaded") come directly at the camera, thrown by a young, kneeling Glenn Ford. He makes another pass of the dice. As Johnny Farrell, who narrates most of the film, he scoops up his winnings and leaves the group of suspicious losers hurriedly, walking alone on the Buenos Aires docks until a poorly dressed stranger with a gun tries to rob Farrell of his winnings. An "elegant" stranger with a walking stick concealing a sharp knife prevents the theft, lets the robber go and chats with Farrell, especially about his walking stick, "his most faithful and obedient friend." The man invites Farrell to a gambling casino across town. Farrell arrives there, dons a borrowed tie and begins to play blackjack.

The casino is one of the most fascinating set pieces in noir films, like the one in von Sternberg's *The Shanghai Gesture* (1941). While playing 21, Farrell is caught cheating by the boss of the casino who turns out to be his rescuer, Ballin Mundsen (George Macready).

Mundsen agrees to hire Farrell and flashes his dark eyes at Mundsen in a brief "homo-erotic" moment caught by film director Charles Vidor. Since Farrell would be working for the owner of the "joint," he wouldn't be stealing his own money. Mundsen adores Farrell's insouciance—but one thing he must be sure of: "There is no woman anywhere for gambling and women do not mix."

The end of World War II is celebrated in Buenos Aires. In a matter of weeks, Farrell works his way up to the top of Mundsen's organization. Mundsen's office is another extraordinary set piece in which he has two sets of folding blinds to secretly view the guests at the club as well as a series of hidden microphones at each table to eavesdrop on his patrons' conversations. Farrell takes charge of the casino when Mundsen must go on a business trip to Montevideo. After Mundsen returns, Farrell is invited to visit his home. Mundsen has married an old flame of Johnny's—the beautiful singer-dancer Gilda. The scene in which he greets Gilda for the first time is probably the most well-known, erotically charged introduction of a female star on screen. As Mundsen asks Gilda, "Are you decent?" Rita Hayworth swoops her hair up from the bottom of the frame and smilingly answers, "Me? Decent?" Spotting Farrell in the doorway behind Mundsen, her smile changes. "Sure, I'm decent." Mundsen notices Gilda's dislike for Farrell. "She, too, was born the night she met me—no pasts, all futures, like the three of us." Farrell gives Mundsen his key to the front door. Mundsen looks puzzled. Farrell says, "Tact."

The scene shifts to the wash room of the gambling casino. Uncle Pío (played by Steven Geray) the attendant says to Farrell after an altercation with Gilda, "You are both young and beautiful—this will be interesting to watch!" Mundsen, Gilda and Farrell dine at the restaurant of the casino and drink a toast to the "three of us" and also to the woman who brought Farrell down because of his belief in the instability of women. "Let's hate her," Mundsen says.

Shortly after Mundsen is called away on business, Gilda begins to flirt and dance with other men. Señor Obregón of the Argentine Secret Police (played by Joseph Calleia) inserts himself into the social equation as Gilda dances and flirts with Captain Delgado (played by handsome Gerald Mohr, star of Columbia's "Lone Wolf" series). Mundsen returns, asks Farrell to retrieve Gilda from the dance floor and inveigles Farrell to "take care of her." Once again, all three are seated at the dining room table and Mundsen makes a toast: "Disaster to the wench who brought down our Johnny."

At home, in their bedroom, Gilda admits she hates Farrell. Her face is photographed in deep shadow as she says this. Mundsen replies, "Hate is an exciting emotion — the only thing that has ever warmed me."

A shooting incident takes place at the casino. Since Mundsen denied a small, mustachioed man an opportunity to continually win at roulette, the latter tries to kill Mundsen but is chased by Farrell and the police into the washroom where he commits suicide. While this occurs, Gilda retreats to the dance floor with a new handsome young pick-up, Gabe Evans (played by Robert Scott). When Farrell retrieves Gilda from the arms of Evans, Gilda protests and says, "Didn't you hear about me, Gabe? If I were a ranch, they'd have named me the 'Bar Nothing.'" To protect Ballin from Gilda's "infidelities," Farrell lies to Mundsen, saying she went to the movies.

Mundsen, shaken by the shooting and suicide, decides to give Farrell the combination to his private safe and reveals he is the head of a "tungsten cartel." By taking Farrell into his confidence, Mundsen cements their relationship. Mundsen is "mad about her," and so Farrell should not come between them. Gilda returns home with Gabe, wearing a stunning Jean Louis evening jacket loaded with glitter. Farrell knocks the slightly drunken Gabe down for flirting with another man's wife and the latter retreats. But Gilda gives Farrell an ultimatum: She'll go anywhere and do anything she wants to but Farrell counters with a proposal that he will take her and bring her back, like "laundry" and not revealing to Mundsen anything about her infidelities.

In a quiet moment, Gilda reveals to Farrell that she is afraid of Mundsen and what he may do to her and that she should never have married on the rebound. But Farrell will have none of it. Farrell lies to Mundsen about going "swimming" with Gilda when she was really elsewhere. Gilda is always hanging around the casino because Farrell still interests her sexually and her husband does not.

Two — Columbia Pictures and *Gilda* (1946)

In a very long scene, the gambling casino is transformed into the setting for a masquerade ball. It is Carnival. After Uncle Pío is fired for insubordination, some Germans arrive to see Mundsen. Farrell is ordered to pick up Gilda at the house and take her to the ball. They dance, and for Gilda dancing is a metaphor for sex. Gilda carries a whip. "You're out of practice. Dancing, I mean. I could help you get into practice. Dancing, I mean..." Johnny pushes her away, rebuffing her sexual advances, and Gilda goes off alone to the Hotel Centenario. Back at the ball, one of the Germans is found stabbed to death (probably with Mundsen's "walking stick") and the police take charge. Mundsen does not admit to the crime and orders Farrell to find Gilda and bring her home. Gilda provokes Farrell into kissing her and Mundsen interrupts their tryst, deciding to flee, running out of the house. He heads for the airport. Farrell, in a voiceover, admits his reason for kissing Gilda: "I had to get rid of her for him!" Gilda says to Farrell, his face completely in shadow: "I hate you so much that I think I'm going to die from it."

Farrell and Obregón follow Mundsen to the airport, arriving too late as his plane takes off and proceeds towards Africa. It explodes, but Mundsen, unseen by Farrell or Obregón, parachutes safely into the ocean where a launch is awaiting him. He says to his henchman that he will return to Buenos Aires and attend to "something," referring to Gilda and Farrell's infidelities.

When Mundsen is declared dead, Farrell takes control of the casino and the tungsten cartel which Gilda inherited and the latter becomes his wife! But unknown to Gilda, Farrell wants to keep her faithful to Mundsen. She says: "I never thought one woman could marry two insane men in one lifetime!" Gilda is trapped in a "cage" of Farrell's making. When she tries to seek out the company of other men, they are abducted by Farrell's henchman. When she finally realizes Buenos Aires has become a "prison" for her, she flees to Montevideo.

The scene shifts to a Montevideo nightclub where Gilda is the star performer, singing and dancing to a lovely, exotic and sexy song, "Amado mío." There she is romanced by lawyer Tom Langford (played by Don Douglas) who promises to secure a legal divorce and annulment for her. Unbeknownst to Gilda, Langford is working for Farrell and returns her to a suite at the Hotel Centenario where Farrell is waiting for her. She slaps and pummels Farrell to no avail, collapsing at his feet.

Back at the casino, Obregón questions Farrell about the tungsten monopoly. In the nightclub, Gilda sings the famous song "Put the Blame on Mame," pretending to be a "loose" woman, doing a provocative striptease, with her gloves, necklace, even soliciting help to open her zipper, proclaiming herself a "tramp" so that everyone will now that the great Johnny Farrell got taken when he married her. Farrell angrily retrieves her from the dance floor and slaps her hard. Obregón says to him: "You kids really love each other — the most intense love-hate relationship I've ever seen!" Obregón also tells Farrell that Gilda is returning to the United States — and that she didn't do any of those things he thought she did. It was just an act. It is also interesting to note that Hayworth's song "Put the Blame on Mame" is a song about men who attribute natural disasters to women's sexuality, but critics have argued that her violent treatment by Farrell is due more to his pathological character than her presumed status as a femme fatale.

We finally arrive at the last scene, played at the bar in the casino late one night. The casino will be taken over by the Argentine police and Farrell begs Gilda to forgive him and take him home with her. She agrees: "There's nothing to forgive. We were both stinkers!" But Mundsen returns and wants revenge and his wife. Making a furtive appearance from his office, dressed in a cape and carrying his walking stick and a gun, he says he'll have to kill Gilda, too. Uncle Pío stabs Ballin from behind and admits his guilt to Obregón. The latter says no one is guilty since Mundsen can only die once. Gilda and Johnny walk out the bar, hand in hand.

Rita Hayworth was no stranger to the film noir style. *Gilda* was her first film in that genre and she gave a bravura performance in the title role. She can also be seen in Orson Welles's *The Lady from Shanghai* (1948) in which she plays a "short-haired blonde" femme fatale. With her natural long red hair she appeared with Glenn Ford *Affair in Trinidad* (1952). Most critics agree that with *Gilda,* Hayworth gave the most extraordinary, sensuous, tempestuous performance of all time and deserves the title "Sex Goddess."

Glenn Ford also made four important film noirs for Columbia. In his first, *Gilda,* he plays at both a homo-erotic relationship with Ballin Mundsen (George Macready) and as a swaggering sensual male attracted to the femme fatale. It was the role of Johnny Farrell that catapulted Ford to stardom at Columbia Pictures. In *Framed* (1947), he loses his swagger, playing a good-guy victim to Janis Carter's femme fatale. Re-teamed with

Two — Columbia Pictures and *Gilda* (1946)

Hayworth in *Affair in Trinidad* (1952), he reprises the Johnny Farrell role of *Gilda* but not as odious. However under the direction of Fritz Lang, he gives the most sensational performance of his career in *The Big Heat* (1953), playing a police detective who seeks revenge against the mob and almost loses his badge to obtain it. Although Ford appeared in other noir films, these roles made him into one of the most famous of noir male icons.

Macready is a character actor you will always remember because of a huge scar that nearly covers his entire left cheek and his elegant persona which he exploited in several noir films for Columbia and Paramount, among them *Gilda*, *The Big Clock* (1948), *Knock on Any Door* (1949) and *Detective Story* (1951). Whether playing a criminal-gambler and illegal head of a tungsten cartel (Ballin Mundsen) or a yes-man to Charles Laughton, picking up after the latter's crimes, or a vengeful district attorney or a doctor performing illegal abortions, Macready exuded wonderful portrayals of criminality and evil and never got away with murder.

Joseph Calleia was equally adept at playing good and bad characters in noir films. He was especially notable as a gangster in Paramount's *The Glass Key* (1942) and as the good cop Obregón in *Gilda*. He played a wide range of sinister roles, one of his last in supposedly the last film noir in the American cycle, Orson Welles's *Touch of Evil* (1958).

Steven Geray, of Hungarian descent, played characters in a wide range of films for Columbia; his two most important noirs were a B film, *So Dark the Night* (1944), in which he co-starred with Nina Foch, and the A film *Gilda* as the weak wash room attendant–philosopher Uncle Pío who figures so importantly in the denouement.

Although there were a multitude of other actors in the film from Columbia's stock company of players, the only one worthy of mention is Gerald Mohr, who starred in the "Lone Wolf" series based on the radio plays and appeared in two noir films, *Gilda* and Paramount's *Detective Story* (1951).

Virginia Van Upp was one of two talented women producers in the film industry circa 1945. (The other was Joan Harrison at Universal.) A capable screenwriter in her own right, she guided the career of Rita Hayworth from the latter's starring role in the Columbia Technicolor musical co-starring Gene Kelly, *Cover Girl* (1944), into a starring role as *Gilda*. Van Upp wrote some of the sexiest *double entendre* dialogue heard on the screen in the mid–forties.

Gilda (1946): Rita Hayworth, bathed in a spotlight, sings while doing a striptease.

Two — Columbia Pictures and *Gilda* (1946)

Hungarian director Charles Vidor, no stranger to the noir style, made the pre-noir *Blind Alley* (1939) for Columbia (which was remade in 1948 as *The Dark Past*), as well as the Technicolor musical *Cover Girl* with Rita Hayworth before he decided to direct her in his best noir film, *Gilda*. Although he directed many other notable films in Hollywood, *Gilda* is probably his best remembered film.

E.A. Ellington was responsible for the original story and Jo Eisinger adapted it for the screen. (He was also responsible for the screenplay of the great Jules Dassin Fox noir *Night and the City* in 1950.) Marion Parsonnet's flip, almost cruel dialogue, complete with sexual innuendo, made *Gilda* the startling, mature hit it deserved to be.

The production was also fortunate in having Rudolph Maté as its cameraman. Of Austrian descent, Maté worked in Germany for Fritz Lang and was part of the expressionist movement that gave rise to the film noir style. You can see by his use of shadows covering Hayworth's face what a master he was of the noir style. His use of the key light as Rita sings "Put the Blame on Mame" is also extraordinary. Maté later graduated from cameraman to director, making the extraordinary *D.O.A.* (1949) in which Edmond O'Brien gives his most extraordinary performance. As a director, he made an outstanding noir for Paramount, *Union Station* (1950), but he never achieved the brilliance of his first noir as cameraman, *Gilda*.

The film owes much to its art directors Stephen Goosson and Van Nest Polglase. The former joined Columbia in the 1930s and created interesting effects based upon expressionist style and art deco, notably in *Gilda*; he designed the nightclub interior and the semi-tropical locale of Buenos Aires. He also worked on four other noirs: *Dead Reckoning, Framed, Johnny O'Clock* (all 1947) and *The Lady from Shanghai* (1948). Polglase was an art director at RKO until he was fired for alcoholism but collaborated with Goosson at Columbia, mostly on the casino and nightclub scenes. He was famous for the art deco look of those thirties Fred Astaire-Ginger Rogers musicals.

Of the important stills from the film, the most famous is Rita Hayworth spotlighted, swinging one glove high above her head as she attempts to twirl it out to the audience as she sings "Put the Blame on Mame" in the nightclub–gambling casino. She wears the beautiful strapless gown designed for her by Jean-Louis which permits her to show a lot of her right leg and her high-heeled shoe, standing on the ball of her foot as she swings her hips and continues her fully dressed "strip-tease." The members of the band sit behind her as well as the patrons of the nightclub who urge her on to complete a strip-tease.

The second still shows Macready on the left, spinning the dial of a safe that was hidden behind a painting, seen raised above the safe as Glenn Ford watches smugly and carefully. We are in the home of Ballin Mundsen, and Johnny Farrell is being told that if anything happens to the former, he is to open the safe in which the papers from the "tungsten cartel" are to be found. The cartel is another "McGuffin" like the famous "letters of transit" in the famous Michael Curtiz thriller *Casablanca* (1942). The light is coming from the lamp over the portrait but makes a thrilling, mysterious exposition into noir lighting.

Gilda is a terrific suspense thriller, shot in black and white and having spectacular nightclub scenes loaded with the ambience of Hollywood's idea of Buenos Aires and Montevideo nightlife. Gilda's story is revealed

Gilda (1946): George Macready (left) gives Glenn Ford his household safe's combination with a single noirish light source above them.

Two — Columbia Pictures and *Gilda* (1946)

in the monologues of her lover, a primary key to many noir thrillers without the use of flashbacks. But the underlying sexual repartée between Rita Hayworth, Glenn Ford and other men in Gilda's entourage testify that there a lot of talk about sex and sexual innuendo, but Gilda is not a tarnished woman. She just appears to be. But she is trapped in a convoluted plot, typical of noir films which makes for great entertainment.

Columbia Pictures made some 40 film noirs between 1946 and 1976, if you count Paul Schrader's color *Taxi Driver* (1976) which has more neo-noir qualities than the usual black and white film noir. The best five are the following:

Dead Reckoning (1947), John Cromwell, director. Cast: Humphrey Bogart, Lizabeth Scott, Morris Carnovsky, William Prince. An Air Force vet searches for his best friend and winds up in a labyrinthine nightclub milieu where sex, murders, gambling and gangsterism co-exist.

The Lady from Shanghai (1948), Orson Welles, director. Cast: Rita Hayworth, Orson Welles, Everett Sloane. A dizzying noir about the duplicity of femme fatale Rita Hayworth.

The Reckless Moment (1949), Max Ophuls, director. Cast: Joan Bennett, James Mason, Geraldine Brooks. A mother protects her daughter from a blackmailer whose accidental death she hides by sinking his body in the ocean.

In a Lonely Place (1950), Nicholas Ray director. Cast: Humphrey Bogart, Gloria Grahame, Frank Lovejoy. A screenwriter with a temper is suspected of murder and he loses his lover because of her suspicions about his criminal tendencies.

Pushover (1954), Richard Quine, director. Cast: Fred MacMurray, Kim Novak, Dorothy Malone. Almost a remake of *Double Indemnity* with a corrupt cop seduced by a femme fatale and fatally shot at conclusion.

If I were to choose a runner-up noir from Columbia, it would be *Dead Reckoning* because it has the same elements as *Gilda*—an ex–Air Force soldier falling for a femme fatale while investigating the murder of his best buddy. The metaphor of a parachute opening and descending towards earth indicates the "letting go" or death of Lizabeth Scott.

CHAPTER THREE

Eagle-Lion Studios and *Hollow Triumph* aka *The Scar* (1948)

Eagle-Lion was a small British production company owned by J. Arthur Rank. He acquired Producers Releasing Corporation, a dismally small Hollywood production company that was renamed upon purchase. PRC was one of the most respected makers of Hollywood B-movies on what was known as Hollywood's "Poverty Row." (More about PRC later.) Eagle-Lion replaced the studio in name only since the production values remained virtually the same — adequate at best. Eagle-Lion was also a film distribution company under the name of Eagle-Lion Distributors Ltd. in the United Kingdom and Eagle-Lion in the United States.

In its first year of acquisition, 1948, Eagle-Lion released several film noirs made chiefly by director Anthony Mann (*Raw Deal* and *T-Men*) along with this film directed by Steve Sekely, *Hollow Triumph* aka *The Scar*.

The titles for *Hollow Triumph* aka *The Scar* are placed on cards showing huge, billowy clouds. After we note the director's name, the camera swoops from the clouds through a window into the office of a warden in an Eastern penitentiary. We hear the warden's aide describing John Muller, a criminal who studied psychoanalysis for four years, sold non-existent stocks and bonds, participated in an unsuccessful payroll heist and was sentenced to a term of two years. The warden now interviews Muller (played against type by the aristocratic Austrian actor Paul Henreid) and tells him he has a clerical job waiting for him in Los Angeles at the Michael John Company but cautions him that "he'll be back!"

Three — Eagle-Lion Studios and *Hollow Triumph* aka *The Scar* (1948)

We watch Muller leave the prison and enter a car driven by Marcy (Herbert Rudley). A young woman is sitting in the back seat. "You'll have a lot of lost time to make up for," says Marcy. The scene suddenly switches to a hotel room the next morning where Muller's former gang buddies reunite. The majority of them have become secure in their work and hold down small jobs by which they eke out a living. But Muller has other ideas: He wants to "have the whole world by the tail. Ya gotta take chances, big chances!" His plan is to knock over Rocky Stansyzk's gambling joint for $200,000. But the plan goes awry. The heist is pulled off and a car with Marcy and Muller in it makes a clean getaway but the other robbers' car is stopped by gunfire. One of Muller's men identifies the two who got away after Stansyck punches him in the stomach. Stansyck tells his men: "Get 'em if it takes twenty years, but get 'em!" He then urges the two accomplices to just walk away but Stansyck tells his henchman "Bulls-eye" (played by a very young Jack Webb of TV *Dragnet* fame) to *not* let them get away.

On a speeding train, Marcy tells Muller that he intends to go to Mexico City with his share of the loot to escape the wrath of the gambler. Muller goes on to Los Angeles and his new job at the Michael John Co. for $35 per week. Muller becomes a 9-to-5 working-stiff, stamping invoices at this dull clerical job. Mr. Thompson rides Muller, urging him to quit if this job is "beneath him." One day, he tells Muller to deliver some books to the Medical Building. Muller reluctantly agrees but realizes he is being followed, not by the Stansyck mob but a local dentist (John Qualen) whose office is located in the same building. The dentist tells Muller that Dr. Victor Bartok, a psychologist whose office is also in the building is his (Muller's) exact double, except for a scar. Very curious about this revelation, Muller enters Bartok's office and his secretary, Evelyn Hahn (played snappily by a sexy Joan Bennett) plants a long kiss on Muller's mouth. Realizing her error, she asks, "What can I do for you?" He answers: "It's more than any man can ask!" Curious about Bartok's life and work, Muller decides to date Evelyn.

When Muller returns to work three hours late, he is admonished so severely by Mr. Thompson that he knocks the latter out and is fired from his job. Just as he is about to leave, he is told there is a message from his brother Fredrick (Eduard Franz) who is staying at the Hotel Frazier. Fred shows Muller a headline about Marcy being killed in Mexico City. Realizing that Stansyck's men must have followed him, Muller is almost caught by Bulls-eye and another mobster as he flees the hotel. There are some exciting location shots at night on a local trolley as Muller pushes one of the thugs on to the tracks. Muller retreats to his hotel room and, while staring into the mirror, we hear a voiceover: "I might be able to get away with it, becoming Bartok!"

The scene switches to a sunny day at the zoo. Muller is dating the cynical Evelyn, but suspects he is trying to put something over on her. She invites him in for coffee anyway and he asks her to look at Bartok's files. There is real chemistry in their last kiss that Sunday evening. On the following day, Muller shows up unannounced at Bartok's office and steals a check with Bartok's signature from a file room, covering up his discovery with another kiss for Evelyn. He must have also taken some tape recordings of Bartock's voice. Muller follows Bartok to the Clover Garage where he keeps his private car, and studies his movements at a concert. Muller is about to make his move and *become* Victor Bartok! He visits Evelyn, gives her an elaborate necklace of real jewels and says he is going off to Paris. Evelyn confesses that she is really in love with him and asks if they could make some kind of life together. Muller leaves and Evelyn breaks down crying alone in the kitchen.

Muller arrives at the Clover Garage, wearing a mustache and looking for a job. He becomes a night attendant, exactly the kind of job he wants. On the next day, he photographs Bartok on the street. Smoking a cigarette and looking directly into a mirror with Bartok's newly developed photo in his right hand, Muller sees that Bartok's scar is on his left cheek. After performing the necessary mutilation to his face, Muller realizes the photo shop forgot to return the negative. He hurries back there, demands the negative and abruptly leaves. Artell, the manager of the shop (Sid Tomack) tells his assistant Aubrey (Charles Arnt) that he did not have time to tell him about Aubrey's *flipping* the negative. And so, the scar should really be on the *right* side of the face!

Muller returns to the garage to his new job. The gangsters sent by Stansyck show up in a car, order some gasoline, have him check the oil and ask Muller about storing the car for the night, all these questions while Muller tries to avoid being seen by Bull's-eye. After they pull out of the garage, Muller arms himself with a heavy wrench from the garage tool box and, later that night, he kills Bartok with a blow to the head. (We hear the thump but not the actual murder, *a la* the murders in *Double Indemnity*, 1944 and *The Postman Always Rings Twice*, 1946.) As Muller drives up to

Three — Eagle-Lion Studios and *Hollow Triumph* aka *The Scar* (1948)

a siding on a bridge to dispose of the body, he realizes, holding Bartok's dead face within his hands, that the scar is on the *left* side and his surgically inflicted scar is on the *right*! Nevertheless, he must go through with the charade.

The next morning, Muller begins to pose as Dr. Bartok, consulting psychologist. From that point on, Muller passes himself off as Dr. Bartok, listening to patients, helping them with their problems. Even Evelyn does not catch on ... yet.

In Bartok's apartment, Muller reviews the doctor's bank statements, his declining income and frequent sale of stock certificates. A woman calls on his private phone and he encourages her to meet him at the Hotel Wellington and to buy herself an orchid so that he may recognize her. She turns out to be Virginia, who is probably a shill for Maxwell's, a gambling establishment. Since he doesn't know where the place is, he lets her drive his car there. Apparently Bartok was at Maxwell's two or three times a week and is a compulsive gambler!

The following day at work, Evelyn seems to be watching Bartok. He says, "I know you've been seeing somebody. You're a bitter little lady, but I'll never let you go, Evelyn." While Muller is seeing a patient, his brother enters the office. Frederick Muller shouts out, "There he is, that's my brother!" Evelyn realizes the truth, that Muller killed Bartok. Muller asks Evelyn reluctantly until he talks to his brother in his office. She tells Frederick that John Muller went off to Paris and that's all she knows. "Bartok" advises Muller to let John go; he can take care of himself. Frederick tells Bartok that the mob is no longer after him, since Rocky Stanzig is being deported for tax evasion and is no longer a threat. Meanwhile, Evelyn leaves the office, buys a ticket for a cruise to Honolulu for midnight that night and packs her bags. Muller goes back to her apartment and tries to convince Evelyn that they can now cash in on Bartok's practice and identity. He slaps her hard, but he cannot convince her to join him — and so, decides to go with Evelyn to Honolulu.

As he plans to meet her on the ship and arranges for other psychiatrists to take over his patient schedule, a cleaning lady asks the good doctor if she is mistaken, but she always thought the scar was on the left side. Muller/Bartok blesses her for her perception as he says goodnight and jumps into a waiting taxi. Meanwhile, Maxwell's "boys" follow the doctor to the pier unbeknownst to him. Evelyn waits on the deck, looking for Muller who is side-tracked by the two thugs looking for Bartok. He explains to them that he is Muller, not Bartok and the scar is on the *wrong* side of his face. Muller tries to run and shots are heard. The boat begins to sail and Evelyn walks briskly forward on the deck, lied to again by a man she really loved. Muller looks up at her but dies in the crowd of visitors. Evelyn tearfully moves forward but never sees Muller as he dies. This ending is reminiscent of the great Duvivier film *Pepe Le Moko (1938)*, with Jean Gabin dying in almost similar circumstances. Muller did not realize that Maxwell's would not let him get away from them, owing some $90,000. An ironic ending for a thief trying to escape from his new identity!

The Scar offered Austrian actor Paul Henreid his first opportunity to produce and star in a film. He played a double role *and* he played against the heroic prototype to which he was accustomed. Although Henreid was no stranger to film noir, making *Casablanca* (1942) with Humphrey Bogart and *Deception* (1946) with Bette Davis, he usually played a romantic leading man with scruples. Here as John Muller and Dr. Bartok, Henreid had the unusual opportunity to play both a gangster and a gambler, talking tough and looking very believable in the roles.

His co-star Joan Bennett is considered one of the great icons of film noir, especially due to her friendship with director Fritz Lang. Lang starred her in *Man Hunt* (1941); Lang, Joan and her husband Walter Wanger formed a three-way partnership called Diana Productions which made *Scarlet Street* (1945), *Woman in the Window* (also 1945) and *Secret Beyond the Door* (1948). Although she made *The Reckless Moment* (1949) for Max Ophuls and Columbia Pictures, her greatest success will always be considered the femme fatale she played in Lang's *Scarlet Street*.

In *The Scar,* Bennett plays Evelyn Hahn, a secretary whose cynicism about men hides her true emotions until they are tested at the conclusion, only to be reaffirmed when Muller does not appear on board the cruise ship. Her eyes seemed to glaze over as she hid her sadness over many disappointments in love. Her portrait of Evelyn Hahn is a realistic one of a victim of circumstances.

Eduard Franz, playing John Muller's brother Frederick, was an American character actor who blends into most roles, sometimes affecting a particular foreign accent. Here he serves to establish the doppelganger and corroborates Evelyn's suspicions that John murdered and has become Dr. Bartok. Franz played a variety of roles for many studios through the 1970s.

John Qualen, who played the dentist, was a very well-known character actor of the thirties and forties. Of Canadian-Norwegian origin, he usually used a Nordic accent when playing his minor roles, the most outstanding of them being John Ford's *The Grapes of Wrath* (1940) in which he played a sharecropper.

Leslie Brooks plays Virginia Taylor, the beautiful blonde who steered Muller-Bartok to a gambling joint and played a considerable role in the latter's downfall. It was probably she who phoned Maxwell's that Bartok was not coming to the casino that evening and had him followed by gangsters. No stranger to noir, Brooks had the title role as an adulteress-murderer in a Film Classics cheapie entitled *Blonde Ice* (1948) in which she gets her just deserts at the end.

Herbert Rudley plays Marcy, the cohort of Muller who tried to welch on Muller by pulling out of the robbery of the gambling joint but courageously throws in his loot with the other robbers. He is killed later on by the mobsters in Mexico City. Rudley played many B-roles throughout a long career in Hollywood.

There are many actors in *The Scar* who had minor roles but the only one who went on to career stardom was Jack Webb, who played Bulls-eye, a deadly shot who won't let Muller's men get away with robbery and who finally tracks down Muller in Los Angeles only to lose his quarry to Maxwell's mobsters. Webb had several supporting parts in Eagle-Lion films as well as for Paramount Pictures before he starred as Sergeant Joe Friday in the NBC-TV series *Dragnet* through the fifties and sixties. Briefly married to singer Julie London, Webb died rather early from cancer in 1982.

Director Steve Sekely had a Hungarian background; his style was mostly distinguished by expressionist lighting and a distinctly Germanic sensibility. He worked in Hollywood since 1938, making low-budget dramas; one of his most successful films was *The Day of the Triffids* (1963), a sci-fi epic in color. Sekely was often compared to his counterpart Edgar G. Ulmer, who was also a specialist in B-noir films for PRC Studios. He died in 1979.

Daniel Fuchs wrote the screenplay for many low-budget thrillers, including *The Gangster* (1947), *Criss Cross* (1949), *Panic in the Streets* (1950), *Storm Warning* (1950) and *The Human Jungle* (1954). He was born in Brooklyn and his screenplays contain a lot of hard-boiled dialogue and some very strong characters. It seems inconceivable he won an Academy Award in 1955 for Best Story for the noir musical *Love Me or Leave Me*

(1955) but no awards for his crime films. Steven Soderbergh thought enough of Fuchs' original screenplay *Criss Cross* to remake it in 1995 as *The Underneath*, although without too much success.

The entire style of film noir owes much to cinematographer John Alton. Besides being one of the most prolific (he photographed most of the classic noir films of the period 1946 to 1955), his style owes much to the German expressionism school. Whether he was in a studio or on location, he exploits the best contrasts between darkness and shadow and did his best work on low-budget black and white films although he was no stranger to the color camera. He was also the first cinematographer to write a book on noir style, *Painting with Light*. The films *The Scar, Raw Deal* and *T-Men* (all 1948 for Eagle-Lion) brought him to prominence. His work for MGM, United Artists and Allied Artists added luster to his career as a noir cinematographer. He died in 1996 at the age of 95.

Hollow Triumph (1948): Paul Henreid stares in the mirror, ready to cut a scar into his left cheek.

Three — Eagle-Lion Studios and *Hollow Triumph* aka *The Scar* (1948)

Sol Kaplan (1919–1990) was a prolific concert pianist and composer and composed scores for many films including *Tales of Manhattan* (1942), *Salt of the Earth* (1954), and *The Spy Who Came in from the Cold* (1965). His career was disrupted because of a run-in with the House of Un-American Activities but he worked till his death from lung cancer. He also did the score for *Niagara* (1952), the movie that made a star of Marilyn Monroe. *The Scar* has several musical themes that thread their way through the plot in a Mickey Mouse fashion which was the style of the times, but generally remains unobtrusive.

Very little is known about art directors Edward Ilou and Frank Durlauf, but one can easily recognize the appropriate style of seediness in the interiors of the hotel scenes and the obvious lacks of luxury in the gambling settings. Since a lot of exterior shooting took place, their work seems appropriate to the film made on an extremely low budget. Durlauf (1893–1984) worked on only nine Hollywood productions, mostly noir films for Eagle-Lion and Warner Bros. between 1949 and 1959. Ilou (1905–1978) worked mostly in TV of the fifties and sixties. Some noir films include *Kansas City Confidential* and *Port of New York* for United Artists, but his major output was for Eagle-Lion Films during the late forties, including *Reign of Terror, He Walked by Night* and *Raw Deal*.

The first still shows the seediness I speak of the above paragraph: Muller (Henreid), holds a razor in his left hand and contemplates how he will make the incision for the scar. The reflection of the hotel room in the mirror is even more seedy than one expects and Alton's spot lighting from the rear bring out the darkness in Henreid's concentration as he wonders if he can get away with becoming Dr Bartok's double. We never see the self-mutilation but we watch a burning cigarette placed on a cheap piece of furniture until it goes out completely — a gross and seedy act in compliance with the thoughts of the character in this almost ugly setting.

In the next still, Paul Henreid (left) grabs Joan Bennett's wrist hard as she tries to get away from him after discovering he has indeed killed Dr. Bartok and taken his place. Note the lighting from the outside through four slats of the blinds that imprisons both of them as well as the scar highlighted on the wrong cheek. In this scene, Muller, dressed in a suit and tries to convince Bennett to stay. Although her clothes by Kay Nelson are appropriate for a secretary and unruffled (note especially her fully but-

Hollow Triumph (1948): Paul Henreid (left) grabs Joan Bennett's wrist in a prison-like, darkly-lit office setting by cinematographer John Alton.

toned jacket), the look in her eyes tells us that she will have nothing to do with Muller or the murder and subsequently runs out of the office to escape his clutches.

Hollow Triumph is a terrific, fatalistic noir, where a criminal attempts to escape his past through murder and impersonation of a lookalike psychiatrist (a creative doppelgänger theme) but dies because he finally outsmarted himself and lost his chance at love. Besides Henreid and Bennett, the other real star of the film is John Alton, the photographer, who made use of authentic Los Angeles locales, filming them with the necessary "darkness" inherent in film noir style.

Eagle-Lion released only six film noirs during its short duration as a company, all very interesting:

Behind Locked Doors (1948), Oscar [Budd] Boetticher, director. Cast: Lucille Bremer, Richard Carlson, Douglas Fowley. A female reporter searches for a crooked judge on the run from the law. The trail leads to a mental hospital.

Canon City (1948), Crane Wilbur, director. Cast: Scott Brady, Jeff Corey, Whit Bissell, Stanley Clements, Charles Russell, De Forest Kelley. The semi-documentary account of escaped prisoners from a Colorado penitentiary.

Raw Deal (1948) Anthony Mann, director. Cast: Dennis O'Keefe, Claire Trevor, Marsha Hunt. A gangster seeking revenge falls in love with two women. An excellent story told in flashback with wonderful lighting by John Alton.

T-Men (1948) Anthony Mann, director. Cast: Dennis O'Keefe, Alfred Ryder, Wallace Ford, June Lockhart. Treasury agents infiltrate a counterfeiting gang with tragic consequences for law enforcers; told in semi-documentary style.

He Walked by Night (1949), Alfred Werker, director. Cast: Richard Basehart, Scott Brady, Whit Bissell. An ex–Navy radio man becomes a criminal and eludes police through L.A.'s storm drain system. Told in semi-documentary style with excellent lighting by John Alton.

If I were to choose a runner-up to *Hollow Triumph*, it would certainly be *He Walked by Night*.

CHAPTER FOUR

Metro-Goldwyn-Mayer and *The Asphalt Jungle* (1950)

MGM, the fifth oldest movie studio in the film industry, was founded on April 16, 1924, in Los Angeles, bringing together Metro, Goldwyn and Louis B. Mayer pictures. Mayer was made the vice-president of the studio and as a collective, MGM released practically one film per week.

Most of the entertainments were glossy affairs, produced by Irving Thalberg, the "boy genius" of the studio until his untimely death in 1937. They were usually "family pictures" or "musicals." After Thalberg died, many producers of films had creative control of their works from then on. Mostly star-geared and family films prevailed until the noir period (1940–1960), during which relatively few films in this style were produced in comparison to other studios—just two dozen or so.

On April 8, 2005, MGM was sold to the Sony Corporation in combination with other corporations that distribute films, theirs and others, but no longer produce them.

The Asphalt Jungle (1950) was made at the height of the film noir period and belongs to a genre of "heist" films, setting the standard for Jules Dassin's *Rififi* (1954), Phil Karlson's *Kansas City Confidential* (1952) and Stanley Kubrick's *The Killing* (1956), among other "caper" films. It is still considered a masterpiece of the cynical noir style in which crime is defined as a "left-handed form of endeavor."

On the latest DVD version of *The Asphalt Jungle*, its director John Huston explains in an introduction that W.R. Burnett's novel deals with the human relationships inside the milieu of burglars and they are viewed "from the inside out." "We all work for our vices..." The Doc's vice is

Four — Metro-Goldwyn-Mayer and *The Asphalt Jungle* (1950)

young girls; Emmerich, the lawyer's, is extravagance; Cobby the bartender's vice is liquor; Hooligan's vice is horses and Doll, the B-girl, likes men, especially the hooligans.

After the roar of the MGM lion Leo, large white letters announce the titles against a grim cobblestone street with a view towards a bridge as Miklos Rosza's musical score swells up into a variation of the "dum, dee, dum, dum" themes he used in Robert Siodmak's *The Killers* (1946) and the later television series *Dragnet*. The music punctuates the title cards, noting especially that the film is "A John Huston Production." The camera moves under the titles off the dock area to a police car cruising into the street of an unnamed mid–western big city circa. (On the poster for this film, under the main title there is the subtitle "The City Under the City" which does not appear in the film titles.)

A very tall blonde man, dressed in a hat, suit and tie, hides behind a concrete pillar as the police car follows him in this crummy neighborhood. Eluding the police car, Dix Handley (Sterling Hayden) runs into a café-bar. He pushes his gun towards the bartender, Gus (James Whitmore), and the latter hides it in his cash register just before the police enter the bar. This is a service that Gus has provided several times before. The police search Dix and decide to book him on a vagrancy charge.

At a police station, witnesses face the accused lineup of suspects. We know that Dix was involved in a stick-up, but the witness is frightened by Dix's stare and refuses to identify him. (Apparently in the old days, face-to-face confrontation was the procedure but not now.) As Dix is ushered out of the lineup, the camera moves to the office of the commissioner (John McIntire) who dresses down one of his detectives, Ditrich (Barry Kelley). The light in the commissioner's office is reflected from the window on the right, with blinds, making it appear that the precinct is sort of a "prison" for lawmen as well. He asks, "Where is Erwin Riedenschneider?" The latter is a master criminal who has just spent seven years in the state penitentiary for a robbery and successfully eluded the men Ditrich sent to follow him when he arrived at the city's main railroad station.

We are next inside a cab taking the elusive Doc Riedenschneider (played by Sam Jaffe) to Cobby's illegal gambling room. Cobby (played by Marc Lawrence) does not know him as "Doc" but when the latter calls himself the "Professor," he instantly welcomes him and invites him for a drink. Doc ogles a calendar of semi-nude girls while Cobby finishes his business with some gamblers. The lighting of the gambling room is fluorescent, very harsh and very fifties. Doc has come to offer Cobby a heist plan worth about a half million dollars. He mentions that he's heard of Emmerich, the lawyer, who has money to invest. Doc needs start-up money to execute the plan and waits for Cobby's response as he repeatedly ogles the pages of the girlie calendar (his vice). Dix shows up during this conversation and wants to make a bet. Cobby says he already owes him $2300 and Dix yells out, "Don't bone me [embarrass me] in front of other players."

Storming out, Dix returns to Gus' bar, where the latter throws out a customer for insulting him (he is a hunchback). Gus stakes Dix the $2300, the latter preferring to owe Gus and repay his debt of honor. Gus warns Dix not to pull another stick-up because the local police are on a rampage — in fact, they just knocked over the Club Regal, a clip joint where Dix's girl Doll Conovan worked. Gus then phones Louis Ciavelli (played by Anthony Caruso), who loans him $1500 to help Dix pay off his debt. Louis is the first "box man" (safecracker) and has a family, and at first refuses to help Dix. But there is complicity among thieves and all of them will soon work together.

The scene shifts to Dix's well-lighted apartment where Doll arrives with a suitcase. She looks and sounds cheap, asking to stay with him because she was locked out of her room. She then breaks down sobbing, pleading. Dix is very wary of her: "Don't ya go gettin' any ideas." One would expect Dix to live in a sleazy room, but that was not the case for the designers of MGM's interior sets. In fact, when the scene shifts to Alonzo D. "Lon" Emmerich's home, it looks like a mansion used in other black and white films of the era. Emmerich is marvelously played by veteran character actor Louis Calhern, who shares star billing with Sterling Hayden.

The big meeting takes place at Emmerich's hideaway home because who would suspect a classy lawyer of setting up a heist? Doc explains that he needs about $50,000 for start-up money to hire a "box-man," a driver and a hooligan. Emmerich wants to handle the fencing of the jewels but Doc does not like the idea. They have a revealing conversation. The lawyer asks Doc what it is like to spend seven years behind bars and Doc answers, "It's a matter of temperament." Emmerich complains he would not make a "model prisoner." Doc says that when he gets his share of the heist money, he intends to go to Mexico and chase after Mexican girls. Emmerich then

Four — Metro-Goldwyn-Mayer and *The Asphalt Jungle* (1950)

walks into another room, leaning over the couch, watching a beautiful blonde sleeping (Angela Phinlay, played by Marilyn Monroe in one of her earliest roles). She awakens, calling Emmerich "Uncle Lon." It's the old story of a younger woman-sickly wife-older man syndrome. Of course, you *know* he's sleeping with her but in 1950, censorship was at its peak and their relationship could only be barely suggested by the dialogue. It is at this point that Emmerich calls in Bob Brannom, a detective (played by Brad Dexter) to collect money owed to him by clients — about $50,000 for the start-up money to pull off the heist.

The scene shifts to early morning in Dix's apartment. The sun comes up brightly into the living room, pouring through the blinds whose slats cast horizontal bars across the far wall — another little urban prison. Doll, who slept in Dix's bedroom, heard the latter talking about Corncrackers, a black colt from Dix's dreams about his youth in Kentucky during the Depression. We realize Dix is a loser and he declares that his "luck has just gotta turn." He desperately wants to return home, "take a bath in a crick — get the city dirt off me." Doll reacts and nervously begins to empty ashtrays because she is part of the city's dirt and Dix might want to get rid of her, too.

Later that afternoon, Dix pays Cobby back the $2300 he owes, throwing a roll of cash at him as the latter apologizes. Doc realizes that Dix would be a good candidate for the hooligan they need to successfully pull off the heist. Doc also reveals that he's found out that Emmerich is broke. At this point, detective Ditrich walks in, sees Doc and hustles Cobby to the side. He tells the latter that his gambling joint is going to be raided but Cobby talks him out of it. When Ditrich leaves, Doc tells Cobby never to trust a policeman — "They're all right until they turn legit!"

Emmerich tells Brannom that he is broke and cannot raise the cash to finance the heist of Belletiers, one of the largest jewelers. But together they can pull a double-cross if Emmerich can persuade the thieves to leave the jewels with him and convince Cobby to finance the operation following Brannom's advice. Meanwhile, Doc interviews Louis the safecracker, and Cobby recommends that Gus drive and Dix be the lookout during the heist. As the plan falls into place, Doll prepares to leave Dix's apartment. Dix calls her back — but only to get her new address. She mistakenly thought he would ask her to stay on.

The scene shifts from the well-lighted rooms of Dix's apartment to the dark basement of Cobby's gambling joint, with a single bulb casting the light overhead as Doc unfolds the plans on a huge table under the light. They discuss entering the Belletiers store through a manhole where Louis can easily saw through a brick wall, cut the alarm wires, open the back door for Doc and Dix, then proceed into the store and blow open two safes to obtain a cache of jewelry worth about $200,000. Doc takes Dix aside and confides to him his distrust of Emmerich. He will get the cash from Emmerich or take off with jewels on his own. Meanwhile, Emmerich at home takes his passport and ready cash from a desk drawer. His bedridden wife calls down to him to play casino. It seems she has been "ill" for years and "Uncle Lon" has outgrown her in favor of the youthful Angela, unbeknownst to his wife.

It is the night of the big caper. The thieves enter Belletiers according to plan, avoiding one electric eye beam carefully. But when Louis blows open the second safe, all the alarms on the block go off. A guard enters the back door and is knocked unconscious by Dix; his dropped gun goes off, wounding Louis in the stomach. They all flee as wounded Louis insists that Gus take him home.

Emmerich is staring at his watch in his home, awaiting with Brannom his "guests." Everyone is surprised to meet Brannom there, and the lawyer admits he sent his detective friend out to recoup some debts owed to him, claiming he does *not* have the money after Doc asks for it. He is "embarrassed" but in two days, he will have it and suggests leaving the jewels with him for safekeeping. Doc is of the opinion that some smart cop will connect the robbery with Emmerich. At that point, Brannom pulls out his gun and threatens to kill Dix. Doc tosses the bag of jewelry towards him. Dix shoots Brannom through the forehead and is slightly winged in the side in a return shot. Emmerich admits he's broke and asks, "Why don't you kill me?" Doc suggests Emmrich can go to the insurance company for at least 25 percent of the jewels' value, thereby providing a function for the duplicitous Emmerich.

The scene shifts to Louis' tumbledown apartment. His wife Marie (played by Teresa Celli) is waiting there with Gus for the gang's doctor. She chastises Gus, calling him a "crooked back with an evil eye," the source of all of Louis' troubles with the law. Although she apologizes to him, he lies to her and says her husband was shot in a fight.

We hear police sirens as we watch Emmerich dispose of Brannom's body off a pier. The thieves meet up in the dead of night. Dix has taken

Four — Metro-Goldwyn-Mayer and *The Asphalt Jungle* (1950)

a bullet, Cobby has invested $30,000 for Emmerich which he may never recover and Gus calls Dix, telling him the cops are out and to go to a "safe house" for criminals along the waterfront. Doc tells the group that Emmerich has come through: The insurance company will pay $250,000 to recover the jewels.

While playing Casino in his wife's bedroom, Emmerich's mansion is invaded by a group of policemen investigating Brannom's killing. Emmerich is asked where he was on the night in question and says he was with Angela Phinlay at his cottage on the river from 11:30 P.M. to 3 A.M. After the police depart, he telephones his mistress, telling her exactly what to say to verify his alibi. His wife calls from their upstairs bedroom, asking to continue card-playing. He tells his wife, who does not like his consorting with criminals, that "crime is only a left-handed sort of human endeavor."

A cab driver shows up at the local precinct station, recognizing Doc's photo and saying he took him to Cobby's gambling house. Meanwhile, a cop recognizes Doc and Dix on the way to Doll's new apartment and both parties exchange blows, knocking the cop unconscious. Doc, who is bleeding from the head and helped by Dix, arrives at Doll's in need of help. Groggy from taking too many sleeping pills, she lets them in. While cleaning up the blood from his face and head, Doc reflects on "blind accident" causing things to go wrong and admits to his own greed when Emmerich promised him extra money for the jewel heist.

Back at the precinct, the commissioner reflects on Emmerich's role: "He's the worst kind of man, using the law to circumvent it." When the commissioner discovers that the cab driver took Doc to Cobby's place, the police cordon off the area, sending in detective Ditrich in to question the latter. Connecting Cobby to the robbery, Ditrich is not going to let Cobby beat the rap and slaps him around until Cobby admits the truth.

At Emmerich's cottage hideaway, the lawyer promises Angela a trip to Cuba. The police gather at his doorway with the commissioner present. He is there to arrest the lawyer for complicity in robbery and murder. Cobby has signed a confession implicating Emmerich, and Angela is advised to tell the truth about her lover's whereabouts. After he urges her to tell the truth, Angela asks, "What about my trip to Cuba ... is it still on, Uncle Lon?" He answers, "You'll have plenty of trips!" Emmerich then asks permission of the police to telephone his wife in another room. He writes a note to his wife at an ornate desk, tears it up and from the top left-hand drawer, retrieves a revolver and shoots himself off camera. We only hear the sound of a single shot and see the note blow in the wind from the revolver.

When Gus is arrested, he sees stoolie Cobby behind bars and tries to choke him to death. The scene quickly changes from the jail to Louis Chiarvelli's apartment as the cops try to enter but realize there is a group of mourners there, by Louis' open casket. When Doc and Dix read about Emmerich's suicide in the newspaper, they agree to split up. Doc offers Dix some of the diamonds but Dix has no use for them. In Doll's apartment, Dix offers Doc money for his escape to Mexico. Meanwhile, Dix is starting to bleed again from the shot Brannom fired into his side. Doc departs by night, hiring a taxi to take him to Cleveland for a big $50 tip; the driver is a fellow German from Munich. Doll buys a car for Dix, who intends to go back to Kentucky alone. She insists on coming with him. Dix does not understand how much Doll loves him and repeatedly says, "I just don't get it."

As the film winds down, we first follow Doc and the cab driver as they stop on the road at a local sweet shop. After eating well and smoking a fine cigar, Doc provides a roll of nickels to a teenage girl who just wants to jitterbug. Doc watches her bust, her hips, fascinated by the movement while two policemen peer through the window at *him*. The cab driver urges him to leave and as they depart, the two policemen trap their quarry. Uncertain at first if it is really Doc Riedenschneider since he does not have a briefcase with the diamonds, they ask to see his overcoat and feel the stolen gems sewn into the lining. When Doc asks how long they have been watching him, one of the cops answers about two to three minutes — as long as it takes to play a single phonograph record, Doc says. How ironic to be caught because of his own vice in such a few moments of time.

The scene shifts to Doll and Dix waiting for a train to pass at a railroad crossing. Dix collapses from losing so much blood. A railroad employee directs them to a local doctor. He puts an IV unit into Dix's arm and telephones the police. Overhearing the doctor, Dix runs out with Doll as the doctor says, "He won't get very far ... there's not enough blood in him to keep a chicken alive."

Before we discover Dix's fate, there is one more scene at the precinct, where the commissioner is speaking. Ditrich, the bad cop, is in jail. The commissioner turns on the sound system where operators are fielding telephone calls, so police can answer cries for help. "If there is just silence, the jungle wins ... the predators take over. We got six [criminals] out of seven. We'll get the hooligan — a man who is a killer without mercy."

Four — Metro-Goldwyn-Mayer and *The Asphalt Jungle* (1950)

In the very last scene, Dix and Doll are driving past white fences somewhere in Kentucky. Dix rambles on about the past, horses, not selling the black colt. He turns into the Hickory Wood Farm, stumbles out of the car, running towards a group of young colts, and collapses. His eyes are wide open, horses surrounding him, nuzzling him. Dix is dead and Doll runs towards the farmhouse for help. We never really meet Dix, the murderer, a killer without mercy in the film. He is for the most part portrayed as a proud Southerner, a stick-up man, a loser, but one with a heart and an appreciation for animals. The End titles and Cast of Characters come up as the camera pulls back in a long shot of Dix lying in the field, surrounded by horses and Doll running towards the farm to the resolution music of Miklos Rosza's resounding final notes of his crime score.

Most of the actors described below are no strangers to film noir; in fact, for most of them, this film may be their initiation into this style of film. Tall, blonde Sterling Hayden, who usually played action heroes in the forties, began his career in noir with *The Asphalt Jungle* playing a tough if not-too-bright hooligan originally from Kentucky with a yen for the country, horses and Doll (played by Jean Hagen). Hayden went on to be featured in noir films throughout the fifties such as *Crime Wave* and *Suddenly* (both 1954) and was excellent in Stanley Kubrick's *The Killing* (1956), where he played another tough guy, Johnny Clay, who plans to rob the proceeds from a race track. But as in *The Asphalt Jungle,* the entire caper goes awry. Hayden's acting career stretched into the 1970s when he made the first color neo-noir and last film, Robert Altman's The *Long Goodbye,* before he retired from acting.

Jean Hagen's only noir role was in this film, departing from her usual comedy roles. (Her best was yet to come in the 1952 musical *Singin' in the Rain.*) She plays against type as Doll Conovan, a nightclub floozie with a Brooklyn-esque accent, desperately in love with Sterling Hayden but unsure of how to express it.

Louis Calhern, who plays Alonzo "Lon" Emmerich, belonged to MGM's stable of stars and appeared in films from the silent era into the 1950's, appearing mostly in comedies. This was his only film noir.

The next group of character actors belong to the supporting category but are easily recognizable as noir icons.

James Whitmore as the hunchbacked bartender, Gus Minissi, appeared in only one noir film, *The Undercover Man* (1949) for Columbia

Pictures, before he signed with MGM for *Asphalt Jungle*. He also played supporting roles in two neo-noirs, *Madigan* (1968) and *The Split* (1968).

Sam Jaffe as Doc Erwin Riedenschneider, the brains behind the jewelry heist, had a long career in films but appeared in only two film noirs: *The Accused* (1948) and *Asphalt Jungle*. He is best remembered for his performance in *Gunga Din* (1939). His clipped German accent, short bow, respectful clicking of his heels and his sensuous staring at young women dancing make him particularly memorable in John Huston's film.

John McIntire as Police Commissioner Hardy made his film debut in this film and appeared in other noirs like *The Phenix City Story* (1955) but is known to most television fans as a detective from the *Naked City* series. He is the *porte-parole* for the film, justifying the police's efforts to bring criminals as well as corrupt cops to justice.

Marc Lawrence usually plays the role of Italian gangsters in the many noirs he has acted in such as *Dillinger* (1945) and *I Walk Alone* (1947). But in this film, he shows a cowardly streak and less menace than in his previous noirs.

Barry Kelley as corrupt cop Lt. Ditrich gives a wonderful performance, especially when he exacts a confession from Cobby (Marc Lawrence), slapping the latter until he breaks down crying. A tough-looking American Irishman, he played both villains and good guys alike in a series of film noirs between 1947and 1952 such as *Boomerang* (1947) and *711 Ocean Drive* (1950).

Anthony Caruso, as Louis Ciavelli, the "boxman" or safecracker, was a well-known Italian stereotyped villain, playing mainly menacing roles. Here he appears as a family man with a young child, happily married but always ready to take on a new safe-cracking enterprise.

The beautiful, luscious Marilyn Monroe, as Angela Phinlay, the mistress of Emmerich, made five forgettable films at 20th Century–Fox before John Huston discovered her "acting" ability in *Asphalt Jungle*. She later appeared in other noirs, including the Technicolor *Niagara* (1952) which brought her fame as a noir icon.

Although there are many other character actors in this film, only a very young Brad Dexter, who made his debut in this film as corrupt private detective Bob Brannom, is worthy of mention. Usually playing tough hoodlums, he reached the epitome of his noir career in *99 River Street* (1953), playing a thug who strangles the hero's wife to cast blame on the latter.

Four — Metro-Goldwyn-Mayer and *The Asphalt Jungle* (1950)

Producer Arthur Hornblow, Jr., had been a Hollywood producer since the 1920s and was usually associated with MGM. His two finest noir productions were *Gaslight* (1944) and *The Asphalt Jungle*.

Director John Huston, the son of actor Walter Huston, had a remarkable career as actor, screenwriter and director. His first directorial effort *The Maltese Falcon* (1941) established his reputation as the first noir director of the first truly noir film based on Dashiell Hammett's novel; it made a star of Humphrey Bogart as the immortal incorruptible detective Sam Spade. Other noir films he directed are *Key Largo* (1948) and the color neo-noir *Chinatown* (1974). His real life was as colorful and dynamic as any of the characters he created in his screenplays.

Screenwriter Ben Maddow worked on two other film noirs, *Framed* (1947) and *Kiss the Blood Off My Hands* (1948). Maddow's source for *Asphalt* was W.R. Burnett's novel.

Burnett was a newspaperman-novelist-screenwriter for most of his career and his gangster novels of the thirties and forties had a direct influence on the film noir style. He made his greatest impact during the 1930s with *Little Caesar* (1930), based upon the life of Al Capone. Other famous noir screenplays he co-wrote were *Beast of the City* (1932), *High Sierra* (1941), *This Gun for Hire* (1942), *Nobody Lives Forever* (1946), and *The Racket* (1951). He also wrote "noir westerns" such as *Yellow Sky* (1948) and *Colorado Territory* (1949).

Cameraman Harold Rosson worked mostly for MGM as an expert in color productions such as *The Wizard of Oz* (1939) *and On the Town* (1949) but worked in black and white on two film noirs, *Johnny Eager* (1942) and *The Asphalt Jungle* (1950). His other claim to fame was his marriage to actress Jean Harlow during the early thirties.

Hungarian Miklos Rozsa is one of the most famous and memorable film composers for the noir style, supplying noir scores for at least ten films including *Double Indemnity* (1944), *The Killers* (1946), *Brute Force* (1947), *Criss Cross* (1949), and many others. Rozsa is better remembered for his exquisite neo-romantic score *Spellbound* (1945) and his use of the theremin which was subsequently used in noir films such as *The Lost Weekend* (1945).

Cedric Gibbons was the chief art director of the film. After coming to California from New York, he worked at Edison Studios from 1915 to 1917; he insisted on using three-dimensional sets instead of painted back-

The Asphalt Jungle **(1950): Tough cop Barry Kelley throttles cowardly crook Marc Lawrence.**

drops for their films. After spending a few years with Samuel Goldwyn Pictures, Gibbons went to MGM. Gibbons is famous because of his extravagant set designs and worked almost exclusively for MGM since 1924 through the mid–fifties and on at least twenty film noirs. He won many Oscars for Art Design and Set Decoration and proved very adaptable to creating the seedy milieu of his film noirs.

MGM's film noir lighting is far brighter than other studios. The first still shows Barry Kelley as a corrupt cop beating Marc Lawrence until the latter breaks down crying and confesses he knew the whereabouts of Doc Reidenschneider. The second still captures the essence of noir: The scene is lighted from a single bulb of a lamp that swings back and forth, casting shadows on (from left to right) Doc (Jaffe), Dix (Hayden), Louis (Caruso) and Gus the bartender (James Whitmore) as they plan their jewelry heist. Source lighting from a single bulb has been done before by John Alton in a variety of his film noirs, so this type of scene is nothing new — but it

Four — Metro-Goldwyn-Mayer and *The Asphalt Jungle* (1950)

***The Asphalt Jungle* (1950): The gang (from left to right, Sam Jaffe, Sterling Hayden, Anthony Caruso and James Whitmore, standing) plans their heist in the bartender's cellar.**

does capture the intensity of the actors and perhaps the doom that awaits them as everything in their well-executed heist goes awry.

The Asphalt Jungle is still one of the best "heist film noirs" ever made and is only rivaled by Stanley Kubrick's *The Killing* (1956) and Jules Dassin's *Rififi* (1954), some critics insist that *Asphalt Jungle* is the quintessential noir heist film. It also evokes a dark universe of fatalistic desperation. *Asphalt Jungle* is an atmospheric film, strong in its details, natural and intelligent in its execution of character and plot, brilliant in its black and white photography and totally engrossing. It also has that moody noir feel and raw dialogue that represents the period. Most of the scenes are interiors, so the ambience is controlled by shadow and artificial light, a sunless world where gray and chiaroscuro blend into reality. *Asphalt Jungle* is a naturalistic film noir, with a feeling of authenticity. It is also a classic noir because of its elements of despair and alienation.

MGM produced noir films from 1932 to 1969, some thirty films if you count *Beast of the City* (1932), made well before the official noir period (1940–1958), and others released after 1958 like *Point Blank* (1967), *The Split* (1968), *Marlowe* (1969) and *The Outfit* (1974) which all belong to the neo-noir period. However, the best five of them are the following:

Johnny Eager (1942) Mervyn LeRoy director. Cast: Robert Taylor, Lana Turner, Edward Arnold, Van Heflin. A gangster makes a play for a society girl but their romance comes to a bad end. Van Heflin won the Best Supporting Oscar for playing Johnny's drunken good-hearted friend.

Act of Violence (1949) Fred Zinnemann, director. Cast: Van Heflin, Robert Ryan, Janet Leigh. An ex–POW seeks revenge against the turncoat American responsible for the deaths of many during an escape from a German concentration camp.

Border Incident (1949) Anthony Mann, director. Cast: Ricardo Montalban, George Murphy, Howard da Silva. Federal agents infiltrate a gang smuggling Mexicans into the U.S. but one meets a violent end; justice is meted out to the gang. Shot in semi-documentary style.

Cause for Alarm (1951) Tay Garnett, director. Cast: Barry Sullivan, Loretta Young, Bruce Cowling. More melodrama than noir: A sick husband plots against his wife, whom he thinks is having an affair with his young doctor. An exercise in paranoia and claustrophobia.

Party Girl (1958) Nicholas Ray, director. Cast: Cyd Charisse, Robert Taylor, Lee J. Cobb, John Ireland. In one of the few color noirs set in the twenties, crippled Taylor falls for dancer Charisse. Their romance is almost foiled by gangster–nightclub owner Cobb.

If I were to pick a runner-up noir after *Asphalt Jungle*, it would be *Cause for Alarm* because the entire film was shot in daylight. It is the darkness in the actors' moods that put this film in the noir category.

CHAPTER FIVE

Monogram Pictures and *I Wouldn't Be in Your Shoes* (1948)

Monogram Pictures, one of the Poverty Row studios, produced and released films on very low budgets between 1931 and 1953 when it became a subsidiary of Allied Artists. When the Monogram logo appeared on the screen, audiences could expect an action, adventure or noir film whose production values were minimal, since productions only took a few days to film. Although it was the launching pad for many future noir actors like Preston Foster and Robert Mitchum, it did create and nurture its own stars like Gale Storm, Frankie Darro and Belita, the British skating star. It also produced series such as Charlie Chan, Joe Palooka and the Cisco Kid. But it has obtained a huge cult following, owing mainly to director Jean Luc-Godard who dedicated his film *À Bout de Souffle* (*Breathless*) (1959) to Monogram, citing the films made by Monogram as a major influence on his work. However Monogram did not attain such celebrity until it released *Dillinger* (1945), a gangster film with Lawrence Tierney, and several film noirs, including *When Strangers Marry* (1944) with Kim Hunter and Robert Mitchum, *Decoy* (1946) with Jean Gillie, *Suspense* (1946) with Barry Sullivan and Belita, *Fall Guy* (1947) with Leo Penn, *The Guilty* (1947) with Bonita Granville and its last noir, *I Wouldn't Be in Your Shoes* (1948) with Don Castle, Elyse Knox and Regis Toomey.

After the Monogram logo appears, the title cards for this film are displayed against a background of a drawing of a hangman's rope with a pair of dancing shoes tied through the bottom of the loop, an ominous note of events to come. A river of raging water passes outside a penitentiary and the camera focuses on one man behind bars on Death Row, the star of the film Don Castle as Tom Quinn. He is known as Number Five. The camera pans left to view the other four prisoners awaiting their fate. Two guards arrive with Number Five's last meal as the latter awaits word from the governor of New York in a last attempt to stay his execution in the electric chair before midnight with only three hours left. Tom looks at his pocket watch which contains a photo of his wife Ann (played by Elyse Knox). Another convict, Number Three, tries to take his mind off the execution by playing a recording of "I'm Always Chasing Rainbows" (really Chopin) and other prisoners ask Tom to tell them how he got to this crossroads in his life. Although he never speaks to the prisoners directly, what follows is a long interior monologue with several flashbacks that explain his plight.

It is a hot summer night in Manhattan. Tom is dressed in pajamas and a robe waiting for Ann to return to their dingy hotel room. Since he cannot sleep, he begins playing the phonograph loudly as a milkman complains on an upper floor about the noise (he has to get up at 5 A.M.). Ann finally arrives from the Ortiz Dance Club where she dances with any man for tips. Their dream is to go to California and dance as a duo in "real nightclubs," not dingy joints. After a short discussion about this, they decide to take to their respective twin beds and get some sleep. Hearing some cats meowing on a fence outside their window, Tom decides to throw his shoes at them. What he did not realize was they were his new dancing shoes with taps, not the old ones his wife threw out the night before. Tom goes out looking for the shoes but comes back empty-handed. Admitting his anger and impulsive behavior to Ann, they kiss good night and get some sleep. When they awaken the next morning, Ann discovers Tom's new tap shoes outside their hotel room door.

Tom decides to look for a job as a hoofer at the local clubs. A shoeshine boy is polishing Tom's shoes when police sirens break into the peaceful neighborhood atmosphere and several detectives enter the basement of Tom's hotel. A reclusive old man was murdered last night; he was known for spending $20 bills that were "out of circulation" and was also reputed to have a fortune of $60,000 or more stashed somewhere in his cellar apartment. Inspector Clint Judd (played by Regis Toomey) discovers a clean shoe print in the mud outside the murdered man's apartment, probably of a dancer's shoe. The police make a concrete impression of the footprint.

At the Ortiz Dance Academy, Inspector Judd dances with Ann. After

Five — Monogram Pictures and *I Wouldn't Be in Your Shoes* (1948)

a fruitless day of job hunting, Tom returns to the hotel and acts very nervously, locking the door and revealing to Ann that he found a wallet full of $20 bills, nearly $2000 worth. He says he intends to turn it over to the police; Ann says they should keep the money or wait for the next several days, watching the "Lost & Found" sections of the various newspapers to see if anybody reports losing the wallet. After this period, they decide to spend some of the money for Christmas gifts and go to California in style.

Back at the police station, the manufacturer of the shoe identifies Tom as the purchaser. The scene shifts to a newsstand owned by Mrs. Finkelstein; Tom is a familiar customer for newspapers and for candies that say "Love" on them, which he habitually gives to his wife. Tom realizes he is being followed, as does Ann. Since no one has claimed the wallet, they decide to use some of the money to buy presents for each other, returning to their hotel room in the evening. The police knock at the door and want Tom to confess to the murder (the money they spent was part of the old man's fortune). Ann recognizes Clint as the man from the dance academy who gave her $5 tips. "Your shoes betrayed you," Clint says to Tom. Clint urges the other policemen to let Ann go and perhaps she will lead them to the rest of the fortune.

Outside the police station, Clint asks Ann to have a cup of coffee with him at a local diner. He admits he decided to "put the moves" on Ann but had no idea she was married. He says her husband is guilty and Ann rebuffs him. The scene changes to Death Row where Tom re-lives his trial in a surreal manner. Witness after witness corroborates his guilt and we hear the word "shoes," "shoes," "shoes" repeatedly on the soundtrack almost deafening the audience. Tom's defense lawyer tries to find evidence that would vindicate him, but the verdict is "Guilty!" On the first Tuesday after Christmas, Tom will die in the electric chair, all based on circumstantial evidence. The lovers kiss goodbye in the courtroom.

Ann blames herself for Tom's predicament and the guilty verdict because she wanted to spend the money they found in the wallet. The news dealer, Mrs. Finkelstein, gives Ann a miniature Christmas tree and Ann opens her Christmas gift — a watch inscribed "To Ann with Love from Tom." Becoming quite emotional, she decides to revisit the crime scene in the hotel basement and finds Judd there. She pleads with him to find the real murderer and, since she is lonesome, makes a deal with him to marry the detective if he can set Tom free. They kiss to seal the bargain.

The scene shifts to a diner where Ann and Judd are having coffee.

Judd thinks of a new angle. Who retrieved the shoes? Judd investigates and the manager gives him a clue about a "Mr. Kosloff" who rented the room just about the time of the murder. It seems Kosloff went to Pittsfield, New Jersey, to see his mother and was on the way into his girlfriend's house for Christmas dinner when Judd arrested him. Apparently Kosloff was and still is unemployed, but came into some money when his mother recently died. Judd's theory is that Quinn's shoes landed in Kosloff's apartment and the latter murdered Otis Wantner (we finally find out the old man's name), planted the footprint and returned the shoes to the front door of the Quinns' hotel room. However, Kosloff had an appendectomy on the 28th of July when Wantner was murdered and could not have done it. His alibi holds up. This is just another series of red herrings that Judd is using to win Ann's attention.

At the penitentiary, Tom muses to Ann in the visitor's room, "If we ever got to California, we would have killed them!" (Dancing, that is.) In a voiceover, Tom says he feels this whole thing is still like a dream. He takes a cigarette from a fellow prisoner back in his cell as we hear Chopin on the soundtrack and watch Tom surrounded by the shadows of prison bars squeezing in on him.

Ann has decided to leave town, but Judd offers her an East Side apartment which he set up for her — 7 Tracey Square on the East River. "Later, it will be our own place; we made a bargain." Ann refuses the offer as he thrusts a $20 bill into her hand, saying he's through with her. Ann runs after him and goes with him in his car, changing her mind. Meanwhile, back at the prison, a priest recites the Lord's Prayer while a fellow inmate breaks his record of Chopin, indicating his own frustration over Tom's impending death.

It is about 11:30 P.M. when Judd and Ann arrive in the apartment (they were supposed to have a drink in a club called the Green Angel) but Ann convinces Judd to go to "her" apartment instead. Ann loves the apartment. He even bought a white piano for her! He admits he loved her before he met her. He went to her hometown in Ohio, spoke to her friends, even saw her prom dress! She now recognizes that Judd is insane and is the prisoner of obsessional behavior. She confronts Judd and says, "You knew our habits and were waiting for a chance to trap [Tom] so you could be a big hero in my eyes. But you gave me that $20 bill — you killed the old man, why don't you admit it?" Just then, the chief inspector and a detective walk in. Judd pulls a gun and is shot to death. Apparently, Ann caught on

Five — Monogram Pictures and *I Wouldn't Be in Your Shoes* (1948)

to Judd's motives and called the police before leaving the dance hall and the latter alerted the governor. A phone call and Tom is saved within the last half hour before his intended execution.

The very last scene shows the young couple sitting together on a train in the coach area on their way to California, happily eating little chocolate candies that say "Love" on them provided by Mrs. Finklestein. The soundtrack closes on Chopin's music as we fade to darkness.

Don Castle was a leading man of the forties relegated to B roles. Handsome, mustachioed, slim, and masculine, he was another of the Clark Gable–John Carroll types who starred in films of the forties although his voice and personality were not as forceful as his contemporaries. Beginning his career at MGM, he was immediately typecast as a juvenile in *Love Finds Andy Hardy* (1938) and later as an action hero in minor roles in *Wake Island* (1942) but became a Monogram star in *The Guilty* and *The Invisible Wall* (both 1947) and *Who Killed Doc Robbin?* and *I Wouldn't Be in Your Shoes* (both 1948), his best film. A limited talent as an actor, he died without much publicity in 1966.

His co-star, Elyse Knox was a beautiful co-ed type also relegated to the B world for her entire career, appearing in films from the early forties into the mid–fifties with titles such as *The Girl from Avenue A, Tanks a Million, The Mummy's Tomb, Mr. Big, Joe Palooka, Black Gold, There's a Girl in My Heart,* and *The Sweetheart of Sigma Chi*. She was married to football player Tom Harmon and her son Mark is now the star of the popular television series *NCIS* (2012).

Regis Toomey (1898–1991), who plays Police Inspector Clint Judd, always played a cop or a victim in the usual B crime dramas and has had a long career on the screen since 1928 as well as on television. He is best remembered for his role as a detective in Howard Hawks' *The Big Sleep* (1946). In this film, he displays his multi-faceted qualities as a sympathetic killer.

Producer Walter Mirisch was one of three brothers who formed one of the first independent production companies when the "studio system" started to break up in the late forties. This film, one of his earliest efforts for Monogram, displays his talent for keeping a 70-minute film in black and white on a tight production schedule.

Director William Nigh (1881–1955) was a capable B artist, making few memorable films but keeping his cast on target, and he worked well with Walter Mirisch.

Screenwriter Steve Fisher was very well known for working on both A and B productions for 20th Century–Fox (*I Wake Up Screaming*, 1941) as well as Monogram Bs. He had wonderful material to work with, especially the novel of Cornell Woolrich who contributed greatly to the noir canon. Although there may be some plot inconsistencies in Woolrich's work, Fisher could clear them up and give the film a straightforward direction. Entire volumes can be written about Fisher, especially his contribution to film noirs in which he specialized with complex narratives, dream sequences, flashbacks and biting dialogue. Among his other famous noirs are *Johnny Angel* (1945) and *Roadblock* (1951) for RKO, *Dead Reckoning* (1947) for Columbia, *Lady in the Lake* (1947) for MGM and *The City That Never Sleeps* (1953) for Republic.

The same could be said for Cornell Woolrich aka William Irish (1903–1968), whose novels and short stories of mystery and suspense were ready-made for the film noir style. Universal, Paramount, RKO, United Artists and Monogram all produced films from his fictions: *Street of Chance* (1942), *When Strangers Marry* (1944), *The Chase*, *Suspense* and *Deadline at Dawn* (all 1946), *Fear in the Night* and *The Guilty* (both 1947), *Night Has a Thousand Eyes* (1948), *The Window* (1949), *Rear Window* (1954) and *Nightmare* (1956).

I Wouldn't Be in Your Shoes (1948) was competently photographed by Mack Stengler in Monogram's cheap noir settings provided by David Milton, the "Cedric Gibbons of Monogram." Whereas the former art director at MGM worked with extravagant budgets and sets of exquisite taste on a few A-films, Milton was often working singlehandedly on twenty or more productions a year. Based on the budgets Monogram allotted to him, Milton developed a spare and angular style, enhanced by inventive lighting and Stengler's camerawork to disguise the minimalism of the sets. Raymond Boltz, Jr., was the set decorator on this film.

The music score by Edward J. Kay is serviceable, relying upon the popular tune from Chopin, "I'm Always Chasing Rainbows," at moments of extreme frustration among the characters but otherwise it resembles the Mickey Mousing techniques of other low, level composers. Derivative, but competent.

The two stills I have chosen for analysis could not be more on target for noir settings. The first shows a prison guard (Ray Teal) on the left, offering solace to Don Castle the prisoner, ready to take the long walk to the electric chair as the clock ticks down to midnight. Note the darkness

Five — Monogram Pictures and *I Wouldn't Be in Your Shoes* (1948)

I Wouldn't Be in Your Shoes (1948): Don Castle (right) and Ray Teal on Death Row.

of the cell, the guard's uniform and the light mostly on Castle interrupted mostly by the bars of the cell.

The second still is of the darkened impoverished hotel room where Elyse Knox is consoling her husband Castle about the loss of his dance shoes and the good fortune he has had in finding a wallet full of money which they can use perhaps to revive their careers together and go off to California. Note the tatty bedspread and the wretched wallpaper in the darkness of the room that has little to offer but a curtained window and a poor gas stove and table on the left. *I Wouldn't Be in Your Shoes* belongs in the category of Monogram's B films but it surprises us with its competently told story and a plot that unfolds with deftness.

A low-budget thriller in the tradition of *Detour*, the film is full of ironies, accidents and absurdities. The characters have little control over their lives, a quality peculiar to film noir narratives. Also, it is the doomed man who, in his narrative of the past, initiates a series of flashbacks on the eve of his execution, creating an atmosphere of fatalism so typical of

I Wouldn't Be in Your Shoes **(1948): In their dingy hotel room, Elyse Knox tries to convince Don Castle to keep the wad of money he holds.**

noir style. In Woolrich's original tale, Tom is left on Death Row with his fate undetermined. Steve Fisher, the screenwriter, changed the ending to put the blame on Detective Judd, modeling his earlier work on the screenplay for Fox's *I Wake Up Screaming* (1941). Elyse Knox, who kisses Judd and promises to marry him if he finds the evidence to let her husband go free, calls the cops who arrive in time to kill Judd as he pulls a gun out. A very cheap ploy in a Monogram cheapie noir!

Monogram Pictures made only seven Grade B film noirs beginning in 1944 and ending in 1948 with *I Wouldn't Be in Your Shoes*. There are five that are available on DVD:

When Strangers Marry (1944) William Castle, director. Cast: Dean Jagger, Robert Mitchum, Kim Hunter. In Greenwich Village, a woman discovers she may have married a murderer.

Fear (1946) Alfred Zeisler, director. Cast: Warren William, Anne

Five — Monogram Pictures and *I Wouldn't Be in Your Shoes* (1948)

Gwynne, Peter Cookson. A student kills his professor but a detective exacts a confession from him.

Suspense (1946) Frank Tuttle, director. Cast: Belita, Barry Sullivan, Albert Dekker. Promoter Barry Sullivan falls out of love with ice skater Belita and tries to kill her by loosening a sword in a hoop. However, she avoids the hoop, the most dangerous part of her act, and survives.

Decoy (1946) Jack Bernhard, director. Cast: Jean Gillie, Edward Norris, Herbert Rudley, Robert Armstrong, Sheldon Leonard. The girlfriend of a dead gangster tries to get hands on his buried $400,000.

The Guilty (1947) John Reinhardt, director. Cast: Bonita Granville, Don Castle, Wally Cassell, Regis Toomey. Based on a Cornell Woolrich story, the convoluted plot involves the murder of a twin sister.

Runner-up: If I were to choose the second best Monogram film, it would be *Decoy* (1946).

CHAPTER SIX

Paramount Pictures and *Double Indemnity* (1944)

In 1916, Adolph Zukor merged his Famous Players Film Company with Jesse Lasky's movie company, and then took over the Paramount distribution company from which the corporation took its name. Paramount grew rapidly and soon became the largest and most successful movie company; their only competition and rival was MGM. Under Adolph Zukor's leadership, Paramount encouraged artistic creativity and individual experiments by many European expatriates in terms of cinematography, production design, etc. Though the studio made a quick and successful transition to sound, it was badly affected by the decline of audiences in the early thirties because of the Depression. When Barney Balaban took over as president of Paramount in 1936, the studio recovered strongly in the forties, the era of the beginning of the American film noir style. Because of great financial difficulties in the sixties, the conglomerate Gulf + Western assumed control of Paramount and the studio flourished. Paramount made a number of noir films and Oscar winners. Michael L. Stephens says, the Paramount noirs were "characterized by inventive pictorial values (deeply influenced by expressionism) and a ... cynical approach to its romantic themes."

There is an interesting backstory to the creation of *Double Indemnity*. James M. Cain wrote the original story in 1935 for George Raft to star. When the movie was finally made in the 1940s, Barbara Stanwyck thought the femme fatale character would ruin her career and Edward G. Robinson considered his role "supporting" rather than a "starring" one. (He had always been given top billing since *Little Caesar* (1930) and would not accept anything less.) And Billy Wilder thought he was just making a "crime film," not a "film noir," and was never consciously aware of the

Six — Paramount Pictures and *Double Indemnity* (1944)

style in which he filmed it. But the American movie public lost its innocence due to World War II and desired more adult films. Cain's *The Postman Always Rings Twice* was written in 1934 and did not emerge as a Hollywood film till 1946. But Wilder felt 1944 was the right time to bring *Double Indemnity* to the screen and revised Cain's original story with co-scenarist Raymond Chandler. Fred MacMurray, a comedian, totally changed his image by playing the role of Walter Neff. At that time, Stanwyck was the highest salaried female star in Hollywood and was risking a lot by taking this role. Robinson also decided to ease into "character" roles and took on the part of the fast-talking insurance investigator Barton Keyes as well as third billing. Wilder must have been Hitchcock-inspired, shooting many scenes in almost pitch-black between the adulteress and the fornicator (Stanwyck vs. MacMurray) and yet leaving room for a relationship between the men. When lighting his cigarette, Neff says to Keyes, "I love you, too." You really cannot decode this line or others like it as "homoerotic," just the nature of closeness between men.

It took a great leap of faith for the producers at Paramount to make this film at all ... and by today's standards, it is the best film noir of them all.

The film opens with the Paramount logo of a snow-covered peak surrounded by a semicircle of stars. We hear Miklos Rozsa's pounding score and watch a man on crutches totally in shadow approach us while the titles run past in white letters until his shadowy figure totally fills the screen and the director's name appears.

The film opens with a dark 1937 sedan wildly weaving on a Los Angeles street, going through a stop sign. Walter Neff (Fred MacMurray) finally stops in front of an office building and is greeted by a janitor–elevator operator man who takes him up to the twelfth floor and the Pacific All Risk Insurance Company where the cleaning staff is working in the middle of the night. Walter walks into his private office, painfully takes off his somewhat bloodied coat, loosens his tie (we notice a bullet hole in the jacket of his left shoulder) and begins to tell his story into a Dictaphone.

"Office Memo. July 16, 1938, to Barton Keyes re: the Dietrichson case ... it wasn't an accident or suicide ... it was murder, check. I killed Dietrichson ... I killed him for money and a woman ... I didn't get the money or the woman. Pretty, isn't it?

"It all began last May..."

The scene switches to bright daylight. In Glendale, Walter parks his car in the driveway of one of those Spanish-style houses that sold for 30,000 bucks. He rings the bell and Nettie the maid stops him at the door since Mr. Dietrichson is not at home. Walter pushes through and sees Mrs. Dietrichson come in from an outside porch where she was sun bathing (probably in the nude), just wearing a towel, a blonde "floozie" housewife. She invites Walter into the living room while she puts on some clothes. Nettie leads Walter into a darkened room with the blinds partially drawn, casting rays of light not unlike prison bars on his jacket. Walter is already a trapped man as the sun filters through the Venetian blinds; he sees photos of Mr. Dietrichson and his daughter Lola among the bric-a-brac. He admits he wasn't thinking about those insurance policy renewals, only the woman upstairs and the way she looked at him.

After several minutes, finally Mrs. Dietrichson (Phyllis) comes down the stairs adjusting the buttons on her dress, but Walter's attention is riveted on the gold anklet on her left ankle. She doesn't get the joke about the two "f's" in Neff's name like in *The Philadelphia Story* and they sit down to discuss the insurance renewals of the policies that Mr. Dietrichson has with his company. He wouldn't like to see them lapse and then remarks, "That's a honey of an anklet," as she uncrosses her legs facing him. She asks Walter if he writes policies on accident insurance. Seems Mr. Dietrichson works in oil fields and you never know when a concrete block may fall on him. Walter asks what is engraved on the anklet. "My name, Phyllis." "I have to drive it around the block a few times to see if I like it, Walter" answers. She asks Neff to come the following evening to see her husband, but Walter admits he's getting over the idea of meeting Mr. Dietrichson after seeing the missus. "Fresh!" she answers. After Walter makes a pass at her, she replies like a motorcycle cop, "There's a speed limit in this state, 45 miles an hour." "How fast was I going, officer?" "I'd say about 90," Phyllis replies. "Then why don't you get off your cycle and give me a ticket?" "Suppose I give you a warning and rap you with my stick on your knuckles," she replies. "Suppose I bust out crying and put my head on your shoulder," Walter counters. "Suppose you try putting your head on my husband's shoulder," she says. "Well, that tears it!" Great dialogue!

Walter asks Phyllis if she'll be there tomorrow night at 8:30 P.M., same chair, same perfume, same anklet. Walter drives away, saying in voiceover, "How could I know the smell of honeysuckle could smell like murder?"

Six — Paramount Pictures and *Double Indemnity* (1944)

Back at the office, Keyes, the claims manager, wants to see Walter. An Italian immigrant named Galopis (played by Fortunio Bonanova) is filing a false claim. Keyes says he has a "little man inside" (probably his "intuition") that can tell whether a claim is false or legitimate. Keyes is upset with the way the company does business. He lights a pipe with a match offered by Neff and throws Walter out of the office. "I love you, too" says Neff and in a voiceover, he repeats it, knowing Keyes has a heart as big as a house. When he reaches his own office, Walter receives a message from Phyllis to meet her Thursday afternoon instead of tomorrow evening. All Walter can think about is that anklet on her leg.

Thursday comes. He rings the bell and jovially leans against the doorway with a big smile on his face, obviously sexually attracted to her. She says her husband will renew the policy and calls for the maid to bring in some cold beer — then remembers that she gave the maid the afternoon off. Phyllis is now dressed very prettily in a print blouse and dark skirt. Walter lights a cigarette and accepts her offer of iced tea. They banter about her husband's job and its dangers and if Walter would also write an accident policy *without his knowing about it*. Walter gets up, begins to leave and says to Phyllis, "You want to knock him off, baby?" She answers, "You're rotten!" and throws him out. Walter drives off, stopping for a beer along the way, realizing how Phyllis has had him all twisted inside and he knew he was holding a hot poker — that this wasn't the end of the line for both of them. He returns to his darkened apartment, where the bell rings at 8 P.M. It's Phyllis, like the most natural thing in the world. He forgot his hat, she says.

It's raining. She takes off her coat and is wearing a white see-through angora sweater showing her brassiere. She tells Walter her husband will be late coming home tonight and wants him to be nice to her. He knows something has happened between them and urges her to go. But she brushes by him and he grabs her and they kiss. They drink bourbon. He tells her about his experiences with wives who tried to get away with murder. Phyllis brings up Lola (played by Jean Heather), Dietrichson's daughter by his first wife, who he thinks more of than her. Phyllis was his wife's nurse and married Mr. Dietrichson out of pity. He is mean to her, never lets her buy any clothes, etc. She dreams of killing her drunken husband, leaving him sitting in the garage with the car motor on and closing the doors behind her. (Ida Lupino succeeded at killing her older husband Alan Hale in the Raoul Walsh film *They Drive by Night* (1940) so she could have

George Raft.) Walter had been thinking for years how to "beat the system" or "crook the house." All he has to do is get Mr. Dietrichson to sign a $50,000 insurance policy with a double indemnity clause. While we are still in Walter's apartment with Phyllis, the camera cuts to MacMurray lying on one side of the couch, smoking a cigarette and Stanwyck on the other putting on her makeup and lipstick. Obviously, time has passed and they had a sexual encounter (off-screen). Walter says, "We're going to do it — perfect — straight down the line!"

On the next rainy evening, Walter gets Dietrichson (played by Tom Powers) to sign two copies for his auto insurance (the one underneath is the accident policy). Lola witnesses everything and argues about going out with a new boyfriend her dad doesn't like, Nino Zachette (played by Byron Barr). Meanwhile, Neff encourages Phyllis to make Mr. Dietrichson go to his Stanford reunion by train instead of driving, for a train accident is so unlikely that the insurance company will pay double — $100,000. Walter stuffs the new insurance policies into his portfolio, winks at Phyllis and goes out to his car. To his surprise, there he finds Lola. She asks for a lift. While talking to Neff, she reveals that her father does not understand her and Phyllis absolutely hates her and so she has to resort to lies to meet Nino. Nino meets Neff when Walter drops her off. Nino is a tough type who does not want anyone to know his business, especially about his romance with Lola. Walter drives off, unperturbed.

The next scene takes place in broad daylight at Jerry's Supermarket in downtown L.A. Since Walter and Phyllis cannot be seen together, she wears dark sunglasses and he slips the double indemnity policy into her bag. Phyllis tells Walter that her husband broke his leg and no longer wants to go to Stanford.

A few weeks go by and Keyes offers Walter a job as his assistant. Walter sees it as a desk job with a $50 reduction in pay. Walter then receives a phone call from Phyllis: She convinced her husband to take the 10:15 P.M. train from Glendale tomorrow night. Walter is to wear a blue serge suit and put a cast on his left leg. He will get in the back of their car before the couple leaves for the station. Phyllis is to drive down a particular dark street and honk three times on the horn while Walter breaks Mr. Dietrichson's neck.

Outside Phyllis' home, Walter gets into the garage and lies on the rear floor of the car. Her husband on crutches is helped by Phyllis into the passenger seat. As planned, Phyllis deliberately drives down a certain dark street and begins to honk the horn — the camera moves to Phyllis' expression of delight as Walter murders her husband. We never actually see the crime. Phyllis and Walter place the dead Mr. Dietrichson in the trunk of the car and drive to the station. Walter assumes the role of Mr. Dietrichson, with a cast on the right foot and wearing his hat way down over his brow. She insists that no one help her husband to Car 9, Section 11. Walter is now on the train and tells the porter he is going out to the observation car for a smoke. As he makes his way out there on crutches, there is another man smoking there, a Mr. Jackson (played by Porter Hall) from Medford, Oregon. Walter says he forgot his cigar case and asks Mr. Jackson to retrieve it from his compartment. Walter now slips off the observation car with crutches in hand. He runs toward Phyllis' car, and they both drag Dietrichson's body to the railroad tracks, placing the crutches near him. Returning to the car, they are ready to make their getaway, but the car won't start. Walter uses the choke to pump in extra fuel to the motor and the murderers are off! This was a wonderful, anxious filmic moment for the characters and the audience alike, perhaps owing to Alfred Hitchcock's influence. As they reach Walter's apartment, they exchange kisses and vows of love. As Walter starts out for the drugstore to grab something to eat, he suddenly feels that everything could go wrong and in a voiceover says, "I couldn't hear my footsteps. It was the walk of a dead man!"

The scene cuts to Walter's office and his voice dictating as he bleeds ("No visible scars — that is, until now..."). We now flash-back to a scene in Keyes' office. "Dietrichson died of a broken neck. Verdict: accidental death." Keyes' boss tells him he is suspicious of the accident because of the double indemnity clause. Mrs. Dietrichson enters the boss's office wearing a veil. The boss suspects her husband committed suicide and wants Mrs. Dietrichson to settle out of court and not expect a double indemnity payment. Phyllis acts insulted and abruptly leaves. Alone with the boss (Mr. Norton, played by Richard Gaines) and Walter, Keyes lectures them both on the knowledge of actuarial tables about suicide — a great speech by Edward G. Robinson, concluding that there could be no expectation of a man killing himself by falling off the platform of an observation car of a slow-moving train.

The scene changes to Walter's apartment. Phyllis is downstairs at a local phone booth, phoning to ask Walter if she can come up. The doorbell rings and it is Keyes, who poses this question to Walter: "Why didn't Dietrichson file a claim for the accident that caused him to be on crutches, unless he didn't know he was insured?" As Walter and Keyes discuss the impossibility of Mr. Dietrichson falling off the train, Phyllis enters the hallway and stands behind the door of Walter's apartment, which opens out into the hall. Keyes says he suspects Phyllis as he walks towards the elevator and then back to Walter for a match to light his pipe. Phyllis tugs on the doorknob, pulling the door further against the wall, hiding herself as Keyes steps into the elevator and Walter signals Phyllis to enter with a quick right hand motion. Walter tells Phyllis they have to separate and Phyllis replies, "It's pulling us apart!" They kiss.

On the next day, Lola comes to Walter's office. She tells him of her mother's death and about the nurse who had a "look in her eyes that she'll never forget." Also, Phyllis was pinning a black veil to a hat some days before her father's death "and she had that same look in her eyes!" Neff then begins to soothe Lola. Since she's not seeing Nino any more, Walter takes her to an out-of-the-way restaurant on Oliviera Street. The next evening, they take a ride to the beach where no one would see them. Back at the office, sitting outside Keyes office is Mr. Johnson, the man on the train who went back to get Mr. Dietrichson's cigar case. Keyes now guesses the solution: "Mr. Dietrichson wasn't on the train. He was killed long before and his body and crutches were placed on the railroad tracks. And now we have Mr. Jackson who would swear it was not Mr. Dietrichson on the train after seeing photos of him." Jackson looks over at Neff, who seems very familiar to him. Jackson wants his expenses paid and a train ticket back to Oregon the following morning so he can see a good "osteopath" that evening. Keyes replies: "Just don't put her on the expense account!" After Jackson leaves, Keyes confides to Walter: "They committed a murder together and it's like a trolley ride ... they can't yet get off at different stops so it's a one-way ticket to the end of the line and then to the cemetery!" Note the lighting in Keyes' office and the Venetian blinds creating bars like a prison that are cast across the back of Walter's jacket.

Walter calls Phyllis that evening and they meet the next day at Jerry's Supermarket. He tells her Keyes is going to reject her claim, and also about Lola's stories. Phyllis sees Walter is going soft and that Lola might find out the truth that he killed her father. "You planned the whole thing; I only wanted him dead," says Phyllis. She continues: "It's straight down the line for both of us."

Back at the office while Walter continues dictating: "It was the first time I thought about killing Phyllis." Cut to a flashback where Walter and

Six — Paramount Pictures and *Double Indemnity* (1944)

Lola are sitting in his car, listening to a Hollywood Bowl Concert. She reveals that Nino has been with Phyllis every night since they broke up. She suspects now that he may have killed her father, but she still loves him. After their date, Walter returns to the office and meets Keyes. "The guy finally showed — Nino Zachette! Or was it him or someone else?" Now Walter is suspicious and after hours when Keyes is gone, he goes into his private office and listens to Keyes' recordings. He hears that he is *not* a suspect and that Nino has been visiting Phyllis on a nightly basis. Walter then telephones Phyllis. "I've got to see you tonight, baby, around 11 P.M. Leave the front door unlocked and the lights off." He now sees that by getting rid of Phyllis, he can clear himself of this whole mess.

In Phyllis' house, all the lights are off as Phyllis comes downstairs holding a gun concealed by a handkerchief and places it under the pillow of a chair in which she intends to sit. You can hear the song "Tangerine" coming in through the windows from a radio down the street. Walter enters the room, goes over to a window with partially drawn blinds and pulls them shut with the cords: "I came to say goodbye, baby." He tells her that he knows about her affair with Nino and that she could work on his jealous rages to take care of Lola. Phyllis is really rotten. Neff walks away from the blinds towards Phyllis ... and she shoots him. "Try again, baby." She walks towards Walter, gun in hand, admits she's rotten to the heart but couldn't fire that second shot. She urges Walter to hold her and then realizes after he does he is going to kill her. Two shots from Phyllis gun ring out and the latter collapses dead into Walter's arms. He places her body on the couch and the light in the room captures the reflection of that "anklet."

Nino walks up the steps to Phyllis' door; Walter has already crept out of the house, hiding in the garden. He calls to Nino and gives him a nickel to call Lola: PL0386. He shouldn't believe anything that Phyllis told him about her.

We have one last voiceover as Walter sits bleeding in his office dictating his confession. Now Keyes is standing at the door listening. Apparently the janitor called him since Walter was leaking blood from the elevator to his office. Their last exchange is marvelous. "Walter, you're all washed up. I'll call for a doctor." Walter stops him. No gas chamber at San Quentin for him. He wants Keyes to give him time to get to the Mexican border. "You'll never make it to the elevator, Walter." Walter, bleeding more, heavily collapses at the entrance of the Pacific All Insurance and Risk Company. Keyes calls for an ambulance and says, "It's a police job."

> WALTER: You know why you couldn't figure this one, Keyes? Because the guy was sitting right across the desk from you.
>
> KEYES: Closer than that, Walter.
>
> WALTER: I love you, too.

Keyes lights Walter's last cigarette. End of the film.

Billy Wilder shot one last scene in the gas chamber with Fred MacMurray standing, looking out, as Edward G. Robinson supposedly watches him die, sitting in the chair. Only photos of the scene exist and Wilder thoughtfully ended the film at the office door with that wonderful interchange of dialogue. Of course, we all knew in the forties that crime didn't pay but why overemphasize it?

Barbara Stanwyck began in motion pictures in 1928, a brunette from Brooklyn until director Billy Wilder transformed her into the quintessential blonde femme fatale in *Double Indemnity* in 1944. Stanwyck played roles where her characters were the equal of her male counterparts, with a kind of sexuality that was subversive, usually tempting men into committing murder for her. After the phenomenal success with Wilder, she went on to play murderesses or victims in a series of films for Paramount and other studios. Consider *The Strange Love of Martha Ivers* (1946), where as a child she kills her grandmother, becomes an heiress and then kills her husband (Kirk Douglas) because he shared her secret. In *The File on Thelma Jordon* (1949), she manipulates a district attorney (Wendell Corey) into losing his case against her for killing her grandmother and stealing her jewels but winds up in a suicidal car crash with her first husband (Richard Rober) whose existence was unknown to the D.A. Not only playing the manipulator, Stanwyck was seen as the victim of ruthless men who she married and wanted her out of the way. Burt Lancaster wants to have a wealthy, crippled Stanwyck killed in *Sorry, Wrong Number* (1948) and Humphrey Bogart, a psychopathic artist who is falling for the younger Alexis Smith, tries to get her out of the way in *The Two Mrs. Carrolls* (1947). In her other noir films, Stanwyck's roles were more subdued. In *Witness to Murder* (1954), she watches a woman strangled to death in the apartment across the way and dutifully reports it to the police who don't believe her. George

Six — Paramount Pictures and *Double Indemnity* (1944)

Sanders plays the killer, a deranged psychiatrist who tries to do her in. Appearing in many films after these essential noirs, she made a series of television appearances in westerns and other genres, but no role could ever top her performance in *Double Indemnity*.

Although Fred MacMurray received star billing over Stanwyck, he never became a noir icon, appearing only in two other crime films. He preferred working in comedies, musicals and Disney family-fare. Originally a saxophone player, he became a contract player for Paramount Pictures. Ten years after *Double Indemnity*, he played a corrupt cop who falls for a femme fatale (Kim Novak in her first film) in Columbia Pictures' *Pushover*, but MacMurray never could duplicate his *Double Indemnity* success.

Edward G. Robinson became a star in 1930 when he played gangster Caesar Bandello in the Warner Bros. film *Little Caesar* and subsequently played characters both sides of the law, especially during the 1930s. In the forties, he easily transitioned into the noir style of film, starring in *Double Indemnity* and then working for German director Fritz Lang in two of his great films, *Woman in the Window* (1944) and *Scarlet Street* (1945), in which he played older men who falls victim to the charms of femme fatale Joan Bennett. By 1946, even though his age was beginning to show, he switched gears and played a Nazi hunter in *The Stranger* which Orson Welles directed and starred as Fritz Kindler, former head of a concentration camp. Reprising his gangster roles but in noir-styled films, Robinson starred with Humphrey Bogart in the 1948 film version of Maxwell Anderson's play *Key Largo* playing an exiled gangster returning to Florida with his drunken, worn mistress (Claire Trevor in an Academy Award–winning role). But Robinson's most interesting noir of this later period was Paramount's *The Night Has a Thousand Eyes* (1948) directed by John Farrow and based upon a Cornell Woolrich novel. Robinson starred as vaudeville clairvoyant John Triton, whose predictions always come true, including his own death. Robinson was a striking performer with a terrific machine-gun style of reading his lines and he will always be a compelling noir icon. In his very last noirs, he reverted to more character roles, such as the banker head of a family in *House of Strangers* (1949) directed by Joseph Mankiewicz, *Black Tuesday* (1954), directed by Hugo Fregonese in which he plays an escaped gangster from Death Row and director Phil Karlson's *Tight Spot* (1955) in which he plays a gangster on trial trying to kill a material witness (Ginger Rogers) accusing him of murder. Robinson's career extended well into the early seventies in neo-noir films and character roles, but he was never as interesting an actor as he was in the forties and fifties.

Producer Joseph Sistrom was one of a string of producers who worked for B.G. DeSylva, head of Paramount Pictures and assigned to *Double Indemnity*. DeSylva took credit as executive producer on most noir productions of the forties. Sistrom himself was a workhorse at Paramount and Universal Studios for thirty years and died in the early sixties after working on some thirty productions.

Billy Wilder was an Austrian émigré who moved to Hollywood in 1934 with a portfolio of films he worked on in Germany and France as writer and director. Part of the expressionist movement of the early thirties, he put this stylistic experience to good use at Paramount Pictures especially in the forties when he decided to make *Double Indemnity*. Parenthetically, the novel was based on the real case of Ruth Snyder, a convicted murderess who strangled her husband Albert with the help of her lover, Judd Gray, for his life insurance money and she died in the electric chair on January 13, 1928. Cain tried to work with Wilder on the script for the film but Wilder enlisted the aid of novelist Raymond Chandler after reading the latter's *The Big Sleep,* and gave Chandler his chance to write the dialogue which improved on the original novel. Wilder's Germanic background and sharp sense of humor added to the darkness of the noir film which he co-wrote with Chandler. Wilder parted with the detective novelist because of the latter's constant drunkenness and his inexperience in writing screenplays.

Wilder waited six years to write and direct his next true film noir with Charles Brackett, a writer-producer he always liked working. The film, *Sunset Blvd.* (1950) gave Gloria Swanson, the silent film star, her best talking part in years. The script, about a handsome but luckless screenwriter (William Holden) who becomes the lover of a former silent screen star (Swanson), is as abrasive and satirical about Hollywood and the dream factory. It is an incisive portrait of a former star who wants to return to talking pictures as Salome and turns ugly and possessive, even committing murder before the newsreel cameras finally roll to reveal her tragic paranoia. She is a star heading for an insane asylum.

Wilder's last film noir *Ace in the Hole* aka *The Big Carnival* (1951) starred Kirk Douglas as a luckless reporter who is waiting for a "big" story which will enable him to return to the New York newspaper world. Some-

Six — Paramount Pictures and *Double Indemnity* (1944)

where in the southwest, a man is trapped in a cave-in. Douglas has the drillers take a longer direction to free the man, meanwhile cashing in on the delay by sending day-by-day stories and creating a circus atmosphere until the man dies from lack of oxygen.

Douglas receives his comeuppance from the dead man's wife (Jan Sterling, playing one of the most bitter gold-diggers ever seen on the silver screen). The opportunist Douglas dies, stabbed by Sterling, bleeding to death, and the "carnival" disappears. Wilder intended to expose the tabloid press and its sensationalism and the fate of opportunistic columnists. It is the grimmest of Wilder's film noirs.

Raymond Chandler, billed as co-writer of *Double Indemnity*, was known primarily for his detective novels and the creation of Philip Marlowe, private eye of *Murder, My Sweet* (1944) and *The Big Sleep* (1946) fame. Although he and Wilder did not get along, they completed the screenplay for *Double Indemnity* and Chandler stayed on at Paramount to write the screenplay of *The Blue Dahlia* (1946), his only original work for the screen. It was commissioned by producer John Houseman and starred Alan Ladd and Veronica Lake. He also co-wrote *Strangers on a Train* (1951), based on Patricia Highsmith's wonderful novel, and authored a series of novels that were made into popular films of the forties: *The Brasher Doubloon* (1947), based upon his novel *The High Window* for 20th Century–Fox, and *Lady in the Lake* (1947) for MGM in which he reprised Philip Marlowe, played respectively by George Montgomery and Robert Montgomery. Chandler worked as a screenwriter only for the money but preferred and relied on the novel for his reputation.

John F. Seitz was *Double Indemnity*'s cinematographer and one of many who was a noir specialist. He also shot *This Gun for Hire* (1942), *Calcutta* (1947), *The Big Clock* and *The Night Has a Thousand Eyes* (1948), *Chicago Deadline* (1949), *Sunset Blvd.* (1950), and *Appointment for Danger* (1951), all for Paramount, and *Rogue Cop* (1954) for MGM. Much like John Alton, he mastered the use of light and shadow, fog, rainy land and cityscapes as well as night photography as we shall see in the stills.

Miklos Rozsa was no stranger to providing noir music scores and done so for more than ten films. An immigrant from Hungary, he came to the U.S. in 1940 and became a leading composer for noir films, romantic film and epics. He won Academy Awards for *Spellbound* (1945), *A Double Life* (1948) and *Ben-Hur* (1959) at different studios. His musical contributions to film noirs, especially his films for Universal, draw much attention: *The Killers* (1946), *Brute Force* (1947), *The Naked City* and *Secret Beyond the Door* (1948) and *Criss Cross* (1949). He also scored two for MGM's *The Bribe* (1949) and *The Asphalt Jungle* (1950). He worked well into the eighties and provided music for a film noir parody for Paramount; *Dead Men Don't Wear Plaid* (1982).

Hal Pereira and Hans Dreier provided the art and set direction for the majority of Paramount films, often collaborating till Dreier retired in 1950. Pereira's career, especially in noir films, spans from 1943 to 1958; he worked mostly in black and white with the exception of Alfred Hitchcock's, *Rear Window* (1954) *and Vertigo* (1958). Otherwise he worked in black and white for Paramount on such noir productions as *Ministry of Fear* (1944) for Fritz Lang and *Detective Story* (1951) for William Wyler.

Hans Dreier, much older than Pereira, began working in film in Germany in the silent era, especially for Fritz Lang, beginning as an architect for UFA Studios. In 1923 he emigrated to Paramount where he worked on a variety of films: Ernst Lubitsch comedies for which he designed the art deco sets and Josef von Sternberg's melodramas. With Pereira he designed sets for Paramount Pictures exclusively from 1942 to 1955. His catalogue of films include most of the famous noir style films of the forties and early fifties, from *The Glass Key* (1942) to *The Desperate Hours* (1955). Dreier's noirs had a particular "Paramount look," a glow and an opulence that noirs from other studios did not possess. Paramount could afford the set decorations that Dreier provided. He believed every film of his should contain extravagant visuals and at least one elegant, memorable shot. He won the Academy Award for *Sunset Blvd.* (1950); who could forget Gloria Swanson as silent star Norma Desmond walking down that huge winding staircase as Salome with the sound cameras rolling at last?

My first selected still from *Double Indemnity* takes place in Walter Neff's darkened apartment. There is a lamp at either end of the couch in Walter's living room. Phyllis Dietrichson sits there, wringing her hands, confiding to Walter that she cannot stand living with her husband. She wears a white see-through angora sweater, her brassiere entirely visible. Walter is sitting on a table opposite, toying with a pillow and with Phyllis. This scene takes place just before Walter admits his love for Phyllis and that they are going to kill her husband.

In another still, we have a two-shot of Phyllis lying on the couch in her living room, placed there by Walter (he has just shot her). The lighting

Six — Paramount Pictures and *Double Indemnity* (1944)

Double Indemnity (1944): Barbara Stanwyck, holding a drink, seated across from Fred MacMurray before a sexual seduction scene played off-screen.

is extremely dark. He still holds her gun in his right hand. Phyllis lies there with both slippers on and one could see the gleam of that famous anklet on her left leg in the narrow light as Walter surveys her corpse on his right knee, ready to get up somewhat shakily.

By fashioning *Double Indemnity* into a murderous melodrama with sexual innuendo, with naturalistic and hard-bitten performances, Billy Wilder created a realistic noir crime triumph, a classic of the noir cycle of visual and aural style, uniting all the elements in the aggregate that make up the style of film noir. In Silver and Ursini's latest book *Film Noir* (2012), they state, "[C]onspiracy and betrayal, love and sex, murder and the perfect crime — all are part of the plot of *Double Indemnity* — all are linchpins of film noir."

Paramount Pictures produced some 34 film noirs between 1928 and 1973, but I am going to stress the leading five made during the acknowledged critical noir period made between 1940 and 1958. They are the following:

Double Indemnity (1944): Fred MacMurray has just shot Barbara Stanwyck to death and gently placed her body on her living room couch. Note the darkness of the scene during daylight.

Fear in the Night (1947) Maxwell Shane, director. Cast: Paul Kelly, DeForest Kelley, Ann Doran. A man suspects he was hypnotized into committing murder, re-living it until he finds the real killer. A wonderful B-noir written by Cornell Woolrich, it was remade in 1956 for United Artists as *Nightmare*. Maxwell Shane again directed; it starred Edward G. Robinson and Kevin McCarthy.

The Big Clock (1948) John Farrow, director. Cast: Ray Milland, Charles Laughton, Maureen O'Sullivan, Rita Johnson. Laughton, publisher of a magazine, murders his mistress and has Ray Milland investigate the crime. Twisty plot with predictable ending.

Sunset Blvd. (1950) Billy Wilder, director. Cast: Gloria Swanson, William Holden, Nancy Olson. A screenwriter meets up with a silent film star and agrees to write a new version of *Salome* for her in the sound era. The writer becomes her lover, leading to disastrous conclusion for everyone. The story is told in flashback from the dead writer's point of view.

The Big Carnival (1951) Billy Wilder, director. Cast: Kirk Douglas, Jan Sterling, Robert Arthur. A conniving journalist contrives a plot to deter workers from saving a trapped miner to give himself newspaper exclusives. The "carnival" ends tragically for all.

Detective Story (1951) William Wyler, director. Cast: Kirk Douglas, Eleanor Parker, George Macready. A day in the life of a detective in a New York City police precinct. Searing drama with tragic ending.

If I were to choose a runner-up film to *Double Indemnity*, it would be *Sunset Blvd.* (1950).

CHAPTER SEVEN

Producers Releasing Corporation and *Detour* (1945)

PRC was known as the "skid row" of the Poverty Row studios and featured actors who were tyros or has-beens. The budgets for PRC films were terribly low, but with these restrictions came the freedom for directors who were on their way up to invent the kind of films they wanted as long as they stayed within their budget limitations. In the late forties, PRC was bought by a British corporation and renamed Eagle-Lion (see Chapter 3). Three great film noirs were made under the PRC banner: *Detour* and *Strange Illusion*, both directed by Edgar G. Ulmer in 1945, and *Railroaded* (1947), directed by Anthony Mann. Both directors rose to greater heights with their careers. They say that Ulmer shot his classic film noir on a three-day schedule for about $25,000. The graininess of its film stock and poverty of its set decoration and lighting proves this point, but it is still one of the early masterpieces of film noir because of Ulmer's ingenuity and his actors' abilities.

PRC's main product was a series of western films starring actors like Tim McCoy, Bob Steele and Buster Crabbe. There were also "jungle films" with "Crash" Corrigan and horror films with George Zucco, all with very forgettable titles. In fact, some in the Hollywood community of actors, producers and directors said its initials stood for "Pretty Rotten Crap." But some PRC films have achieved cult status such as the three film noirs cited above as well as *Apology for Murder* (1945), a virtual re-make of Billy Wilder's *Double Indemnity* (1944). It starred Ann Savage in the Phyllis Dietrichson role and Hugh Beaumont in the Walter Neff role and was directed by Sam Newfield. Another film that achieved cult status is Frank

Seven — Producers Releasing Corporation and *Detour* (1945)

Wisbar's *Strangler of the Swamp* (1946), a ghost story about an innocent man who was hanged and now is the ghostly "strangler" of the title. It was made with such care by its German director that because of its low-key lighting, use of fog machines and atmosphere of darkness, keeping the face of the murderer always in the dark, that it could almost be counted as a "horror noir." But *Detour* is the single film noir that revels in its B atmosphere and will probably be remembered as the best of its kind for PRC.

> *de*-tour *n.* an indirect way replacing part of a route (Merriam-Webster Dictionary).

The film begins with the PRC logo, white letters against a black background. A car is speeding on a two-way highway westward bound. After the director's name appears, there is darkness and a voiceover. An unshaven man (Tom Neal) is picked up by a truck driver somewhere in Southern California and says he is heading east. He is let off at the Nevada Diner run by a gruff woman (Esther Ralston) who serves him coffee. Another truck driver puts a nickel in the juke box and we hear a woman singing a jazzy version of "I Can't Believe That You're in Love with Me." The unshaven man reacts badly to the choice of song but to no avail. Then he turns to us and with a simple flashlight lighting up his eyes, while he drinks his coffee, in a voiceover (or interior monologue), the scene flashes back a few months to New York City and a nightclub called the Break o' Dawn on Riverside Drive and West 73rd Street. The narrator, a piano player named Al Roberts, is obviously in love with the singer Sue Harvey (played by Claudia Drake) as she sells the crowd the song on the recording while everybody dances to a slow foxtrot.

The club empties out about 4 A.M. and Al is playing some classical music on the piano waiting for Sue. As they leave the club, she says, "You'll have your turn at Carnegie Hall someday," and they walk on to a foggy Riverside Drive. Director Edgar G. Ulmer is fond of cutting to the next scene using wipes. On the street we cut to Al asking Sue to marry him, but she replies, "Not now," and tells him her intention to go out to California. Another wipe. They argue. The scene cuts to the next evening at the nightclub. Al plays classical music during an intermission and then goes into a boogie-woogie version of the song for which he receives a $10 tip from a patron. Al's reaction: "Money: a piece of paper crawling with germs." Sue has already left for California so Al decides to spend the $10 on a long distance call to California: Crestview 6-5723. We watch as the call goes from New York to California over a network of wires across the country. Speaking to Sue, he finds she's working as a waitress in a hash-slinging café and he tells her he'll come out to California and then they'll get married. Since Al has no real money, he decides to hitch-hike all the way.

While thumbing rides, in a voiceover, Al says that it is dangerous and "if I knew what I was getting into" on that day in Arizona when he is picked up in a Cadillac convertible by Charles Haskell, Jr., his life would be changed forever. Haskell is a portly man, intermittently taking pills (perhaps nitrate pills for a heart condition) and is heading straight to Los Angeles, Al's destination. Al notices deep scratches on the driver's right hand and Haskell says it was done by the most dangerous animal in the world — woman! Apparently he made a sexual advance and was repelled. Haskell shows Roberts a real scar above his wrist from dueling when he was a child. After taking another pill, they stop at a café where Haskell treats Al to a meal. He then reveals that the "duel" took place 15 or 16 years ago when he put the other boy's eye out and then ran away from home; he has been on the run ever since. We also discover that Haskell plays the horses and is a bookie out of Miami who lost $30,000 there.

The scene cuts to Al driving while Haskell sleeps. The camera moves towards Al's eyes reflected in the rear view mirror and we see a flash forward of Sue singing in front of three instrumentalists in shadow. The scene returns through the mirror to Al's eyes and it begins to rain. Al asks Haskell to stop so he can put up the top to the convertible. Haskell does not awaken, so Al pulls open the door on the passenger's side. Haskell falls out of the car and hits his head on a large rock. Apparently he died from a stroke and Al believes he can be identified. So he drags the body into a gully by the side of the road; as he returns to the car, a motorcycle cop pulls over, warning Al not to park partially on the highway. After he leaves, he throws Haskell's suitcase into the same gully but takes Haskell's wallet, his bankroll and his identification. When he is stopped at the California border, he shows Haskell's ID and is waved on, stopping at a motel to sleep during the day. Wearing striped pajamas (the mark of a prisoner), he dreams in flashback about Haskell's death until a knocking at the door awakens him. It's the maid wanting to clean his motel room. The slats of the blind are partially closed, creating a "prison" effect for Al and the audience.

Seven — Producers Releasing Corporation and *Detour* (1945)

Going through Haskell's wallet, he finds a letter to his father in California. Al believes Haskell to be a con man, trying to rook his old man out of some cash in a scheme to sell Bibles. Showered, shaved and dressed in Haskell's suit, Al hits the road again but this time picks up a woman, wearing a tight button-front sweater and black skirt. Al describes her as about 24, with a kind of homely beauty that made her look as if she was thrown off the crummiest of freight trains. He asks her name. "Call me Vera," she responds and then falls into a deep sleep. Awakening suddenly, she asks Al, "Where did you dump his body?" It seems Haskell picked Vera up in Shreveport, Louisiana, and he tossed her out of the car after making a sexual advance. She must have gotten another ride and passed Al in the night while he caught up with some sleep in that motel just over the border of California.

Al thinks about the situation and gives out with one of the classic existential statements about his predicament: "That's life. Whichever way you turn, fate sticks out a foot to trip you." Al realizes that Vera (played with extraordinary acidity by Ann Savage) is the mean-hearted woman who scratched Haskell and by coincidence he picked her up hitchhiking — a thousand-to-one long shot.

While on the road approaching San Bernadino, she suggests selling the car and taking 100 percent of the profit. But just before, they decide to rent an apartment in Los Angeles. She'll take the bedroom and Al will take the fold-out bed from the closet. "You know how to work it," asks Vera. "I invented it," Al says cynically. They drink, they smoke, they talk about death, and when Al mentions Vera's mean cough, she minimizes it. "That's what Camille said, the dame that died of consumption," Al says. "You don't like me," Vera says and Al replies insultingly, "I love ya..." Vera tries to come on to Al sexually but he refuses her advances because he doesn't like being a prisoner. He calls Sue when Vera goes to sleep; he hears Sue's voice on the telephone but doesn't respond.

The next day, Vera treats Al just as badly as she did the evening before. She dresses attractively and they (she) decides to sell their car. She goes through the glove compartment and just as Al is about to close the deal for $1850, she walks into the office and nixes the deal. The screen wipes to a drive-in and Vera reads a newspaper article to Al, saying that millionaire Charles Haskell, Sr., is about to die and is looking for his son. Vera is more concerned about this death watch, since it may net them 15 million dollars, but Al refuses to pretend to be Charles Haskell, Jr. Back in their

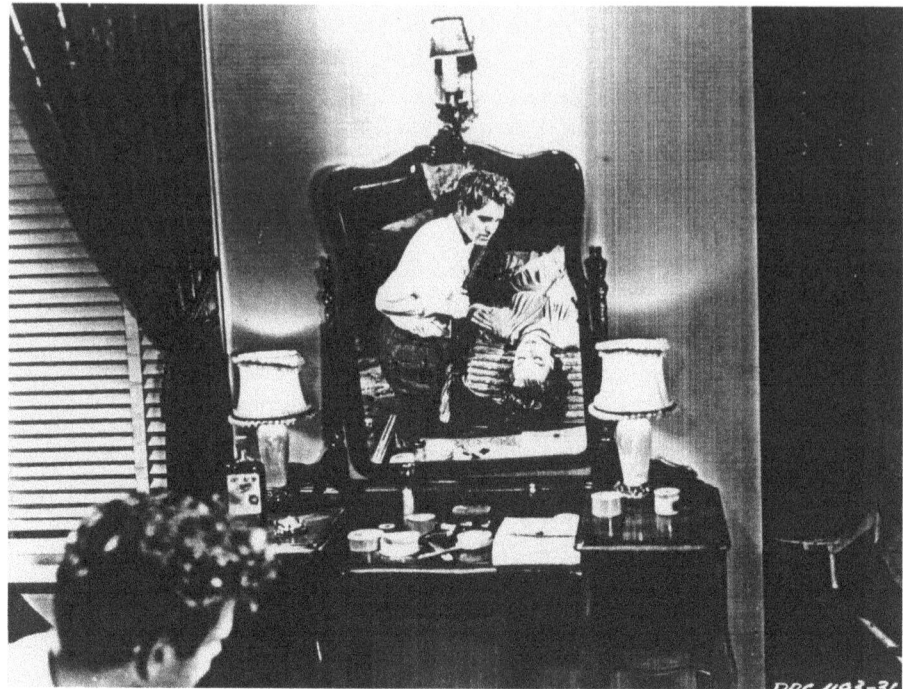

Detour **(1945): Tom Neal breaks into Vera's locked bedroom and finds that he has accidentally strangled her with the telephone cord. The strangulation scene is entirely captured in Vera's mirror with only lamplight lighting the scene.**

sleazy apartment, she drunkenly threatens to call the cops. While Al goes to open a window, Vera takes the phone with her into her bedroom and falls on to the bed with the telephone cord wrapped around her neck. From the other side of the locked bedroom door, Al vainly pulls at the cord to stop her from making a call to the police and when bursting open the bedroom door, he realizes he has accidentally strangled her. In a voiceover, he predicts he'll be convicted of her murder. The camera goes in and out of focus, expressing Al's temporary derangement. He hangs up the telephone and listens to the saxophone playing outside in another apartment. "It's not a love song but a dirge!" Al picks up his jacket and leaves the apartment.

In a voiceover back at the Nevada Diner, he concludes the police think Al Roberts is dead, believing the man he threw in the gully was Al

Seven — Producers Releasing Corporation and *Detour* (1945)

since he assumed the identity of Charles Haskell, Jr. He couldn't go for help to Sue with all those deaths hanging over his head. Al couldn't go back to L.A. for someone might recognize him as Charles Haskell, Jr., whose wife he strangled in that apartment. They would assume Haskell was the murderer. While in Bakersfield, he finds out the police are looking for Haskell, who is already a dead man. Roberts knows his life would have been completely different if Haskell had not picked him up that day in Arizona. Leaving the diner (where the voiceover and film began), he hoped Sue would find happiness and while walking down a dark road to nowhere, he thinks, "Someday a car will pick me up that I never saw before." In this case, it's the Highway Patrol. Al willingly gets into the car, guided by a patrolman. Al's last words: "Fate or some mysterious force would put the finger on me for no good reason at all." End titles as the police car whizzes off with Al.

Tom Neal was an athlete, a graduate of Harvard Law School and a very handsome man who starred mainly in B movies and played some supporting roles in A films at MGM and RKO since 1938. Besides giving support to major actors in smaller action roles, he is still best known as Al Roberts in Ulmer's classic *Detour*. Like the anti-hero of that film, Neal's life took a serious detour: He beat up actor Franchot Tone in a love quarrel over Barbara Payton who then married Tone, divorced him within two months and married Neal. Unemployable after this incident, he became a gardener and in 1965, he was jailed for shooting his third wife and spent seven years in jail for involuntary manslaughter, dying of heart failure in the early seventies. His son Tom Neal, Jr., born in 1957, is the spitting image of his father and appeared in Wade Williams' 2003 color remake of *Detour*, which had a limited release.

Ann Savage worked mostly in B movies at Poverty Row studios. Apart from her work with Tom Neal, she appeared in another film noir, *Apology for Murder* (1945), a rip-off of Billy Wilder's 1944 classic *Double Indemnity*. A talented actress, but not as pretty as Barbara Stanwyck, Savage excelled in playing bitchy femmes fatales. She could still be seen in supporting roles as late as 2007.

Blonde and beautiful Claudia Drake worked in supporting roles at minor studios throughout the forties and fifties and finished her career on television. *Detour* was the only film noir in which she starred. Edmund MacDonald. also worked in supporting roles throughout the thirties and forties as a character actor and mostly in B films. *They Made Me a Killer* (1946) and *Shoot to Kill* (1947) were the only other crime films in which he appeared.

Leon Fromkess and Martin Mooney, producers at PRC, hired Ulmer to direct *Detour* which was supposedly made in two days on a sparse budget of $20,000, but giving Ulmer the chance to direct freely and without interference. Ulmer had a previous reputation before coming to Poverty Row and made films since the early thirties, beginning with Robert Siodmak in 1930 with *People on Sunday* and ending his career at studios like Allied Artists with *Murder Is My Beat* (1955), his only other film noir. Because of difficulties with studio executives, he was blackballed by major studios until arriving at PRC. But because of his German expressionist background and misanthropic noir themes, Ulmer's film gained a cult following. Also for PRC, he made another 1945 noir called *Strange Illusion* with James Lydon, Regis Toomey and Warren William which owed more to William Shakespeare's *Hamlet* than to any other source. It's worth seeing as an interesting experiment in noir stylistics.

Screenwriter Martin Goldsmith produced this original story and was known for his other noirs such as Columbia's *Blindspot* (1947), Universal's *Shakedown* (1950) and RKO's *The Narrow Margin* (1952). All his screenplays had a great amount of tension, action and well-conceived plots and dialogue that made them exciting film fare.

Benjamin H. Kline the photographer worked on over 300 films since the 1920s up through the 1970s when he shot television films. He was very well known in the motion picture industry and understood the wishes of noir-expressionist directors such as Ulmer and also photographed his *Strange Illusion.*

Leo Erdody was music director for PRC. He liked to be known by his last name. His scores were most appropriate for Ulmer and the film noirs he directed. He also delighted in using source music, like the song "I Can't Believe That You're in Love with Me" in *Detour.*

Edward C. Jewell and Glenn P. Thompson were the art and set directors for *Detour*. The former specialized in the shadowy art direction required for noir films like the Ulmer canon and others like *Repeat Performance* (1947). Thompson decorated the sets for noir films appropriately as well as specialized in "horror noir" like PRC's *Strangler of the Swamp* (1946). Both directors got their early experience in Poverty Row studios and went on to more lucrative careers and other studios and in television in the fifties.

In the first still, it is 4 or 5 A.M. as Sue and Al leave the Break o' Dawn nightclub. Note the club's cheaply painted sign, not even in lights. On to the right are two covered garbage cans placed on the sidewalk, indicating city life. Al lights up a cigarette as Sue seriously looks at him, intending to reveal the news that she is going off to California to try her luck at a Hollywood career.

In the second still, Al Roberts is seated on a couch with Ann Savage, who wears a bathrobe; she is trying to seduce him, but Al is unresponsive. She changes into a negligee and grabs the telephone, already a bit drunk.

Al portrays himself as a total loner, tripped up by fate. In fact, fatalism is the key noir theme of this film. Al is a morally bankrupt person, one of the weakest cynics of all film noirs, perhaps deserving of his fate. It is still amazing that for all of its 69 minutes, this film noir packs a hell of a wallop as the embodiment of the guilty soul of film noir. Critic Spencer Selby makes an interesting point: "[As] the film ends, Roberts imagines his eventual capture by the police ... and that fear has been the source of his ongoing fate." Selby also suggests that it is Al's pessimism that brought him to his doom. Perhaps the "detour" is really the road Al wanted to travel to get away from a claustrophobic life with Sue and an equally menacing one with Vera. As Silver and Ursini say in their book *Film Noir* (2012), Al's world "is a fatalistic nightmare world, filled with odd synchronicities, unexplained and chance encounters, creating a chain of events that ultimately drags its unlucky protagonists to their foreshadowed end" in an atmosphere of the absurd. Ulmer is a noir director who utilized that same sense of the absurd in his classic *Detour*. And there is no other film that compares to its fatalistic nightmare story in the film noir canon of American noir cinema.

According to Silver & Ursini's *Film Noir*, Third Edition, PRC produced and released only three film noirs, the others being *Strange Illusion* (1945) and *Railroaded* (1947).

Strange Illusion (1945) Edgar G. Ulmer, director. Cast: James Lydon, Warren William, Sally Eilers, Regis Toomey. A lecherous cad wants to marry beautiful widow but is foiled by her teenage son. The plot resembles *Hamlet*.

Detour (1945): Tom Neal lights a cigarette on a foggy morning as girlfriend Claudia Drake watches him under the canopy of the Break o' Dawn Night Club on Riverside Drive.

Seven — Producers Releasing Corporation and *Detour* (1945)

***Detour* (1945):** Tom Neal is seated on a couch as Ann Savage puts the moves on him, but he will have none of it.

Railroaded (1947) Anthony Mann, director. Cast: John Ireland, Sheila Ryan, Hugh Beaumont. An eccentric gangster who perfumes his bullets uses a beauty shop as a front for gambling activities and leaves many corpses until a brother-and-sister team track him down.

If I had to pick a runner-up to *Detour,* it would be *Strange Illusion.*

CHAPTER EIGHT

Republic Pictures and *House by the River* (1950)

Republic Pictures was founded in 1935 by a former tobacco executive, Herbert J. Yates. It was considered one of the best of the Poverty Row studios. It was the result of a union of five smaller studios that were heavily in debt to Yates' Consolidated Film Laboratories. They were Monogram Pictures, which had a national distribution system; Liberty Films, from which Republic took its original "Liberty Bell" logo; Chesterfield Pictures, Invincible Pictures and Mascot Pictures. The latter had been making serials and westerns since the mid–twenties and owned a first-class studio, the Keystone lot in Studio City. Thus, Republic began to function with a complete production staff, distribution system and studio. Republic mainly produced westerns and serials. The westerns usually starred Roy Rogers or Gene Autry. Yates also made many features that starred Vera Hruba Ralston, a former Czech ice-skating star who became the second Mrs. Yates in 1949. During those years, Republic produced some A features like Lewis Milestone's *The Red Pony* (1949), John Ford's *The Quiet Man* (1952) and Nicholas Ray's *Johnny Guitar* (1954). Yates was lucky enough to hire Orson Welles in 1948 for his production of *Macbeth* and Fritz Lang in 1950 to make *House by the River*, both films in black and white which allowed the directors the freedom to make extremely personal films without studio interference. Republic made several film noirs, among them W. Lee Wilder's *The Pretender* (1947), Frank Borzage's *Moonrise* (1948), and John H. Auer's *The City That Never Sleeps* (1953) and *Hell's Half-Acre* (1954). Republic was shut down in 1958 and its library of films was sold to National Television Associates (NTA).

House by the River is one of Lang's truly personal films. *Cahiers du cinéma* declared, "Lang's main erotic obsession is displayed more clearly

Eight — Republic Pictures and *House by the River* (1950)

than in any other of his films." The Republic logo, an American eagle, precedes all the main titles in white letters against the background of swirling water, a dark river on whose banks sit a series of 1890s style mansions. Stephen Byrne (played by Louis Hayward), a moderately successful novelist, is first seen dressed in a smoking jacket at a table in his outdoor gazebo while writing his latest novel, *The River*. His neighbor, Mrs. Ambrose, gazes into the water and watches garbage and dead animals float by and complains to Stephen that something should be done to clean the river. Maidservant Emily Gaunt (played by the beautiful blonde Dorothy Patrick) brings out Stephen's mail — another manuscript has been rejected by a New York publisher. Stephen writes like an author with a troubled mind. The maid asks if she could use the upstairs bathtub since the downstairs one is not working and the plumber has not yet come. Stephen gives her permission to do so.

The camera cuts to Emily as she stands nude gazing into a steamed-up mirror. We watch the swirling water empty in the bathtub, almost anticipating the swirling water in Alfred Hitchcock's 1960 thriller *Psycho*. Emily dresses in a robe and comes down the staircase in this very dark house where the only source of light is a lit candle. Stephen is waiting for her after drinking a shot of whiskey. As Emily walks down the stairs wearing his wife's peignoir, the camera concentrates on her nude legs, quite an erotic show. Stephen does not let her by on the bottom landing. He kisses her on the mouth, but Emily is frightened and screams. A neighbor hears her scream but does not give it any attention. Stephen stifles Emily's screams and accidentally chokes her to death. There is a knock at the door. It is Stephen's brother John (played by Lee Bowman); Stephen tells him that Emily's death was an accident: "She fell down the stairs. They'll blame me!" But John sees Emily was strangled and that it is murder! Stephen pleads with John to help him dispose of the body before his wife Marjorie (played by Jane Wyatt) returns. John refuses but Stephen asks him to do it for the sake of his marriage and Marjorie, who is going to have a baby. Stephen helps John stuff the girl in a burlap sack and carry it out the front door only to be interrupted by Mrs. Ambrose. John hides in the bushes with the sack. After Stephen finishes his conversation with the busy-body neighbor, they proceed to their private dock. John ties an anchor to the burlap bag and they row out on to the river. As they lower the body into the water, a fish jumps out, but only Stephen sees it.

The camera cuts back to the staircase and Stephen thinks, somewhat deranged, "It's Emily coming down," but its Marjorie's legs he sees. Lang's fetish for nude legs and Stephen's guilt-stricken face almost give the show away. But Stephen realizes in time it is his wife, and she demurely asks if Emily is about to help her dress for tonight's party at the home of Mrs. Ambrose.

The camera cuts to the party scene. It is square dance. Stephen is the life of the party, while brother John looks sad and subdued. John does not dance much because of a game leg, doesn't want to drink the punch that Stephen offers him and tells Marjorie that "he's a wet blanket." (Some of the colloquialism seem too modern for a Victorian era film.) The party is Stephen's alibi — he's protecting himself and his brother. The housekeeper complains that Emily is not home yet. Marjorie sees that none of her dresses are missing. On the next day, the local newspaper reports "the disappearance of a human being." Emily Gaunt had a bad reputation, always gallivanting around. Stephen calls Emily a thief and a trollop and after further investigation, Marjorie says a hat, dress and a pair of opal earrings (a birthday gift from Stephen) are all missing. His wife also notices that Stephen looks "odd" whenever Emily's name is mentioned. Stephen's photo appears in the local newspaper, Marjorie discovers, taken out of their own family scrapbook. Suddenly Stephen is a celebrity. *Night Laughter*, his last novel, becomes a local bestseller and Stephen is seen at a book signing. Asked about his new novel *The River*, Stephen says he writes from his own experiences. Emily's disappearance provided Stephen with the opportunity for some publicity. But Stephen is still jealous of his brother John. "He's just a bookkeeper, not an artist," he proudly tells the public.

At John's house, his maid asks him about the "wood sack" that is still missing, with John's name stenciled on it with India ink. John realizes he has become involved in murder by using the very burlap sack he loaned to him. Another day passes and Stephen spots the "burlap sack" in question floating by his house on the river. Mrs. Ambrose also sees it and its sight frightens Stephen so that he takes out his boat out to try to overtake the elusive sack and the body hidden in it. John arrives at Stephen's home and finds Marjorie alone. She confesses she does not know Stephen's whereabouts, that he is probably boating on the river. She treats John as a good friend and complains to him about her marriage and Stephen's "freak success" since Emily's disappearance. John had previously given up some of

Eight — Republic Pictures and *House by the River* (1950)

his inheritance for Stephen and now asks Marjorie if she is going to have a baby. "Not true," she replies. He must have misunderstood Stephen, he responds. Stephen lied to him to save himself!

Stephen rows frantically along the river. Night has fallen and he cannot find the burlap sack. John returns to his home and argues with his maidservant about the sack. She is not appreciated by John and so she decides to leave his employ. Stephen spots the sack and tries to grab it with a stick from the shore. He succeeds in opening the top of the sack and sees Emily's long blonde hair floating on the water, a scene very reminiscent of Shelley Winters' underwater scene in Charles Laughton's *The Night of the Hunter* (1955), where her long, blonde hair waves with the current. Then Stephen sees the white fish jumping again near the sack, perhaps a reminder of his guilt. The sack floats on by and Stephen cannot grab it.

Stephen tells John of his experience on the river and John thinks they'll trace Emily's murder to him because his name is stenciled on the sack. A policeman calls at Stephen's house and shows him a dry, folded burlap sack. Stephen says it was stolen from his cellar four weeks ago. Of course there will be an inquest into Emily's death.

At the inquest, Marjorie testifies that after Emily went missing, she noticed a hat, dress, some lingerie and her opal earrings were missing. John's maidservant testifies that it was John's burlap sack and tries to pin Emily's murder on him because he fired her. Stephen is asked by the prosecutor if he had known Emily "intimately" and he replies in the negative. Mrs. Ambroses' unsolicited testimony breaks open the case regarding John and suspicion that he murdered the girl because his maid was jealous of her and secretly in love with her employer. The verdict: "Emily took a secret trip and was murdered by an unknown assailant." After the inquest, Stephen is called back by the prosecutor and tells him that he is fully convinced his brother is innocent.

Returning to their mansion, Stephen seems irritable. Marjorie tells him that she keeps running into a detective everywhere she goes. But now Stephen starts to blame John for her murder: "It's not hard to blame him, after all he is a cripple and he probably forced himself on a servant girl." Marjorie accuses Stephen of having a "filthy mind" but Stephen goes on: "Cheap perfume and a scantily dressed woman can be exciting!"

"You swine," she answers.

Marjorie goes to visit John and realizes he is protecting his brother.

"The townspeople are vicious," she says. Since people are closing their accounts with him and her own support of John can cause gossip, he sees Marjorie home. Clearly, John is in love with Marjorie. In a conversation with Stephen, Marjorie suggests that the latter look after his brother because his anxiety may cause him to commit suicide. Stephen agrees and pretends to leave the house, but instead goes to his desk and opens a secret compartment where he hid the opal earrings, supposedly stolen by Emily. The director uses many long shots of Stephen walking down shadowy, windy hallways with curtains blowing everywhere. He goes directly to John's house, enters through a window and plants the opal earrings in the bottom of John's hall clock. Then he sees John at the end of the pier. Stephen has become more courageous after committing a murder. The event has turned him into a "real writer." The brothers face each other and John admits his love for Marjorie and says he is going to the police. Stephen grabs a chain off the dock and knocks John out with it from behind, then pushes his body off the pier into the river. Meanwhile, Marjorie is at their home reading Stephen's new manuscript, *The River*. She realizes Stephen is a murderer. Furious at her for reading his work, Stephen tries to choke her to death. But we hear the footsteps of a lame man coming up the staircase. It is John or perhaps the "ghost of John," Stephen thinks. Stephen flees down the dark hallway out of Marjorie's room, becomes entangled in the curtains caught by the wind and falls over the banister to his death. The title of his newest work that Marjorie was reading is *Murder on the River*.

Although *House by the River* is a unique Lang film set in the Victorian era, its characters are extremely modern and speak in common English. There is no memorable dialogue and the themes of adultery and marital and family betrayal are very familiar. The look of the film is very noir with its slow, dreamy sequences and heavy shadows, haunting long shots and ethereal music. The stars are all very good in their roles, especially Louis Hayward as the mad author. Lee Bowman seems rather weak in his supporting role. Jane Wyatt looks too good and innocent to understand her husband's carousing and weakness for loose women and cheap perfume. His nightly jaunts out on the town for sex and drink should have disturbed her earlier on. It is only Louis Hayward who makes the film come alive, trying to be an adulterer, sweating, artistically talented as a writer and always in a panic that he might be discovered as the murderer. Lang's

Eight — Republic Pictures and *House by the River* (1950)

obsession for nude legs and long billowing hair even photographed in this expressionist style of noir make it a personal film, but not one of his best. As a Republic Picture, it was a very unusual artistic production for its studio and its time.

Hayward, of South African descent, was mostly known for his heroic roles in costume dramas like *The Man in the Iron Mask* (1939), *The Black Arrow* (1948), and *Captain Pirate* (1952). He also appeared in several film noirs, like Edgar G. Ulmer's *The Strange Woman* (1946) and *Ruthless* (1948). But his most noirish role was as Stephen Byrne, the demented writer in Lang's film where he accidentally chokes the scantily dressed blonde maid to death in an orgasmic moment as the upstairs bathtub empties with a gurgling sound. Hayward was especially good at playing mentally crippled souls in contrast to his brother John (Lee Bowman) who was crippled physically (a game leg).

Bowman was an mustachioed actor of the thirties and forties who had a minor career in films and enjoyed brief successes at Columbia Pictures, especially playing the guy who doesn't get the girl in Rita Hayworth Technicolor musicals like *Cover Girl* (1944) and *Tonight and Every Night* (1945). His best dramatic role was as singer Lillian Roth's husband in the almost-noir biography *Smash-up, the Story of a Woman* (1947) which starred Susan Hayward, directed by Stuart Heisler.

Jane Wyatt is best known for her television roles, especially as the mother Margaret Anderson in the ABC series *Father Knows Best* (1954–1960). She appeared in some early film noirs such as Elia Kazan's *Boomerang* (1947) and Andre de Toth's *Pitfall* (1948), as the wife of a Connecticut lawyer (Dana Andrews) in the first and the supportive wife of errant husband Dick Powell in the second. It was rare for her to step out of her "wifely" roles although she was a leading lady for nearly forty years in film and television.

Blonde Dorothy Patrick was mainly a supporting actress in mostly low-budget films from the early forties through the nineties. She appeared in noirs such as *Follow Me Quietly* (1949), *711 Ocean Drive* (1950) and *Violent Saturday* (1955). In *The View from Pompey's Head* (1955), a romantic drama, she competed with Dana Wynter for the affections of Richard Egan.

Screenwriter Mel Dinelli worked on many film noirs for various studios, especially RKO. He adapted various novels into screenplays beginning with *The Spiral Staircase* (1945), his best noir which starred Dorothy McGuire stalked by a serial killer of women with "imperfections." He also wrote the screenplays for *The Window* and *The Reckless Moment* (1949), *Cause for Alarm* (1951), *Beware, My Lovely* (1952) and *Jeopardy* (1953).

Edward Cronjager worked some forty years in the film industry, photographing mostly in color. His first color noir was Hal B. Wallis' Paramount production *Desert Fury* (1947) starring John Hodiak as a gangster competing with Burt Lancaster, the local sheriff, for the attentions of femme fatale Lizabeth Scott. Noir was not his specialty and it shows up particularly in this Lang film of "Victorian" noir, where the sets are lit too brightly and not enough menace is brought into the atmosphere of the film, except for those "Lang" touches of the rolling dark river scenes, the murder and the conclusion with the death of Hayward, caught in a long hallway of swirling drapes in which he is trapped, hanged and thrown over a staircase to his death. Cronjager ended his career photographing for television although he was a seven-time nominee for the Oscar for cinematography.

The music score by George Antheil was perhaps one of the best elements in Lang's film. Antheil lived in Paris during the era of Surrealism and his scores had a modernist, atonal touch. He only worked on three film noirs, *House by the River*, *Knock on Any Door* (1949) and *The Sniper* (1952), films about dangerous men who wind up dead at the conclusion. Although he was a concert pianist by profession, he worked on film scores from 1937 through 1959, the year of his death.

Art director Boris Leven worked on several noirs including *Criss Cross* (1949), *Quicksand* and *Woman on the Run* (1950) and Joseph Losey's *The Prowler* (1951). His film noirs possessed an elegant art deco style as well as the dark style of expressionism. His earliest work was for Josef von Sternberg, *The Shanghai Gesture* (1941), and his last noir was the Joan Crawford "woman in distress" starrer *Sudden Fear* (1952) in which Jack Palance made his debut as her menacing actor-husband who succumbs to that "bad girl of film noir," Gloria Grahame.

The first still is the most noirish scene in the film, lit by candle from above the stairs. Stephen (Louis Hayward) in smoking jacket in a semi-drunken state has just strangled Emily. This is a key still in the Langian portraits of "accidental" murder, darkly lit and showing great emotion on Stephen's sweaty brow.

Eight — Republic Pictures and *House by the River* (1950)

Strangler Louis Hayward holds the dead body of maid Dorothy Patrick in *House by the River* (1950).

The second noir still was taken near the conclusion of the film. Marjorie (Jane Wyatt) has been hurled to the floor by Stephen, who blocks the door after she told him she had read his manuscript. Note the attempt at Victorian settings: flowery wallpaper, a breakfront full of odds and ends on the left and the room lit by lamplight to the right with a comfortable easy chair with Queen Anne legs to the far right.

House by the River is one of Lang's darkest, bleakest noirs. Made as a B film, it is an unsettling work because it presents a "dirty" world, symbolized by the garbage thrown into the river that is the repository for hidden crimes. The protagonists move in a claustrophobic society, with trashy values. After all, they read lurid crime stories written by one of their own elite members, but do not realize that Stephen's new novel *The River* contains autobiographical details of his deceptions, his lurid (be it accidental) murder and his unsatisfied eroticism and frustrations, both with women and his career as an author, two very important noir qualities that elevate this film.

House by the River (1950): Louis Hayward stands against the door after knocking down Jane Wyatt, who discovered that he was a murderer.

Eight — Republic Pictures and *House by the River* (1950)

Republic was not a studio that made many noir thrillers; in fact, it only produced four in its entire history. They were *House by the River, The Pretender* (1947), *Moonrise* (1949), and *City That Never Sleeps* (1953). *House* was most atmospheric and suspenseful because of its noir style, but becomes more melodrama than noir unlike its predecessor *The Spiral Staircase*, a superior gothic Victorian noir also written by Dinelli and directed by Robert Siodmak.

Here are more details about Republic's other three noirs:

The Pretender (1947) W. Lee Wilder, director. Cast: Albert Dekker, Catherine Craig, Charles Drake. A middle-aged embezzler hopes to marry an heiress and cover up his crime of having her fiancé killed as well as his mismanagement of her estate. Wonderful lighting by John Alton.

Moonrise (1949) Frank Borzage, director. Cast: Dane Clark, Gail Russell, Ethel Barrymore. A somber story of a young man's memories of his murderous father and of childhood fears that drive him to violence. It is set in a swampy setting where he finds love and justice.

City That Never Sleeps (1953) John H. Auer, director. Cast: Gig Young, Mala Powers, William Talman, Edward Arnold. A semi-documentary police procedural set in Chicago, telling a love story about a cop and a stripper.

If I had to pick a runner-up film, it would be *City That Never Sleeps*.

CHAPTER NINE

RKO Radio Pictures and *Out of the Past* (1947)

Driven by the success of Warner Bros.' talkie *The Jazz Singer* (1927), David Sarnoff, general manager of RCA, approached multi-millionaire Joseph Kennedy about purchasing the Keith-Albee-Orpheum (KAO) circuit of theaters. By 1929–30, after various stock transactions, RKO Radio Pictures became a studio in its own right, headed by William LeBaron, first producing musicals and then later quality A productions under the ageis of Pandro S. Berman. The Fred Astaire-Ginger Rogers musicals of the thirties gave the studio financial stability. By the time Berman left for MGM in the early forties, the studio underwent a change of heads and producers. The hiring of Val Lewton to head up his own production unit which led the way for filming many film noirs by other directors.

Although Lewton was a specialist in "horror noir," his B productions were always a delight to watch, especially *Cat People* (1942) and *I Walked with a Zombie* (1943). Lewton was responsible for bringing a whole group of artists (d.p. Nicholas Musuraca, lighting man John Alton, directors Robert Wise, Mark Robson, Robert Rosson, Edward Dmytryk and Jacques Tourneur to the RKO lot.

In my earlier book *Noir, Now & Then* (2001), I theorized that film noir was a style, *not* a genre, and that RKO was the principal studio that began making noir-styled pictures in the early forties with Boris Ingster's original *Stranger on the Third Floor* (1940); Orson Welles' monumental *Citizen Kane* (1941), which contained many noir elements in its lighting and photography by Gregg Toland; Alfred Hitchcock's *Suspicion* (1941); Welles' *Journey into Fear* (1943); Jacques Tourneur's *Experiment Perilous* (1944); Fritz Lang's *Woman in the Window* (1944); Edward Dmytryk's

Nine — RKO Radio Pictures and *Out of Past* (1947)

Murder, My Sweet (1944), and many other famous noir-styled films made up through 1956. But the cinematic high point of noir came in 1947 with Tourneur's *Out of the Past*, based upon the original novel "Build My Gallows High" by Geoffrey Homes (pseudonym for Daniel Mainwaring).

This is the archetypal film noir with the destructive femme fatale, the corrupt protagonist-detective, the existential plot pushing the characters to their doom, all filmed in Tourneur's expressionist noir style. After watching Billy Wilder's *Double Indemnity* (1944), where the principals and familiar noir elements became a cohesive unity, *Out of the Past* brings noir to its heights of style, existential philosophy and sophistication. This one is essential viewing.

After the RKO logo disappears from the screen, we are riding in car driven by a man in a black coat in daylight. White titles appear against California mountainsides and roads as the camera tracks behind the driver leading us to a Bridgeport gas station. Stephanos, the driver (played by Paul Valentine), stops for gas and notices a deaf and dumb teenager (played by Dickie Moore) repairing a tire. The former points to a sign, "Bailey's," and asks the teenager where the owner is and if he's coming back today.

At Marnie's Café across the street from the station, Stefanos orders a cup of coffee. In walks the local town sheriff Jim (Richard Webb) as Marnie sounds off about Bailey and the sheriff's girlfriend Ann (played by Virginia Huston) always going fishing afternoons together, insinuating a love triangle. So the lingering question is, where is Jeff Bailey right now?

The scene cuts from Marnie's Café to a bucolic, brightly lit river fishing scene in the California mountains where Jeff proposes marriage to Ann just as the mute boy shows up and tells him in sign language that a mysterious man from the city is waiting to see him at the gas station. Bailey (played by Robert Mitchum) reels in his catch and tells Ann a "man want to see him" in town. Joe Stephanos and Jeff meet and talk, Stephanos telling Jeff "that man" Whit (played by Kirk Douglas) wants to see Jeff again at his home in Lake Tahoe. Apparently Jeff blew the best job Whit had ever given him. Jeff picks up Ann at her home. (Her parents don't approve of him.) Jeff asks her to ride with him to Lake Tahoe and reveals his true identity after Stephanos shows up, a man "out of the past."

First Jeff tells Ann his real name is Markham but he uses the name Bailey in California. Then his story to Ann results in a flashback to New

York City where Jeff worked as a detective with a partner named Jack Fisher (played by Steve Brodie). Whit had been shot four times by a woman, who made one of the shots good but ran out on him with $40,000. All Whit Sterling wants is the woman back and he will pay Markham $5000 plus expenses and $5000 when she is returned to Sterling. Jeff and his partner accept the job since Jeff is a smart and honest detective. The woman is named Kathy Moffet, played beautifully by Jane Greer.

The next scene takes place at a Harlem jazz club where Jeff asks Kathy's former maid, a black woman named Eunice Leonard, a few questions. Apparently her ex-employer got sick from the vaccinations she took and was looking for a place in the sun, perhaps Florida, with baggage that weighed over 131 pounds, 90 pounds in excess. Jeff deduces that Kathy went to Mexico City and traces her to Acapulco. He winds up sitting for days in a bar called La Mar Azul. "And then I saw her coming out of the sun and I knew why Whit didn't care about the $40,000," Markham says in a voiceover. As Kathy enters the bar in a large hat and sheer light-colored cotton dress, she orders a cuba libre. Jeff joins her and she says she sometimes goes to a cantina down the street where they play American music "like you hear in a New York bar on 56th Street." There is an immediate sexual attraction between them. She leaves and Jeff "grinds it out," sitting in that cantina. Then one evening, she walked in out of the moonlight and the "love theme" by Roy Webb is heard whenever they meet. Kathy offers to take Jeff to a gambling casino in Acapulco. She is curious as to why he never asked her name. They kiss on the beach against a background of moonlight sky and fisherman's nets and then she asks Jeff, "When are you taking me back?"

Jeff answers, "Whit didn't die."

"I hate him," she replies. She was glad it was Jeff who found her and confides in him that she did not take the $40,000. "Don't you believe me, Jeff?" He answers, "Baby, I don't care," since he has fallen in love with her. "I never saw her in daytime — we seemed to live by night. We seemed to meet only what was left of the day went away, "like a pack of cigarettes you smoked to the end." She'd come along like school was let out. "Miss me," Kathy asks. "No more than my eyes," Jeff replies. Kathy now takes Jeff to her cottage in Acapulco through the rain. The love theme music fades in and as they dry each other's wet hair, Jeff throws the towel at a lamp, the only source of light, and the camera tracks out the front doorway into the rain. We assume there is a time lapse and that a sex scene takes place off-camera. In a voiceover, Jeff says, "There was something that always got me about her—that magic." Jeff invites Kathy to go to San Francisco since he is sincerely in love with her. They plan to meet the next morning at his hotel.

The following day, Sterling shows up with Stephanos and they enter Jeff's room. Jeff notices Kathy's jewelry on a table and quickly stuffs it into his pocket with a pack of Chesterfield cigarettes. Jeff says he didn't find her. They decide to go down to the bar. Whit says Jeff "blew it" and Jeff claims Kathy took a boat to Guatemala. Thinking he sees Kathy at the lobby entrance, Jeff spills a glass of liquor and Whit notices Jeff's attack of nerves: "You missed her and you feel bad." Sterling leaves with Joe for Mexico City where they intend to buy a horse. Kathy and Jeff take a ship in the opposite direction to San Francisco. The scene cuts back to the present when Jeff tells Ann in the car that is taking him to Whit's home: "What was important to me is that I had *her*!"

The scene flashes back to San Francisco where Kathy and Jeff hid out at small theaters, out-of-town bars and clubs, lived in the country until one day, they decided to go to the racetrack. Fisher, Jeff's ex-partner, spies Jeff at a betting window. ("It was a chance in a million, but he was an excellent gumshoe, if nothing else.") Jeff thinks he lost Fisher by driving circuitously before coming back home to their cabin, but Fisher had apparently followed Kathy. He walks into their cabin with a blare of headlights behind him. Fisher demands half of the $40,000. "Pay me off," he insists. "Break his head, Jeff," says Kathy. Jeff and Fisher fight and suddenly a shot rings out. Kathy no longer has that impassive smile on her face but a sadistic one as she shoots her gun at the writhing bodies of the two men fighting in shadow. Kathy has killed Fisher, and says, "He'd always be against us ... he would have gone to Whit." Jeff's eyes show surprise and as he turns Fisher over. Kathy escapes, leaving in Fisher's car. And it is precisely at that moment that Jeff finds Kathy's bankbook with a balance of $40,000.

Another flashback to the present. Ann asks Jeff, "Do still want to see her?" Jeff answers no. "It's all past," Ann says. She wants Jeff to return to Bridgeport. After recounting the past life of Jeff Markham–Bailey to Ann, they reach Whit's Lake Tahoe estate. The doors of Whit's estate shut behind Jeff and he returns to the past. Ann drives back alone. Now the story takes place in present time.

Jeff is greeted heartily by Whit, who needs his help. Jeff owes him. Apparently Whit has tax problems, $200,000 worth. He paid a lawyer–

accountant named Leonard Eels (played by Ken Niles) a great amount of money, but the man wants more. Whit wants Jeff to steal the income tax records.

At that moment, Kathy comes in for breakfast. "She's back in the fold, Jeff," says Whit. "Besides, you owe me!" Jeff sends a note off to Ann that he has business in San Francisco and won't be back for a while. After breakfast, Kathy enters Jeff's room and explains to him that she had to come back, she had nowhere to go. Jeff says, "You're like a leaf that blows from one gutter to another." She says she didn't tell anything about Fisher's death but Jeff doesn't believe her and throws her out of his bedroom. "I have to sleep in this room!" Obviously Kathy wants Jeff's sympathy.

The scene shifts to urban San Francisco in daylight. Jeff is sent to Meda Carson's luxurious apartment on Telegraph Hill (Meda is played by voluptuous redhead Rhonda Fleming) by Whit and Kathy. There she asks Jeff to find his way to 114 Fulton Street, Leonard Eels' apartment, have cocktails with her boss and her favorite "cousin" Jeff while Meda arranges to steal Whit's tax papers from Eels' office safe. Jeff runs into an old friend, Petey, who drives a taxi and confides to him that "he's in a frame-up but cannot tell what the picture is." While Meda introduces Jeff as her cousin to Leonard in his apartment, he tells Eels about "leaving his fingerprints on martini glasses" and that she is not his cousin *and* suggests he was sent by Sterling from Lake Tahoe. "I'm the patsy and you're on the spot," Jeff tells Eels. Jeff leaves, following Meda to the Mason Building and Eels' office. She exits with a portfolio of Sterling's tax papers and has his taxi driver friend follow her.

Jeff returns to Eels apartment and finds him shot dead on the floor. Jeff drags Eels' body to the unoccupied apartment next door. Leaving Eels' apartment building, he waits in the shadows for his taxi driver friend who "ran a light" and lost Meda after being stopped by a cop.

It is still late evening. Jeff returns to Meda's apartment where a party is in progress. He hides in the next room while Kathy dials Eels' apartment house; the clerk tells her that Eels is not there. "But he must be," she screams into the telephone. At that point, she telephones again asking for Joe Stephanos. Jeff surprises Kathy, accuses her of a slip-up in plans, and that Jeff would take the blame for the murder since there is an affidavit in Eels' safe saying Jeff had killed Fisher, signed by Kathy, giving Jeff a motive to murder Eels. Jeff would be the fall guy. But Kathy comes on to Jeff, telling him he knows he hates her now for what she has done, but they

Nine — RKO Radio Pictures and *Out of Past* (1947)

can retrieve the affidavit through Meda. Apparently, Meda took the portfolio to a north beach club owned by Sterling; the manager is named Baylord. Jeff runs out on Kathy, seeking the tax papers while Joe Stefanos returns to her saying he had killed Eels. "But he wasn't there!" They both jump to the conclusion that it was Bailey's interference that jinxed the plot.

Bailey enters the manager's office of the Sterling Club, knocks him out, steals the tax papers, hides the portfolio under his trenchcoat and sends it off parcel post to an address known only to him so he can retrieve it. Jeff is then waylaid by the manager's henchmen at the Sterling Club but in the portfolio, Baylord discovers a copy of the November 1946 telephone book for San Francisco. The manager questions Kathy about Jeff's knowledge of the papers' hiding place. Suspicion falls directly upon her but she diverts it to Meda. Kathy calls Steling in Reno and tells him not to go to Lake Tahoe.

The scene cuts back to Bridgport and Ann's small frame house in the evening. Her father is reading the newspaper headline: "Jeff Bailey is wanted for two murders!" Ann does not believe it or will not believe it. The newspapers also say that Bailey took a plane to Los Angeles and might return to Bridgeport. The local sheriff, Jim, says to Ann that he will not help Bailey get away.

The locale changes to Whit Sterling's home in Lake Tahoe. Whit is not there but Kathy is sending for Jeff through the mute boy. Stefanos follows the mute boy by car to the California mountains, stops his car and follows the boy to where Jeff is fishing in the East Walker river. The mute boy sees Stefanos pull out a gun and hooks the sleeve of his black overcoat as the latter fires his gun, causing Stefanos to fall off the cliff to his death. Jeff returns to Tahoe, wakes Kathy and tells her Joe is dead. "Can't you find some tears for him?" Jeff asks. Kathy lies; she didn't send Joe. Whit enters and Jeff asks him "to take the frame off me. I want $50,000 and an airplane to get me out of the country. Let Kathy take the rap for Fisher's murder."

In the next room we find Sterling alone with Kathy. He slaps her hard in the face. "You're going to take the fall. If you don't, I'll kill you and you won't know when it will come and it won't be quick or pretty." Jeff arranges to mail the tax files to Whit and says, "Cheer up, Kathy, you'll get out of it all right."

The scene shifts to Bridgeport. Jimmy is following Ann when she meets Jeff. She asks Jeff about Kathy: "She can't be all bad." "She comes the closest," Jeff responds. As Jeff leaves Ann, Jimmy follows him to his car, but does not pull out his gun. He tells Jeff that "he's loved Ann since he fixed her roller skates and she's not going to have anything to do with your rotten life." Jeff drives off in a huff, saying, "But she still loves me!"

The camera cuts back to Whit Sterling's home. Jeff enters and finds Whit lying dead on the floor of his living room, eyes open and face up. "You can't make deals with a dead man!" She is the only one to make deals now. She enumerates the deaths of Fisher, Eels, Stefanos and now Sterling. Jeff's answer: "Build my gallows high, baby!" Kathy, the bad woman, answers, "You're no good and neither am I. We deserve each other!" "I never told you I was anything but what I am — you just wanted to imagine it." So Kathy and Jeff will take a plane waiting for them in the desert. He asks her to pack some things for him as well as any money. As Kathy goes upstairs to pack, Jeff sidles over to the telephone in the living room. Once in the station wagon, Jeff has trouble starting the car until Kathy pushes in the choke. "We've been wrong a lot for a long time; we deserve a break," says Kathy. "I never told you anything I wasn't. You just imagined it." Jeff is caught by a powerful femme fatale who is in full control of the situation.

They drive away from Whit's home, Kathy notices a roadblock straight ahead. She calls Jeff a "double-crossing rat" and shoots Jeff in the groin. Kathy fires back at the police who retaliate with machine guns. She lies dead in the passenger seat, bills at her feet while a fatally wounded Jeff falls out the driver's side when a policeman opens the door.

Daylight. Ann and Jim are walking away from police headquarters together. She sees the mute boy by Bailey's gas station and asks him, "Was he going away with her?" He nods and so returns to Jim's car and they drive out of town. The mute boy saves Ann from a troubled future as he signals "Goodbye" to Bailey's sign at the gas station. The RKO logo appears in white transparent through this final scene as the music swells to the end title and Cast of Characters. *Out of the Past* has a convoluted plot, yes, but it has all the essentials of great film noir, especially in its daylight scenes where the characters carry their dark, doomed actions to the limit.

Initially Robert Mitchum was a B-actor, working for Monogram Pictures. In fact, his first noir film was a Monogram release called *When Strangers Marry* (1944) with Dean Jagger and Kim Hunter in which he

Nine — RKO Radio Pictures and *Out of Past* (1947)

played a murderous villain. Mitchum played many small parts from the early forties at various studios. In 1945, in Ernie Pyle's film *The Story of G.I. Joe*, playing soldier Bill Walker, he was given a starring role opposite Burgess Meredith (who played Pyle) and he was recognized as "star" material. He graduated to A roles at RKO in a series of noir films all made in 1947 such as *Crossfire, The Locket* and *Out of the Past*. The first, with Robert Ryan, dealt with the subject of anti–Semitism; the second was about a lying female kleptomaniac played by Laraine Day; and the third was his iconic role as a corruptible private detective who is ensnared by femme fatale Jane Greer.

Mitchum played over 100 roles in motion pictures. His other film noirs include *Where Danger Lives* (1950) with Faith Domergue, *His Kind of Woman* and *Macao* (both 1951) with Jane Russell, *The Racket* (1951) with Lizabeth Scott, *Angel Face* (1953) with Jean Simmons, *The Night of the Hunter* (1955) with Shelley Winters and Lillian Gish and J. Lee Thompson's *Cape Fear* (1962), as a sadistic stalker of Polly Bergen. In the late seventies, for Avco-Embassy Films, he resuscitated the role of iconic detective Philip Marlowe (Dashiell Hammett's creation) in two color neo-noirs, *Farewell, My Lovely* (1975) and *The Big Sleep* (1978) but appeared sleepy-eyed and bloated. Mitchum passed away in 1997 and left a vast body of work in all kinds of films, but his most popular ones were the noirs mentioned above.

Jane Greer made some forty films in her career, but is best known for her role as Kathie Moffet in *Out of the Past* and will be forever be remembered as the two-timing, double-crossing femme fatale. Director Tourneur wanted her to wear light shades of dresses at the beginning of the film and then proceed to dark clothing by its end, always looking "impassive." Representing the personification of a beguiling romantic with a heart of stone and totally evil, Greer totally shocks Mitchum in the role of this treacherous, lying woman who kills him in the end. Greer played two other noir roles at RKO, the good girl who is jilted by Robert Young in *They Won't Believe Me* (1947) and a sidekick for Robert Mitchum in a minor noir love story with mysterious pretensions, *The Big Steal* (1949). It was around this time Mitchum was arrested for possession of marijuana and the RKO executives thought the pairing of Greer with him might restore his reputation as an actor. They were correct.

Greer appeared in two other color neo-noirs in minor roles: *The Outfit* (1973) with Robert Duvall and then as Kathy Moffet's *mother* in the awful 1994 remake of *Out of the Past*, *Against All Odds*. An unconvincing Jeff

Bridges played the Mitchum role and Australian actress Rachel Ward played Kathie, with James Woods in the Kirk Douglas role of Whit Sterling. The other interesting noir icon wasted in this film was Richard Widmark, playing a gambler-landgrabber, far removed from his early noir days as Tommy Udo in Fox's *Kiss of Death* (1947).

After some New York stage experience, Kirk Douglas came out to Hollywood and made his debut in Paramount's film noir *The Strange Love of Martha Ivers* (1946) with Barbara Stanwyck and continued working for the same studio in producer Hal B. Wallis' 1948 production *I Walk Alone* with Burt Lancaster and Lizabeth Scott, Billy Wilder's *Ace in the Hole* aka *The Big Carnival* with Jan Sterling and William Wyler's production of Sidney Kingsley's play *Detective Story* with Eleanor Parker (both 1951). He left Paramount for two noir roles that greatly benefited his star status: a corrupt boxer in Stanley Kramer's *Champion* (1949) and Whit Sterling in *Out of the Past*. Douglas was paid $25,000 for the role, more than any of the actors in the same film, and delivered a dynamite, memorable performance. Douglas worked for MGM in a Hollywood noir entitled *The Bad and the Beautiful* (1952), directed by Vincente Minnelli; he played a violent film director who had his way with women and sought to revenge himself through his work to retain his father's status as a bigwig studio head.

After appearing in some 90 Hollywood productions, Douglas appeared with his son Michael in a mediocre comedy, *It's All in the Family* (2003), and made occasional appearances in documentaries about his life and work. Born in 1916, Douglas is alive and well, living in California, and he received an honorary Oscar for the body of his work in 1997. His dimpled, blonde good looks and unique talent for playing in a large variety of films — westerns, dramas, noir films, love stories, etc. — made him one of the most versatile of Hollywood actors of the century.

Rhonda Fleming made over 60 films in Hollywood and appeared in several noir classics, mostly for RKO, but it was Alfred Hitchcock who discovered the red-haired beauty and put her in a small role as an instutionalized nymphomaniac in his 1945 noir *Spellbound*, a David O. Selznick production released through United Artists. Her physical beauty is heightened in Robert Siodmak's noir *The Spiral Staircase* (1946); she is murdered by maniac George Brent, who is jealous of her relationship with his half-brother.

Director Robert Parrish's *Cry Danger* (RKO, 1951) with Dick Powell has her playing a good girl while in Budd Boetticher's *The Killer Is Loose* (United Artists, 1956) she is hounded by Joseph Cotten and Wendell Corey.

She returned to RKO for two final noirs: Allan Dwan's *Slightly Scarlet* (1956), in color with redhead Arlene Dahl, both actresses vying for the favors of John Payne, and back to black and white in a newspaper story, playing the editor's duplicitous wife, almost the victim of a serial killer (John Barrymore, Jr.) in Fritz Lang's 1956 film *While the City Sleeps*. Fleming's role as Meda Carson in *Out of the Past* is one of those career-making "femme fatale" roles, despite the short time she spends on screen with Robert Mitchum, who grabs her left arm and says to her, "I want to come out of this in one piece," to which she replies, "Do you always like leaving your fingerprints on a lady's arm, not that I mind, Mr. Bailey?" It is the sexiest scene in the film.

Virginia Huston, who played the "good girl" Ann versus Jane Greer's "bad girl" Kathie, had a very short career in films. She began at Monogram Pictures and later moved to RKO Her blonde beauty and goodness is the very antithesis of Jane Greer's dark, evil Kathy. Her noir series began with her debut in Edwin L. Marin's *Nocturne* (1946) with George Raft, and continued with *Out of the Past*, *The Racket* (1951), which teamed her again with Robert Mitchum, and *Sudden Fear* (1952), playing the good girl once again in contrast to Joan Crawford's harried wife, pursued by evil Jack Palance. In the "carnival noir" *Flamingo Road* (1949) she also appeared with Joan Crawford. Her career lasted eight years. "Good girls" in film noir may have outlived their rival "femme fatales" on screen but this one did not last very long in Hollywood.

Richard Webb was cast as the boyfriend of Virginia Huston's Ann. He's a bland, honest sheriff who does not want Ann to get tangled up in Mitchum's gangster-detective life even though she loves the latter and not the boy she grew up with. He fell in love with her when he fixed her roller skates at age seven. Other than this film, Webb has very little noir film experience other than a small role in John Farrow's 1948 film for Paramount, *The Big Clock*. Webb spent most of his career playing good guys in television films.

Director Jacques Tourneur, son of the famous silent film director Maurice Tourneur, had a marvelous and varied career in American cinema. He directed several film noirs, four for RKO and one for Columbia Pictures. They are *Experiment Perilous* (1944) with George Brent, Hedy Lamarr and Paul Lukas, *Out of the Past*, *Berlin Express* (1948) with Merle Oberon, Robert Ryan and again Paul Lukas and *Nightfall* (1956) with Aldo Ray.

Previously (in the early 1940s) he worked at RKO for producer Val Lewton, directing *Cat People* (1942) with Kent Smith and Simone Simon and *I Walked with a Zombie* (1943) with Tom Conway and Frances Dee. Although these films are not classified as officially "noir," they possess the same expressionist style — dark key lighting, wet streets, blowing wind. Tourneur was equally happy working in color, for example in Universal's *Canyon Passage* (1946) with Dana Andrews and Susan Hayward. He spent most of his life working on some 70 films at various studios before he returned to live in France and died in 1977 at the age of 73.

Screenwriter Daniel Mainwaring (aka Geoffrey Homes) began his career as a novelist in the early 1940s; his first novel was *Build My Gallows High* which became the celebrated film noir *Out of the Past* for which he also wrote the screenplay under the pseudonym Geoffrey Homes. (Most of his Hollywood scripts were written under this pseudonym till 1955 and thereafter he used his real name.) Under his pseudonym he scripted or co-scripted some twenty screenplays, among them these famous noir films: *The Big Steal* (1949), *The Lawless* (1950), *Roadblock* (1951), *The Tall Target* (1951), *This Woman Is Dangerous* (1952), *The Hitchhiker* (1953), *A Bullet for Joey* (1955), *The Phenix City Story* (1955) and *Baby Face Nelson* (1957). His one science fiction film, Don Siegel's *Invasion of the Body Snatchers* (1956), has many noir elements. He also spent many years writing television scripts for detective series like *Mannix* as well as for television westerns until his death in 1977.

Cameraman Nicholas Musuraca worked on nearly 200 films, mostly for RKO. He attained success very early in the noir style, working for producers such as Val Lewton and directors such as Jacques Tourneur. All of his black and white films are particularly dark with a heavy use of shadows and dark key lighting to emphasize the darkness of the night and the mystery of the unknown. You can call him the "originator" of film noir for RKO studios, especially with his work on Boris Ingster's *Stranger on the Third Floor* (1940) which contains an incomparable surreal dream sequence and a starring role for Peter Lorre as the stranger. Other noirs he photographed are Robert Siodmak's *The Spiral Staircase* (1945), set at the turn of the century with George Brent as a maniacal serial killer of "imperfect" people, Harold Clurman's *Deadline at Dawn* (1945), based on a Cornell Woolrich thriller about a sailor who tries to clear himself of a murder, John Brahm's *The Locket* (1946) with Laraine Day as an incurable kleptomaniac (the film contains multiple flashbacks in dark noir style), and the

Laraine Day-Robert Ryan thriller *The Woman on Pier 13* aka *I Married a Communist* (1949) which was a "waterfront noir" dealing with the "Red Scare."

Musuraca also made his style evident for Howard Hughes, who took over RKO in the late forties and produced a group of noir thrillers. One was *Where Danger Lives* (1950) featuring Faith Domergue as the murderess of husband Claude Rains, involving Robert Mitchum in her plans. *Roadblock* (1951) is a B-noir with Charles McGraw playing an insurance investigator and the next three are A noirs: Fritz Lang's *Clash by Night* (1952), a moody love story with Barbara Stanwyck as the focal point of Robert Ryan and Paul Douglas' affections. Musuraca worked again with Lang in his 1953 film *The Blue Gardenia,* about a woman (Anne Baxter) who loses consciousness during an affair with Raymond Burr and finds him dead in the morning. Newspaperman Richard Conte helps her solve the case. Musuraca had a very difficult time photographing The Filmmakers story *The Hitch-Hiker* (1953) since the film starred three men, Edmond O'Brien and Frank Lovejoy as fishermen on a Mexican vacation who pick up William Talman on the road; he seeks to murder them and take their car. Ida Lupino directed. Shooting scenes at night proved somewhat difficult for actors and cameraman alike. Musuraca spent the rest of his career working in television, outside the noir style.

Roy Webb composed scores for nearly all important RKO film noirs mentioned in the above paragraphs and over 262 scores in all since the 1930s "The First Time I Saw You" was a song he used in another RKO production, *The Toast of New York* (1937), starring Frances Farmer. In *Out of the Past,* Webb used this song to introduce Kathy as she strides into a bar where Jeff is waiting for her. The noirish mood of the film switches to a romantic one. Webb's score for Alfred Hitchcock's *Notorious* (1946) deserves special praise for his innovative use of samba motifs and dark chords as Claude Rains disappears into his home in a final scene where his fellow Nazis wait to kill him. Webb's music fuses with Hitchcock's action beautifully with the samba.

Albert S. D'Agostino spent practically his entire working life at RKO studios from 1936 to the studio's demise in 1958. He was known for the "gothic style" he developed for Universal in the early twenties; when he switched to RKO in the 1940s, he immediately adapted to the film noir expressionist style shown in the Val Lewton films and the low-budget thrillers that were RKO's métier. He worked with many great directors and his art direction helped to produce the seminal film noir look for the studio. He worked on over 300 RKO films and ended his career in 1958 as art director for the color film *The Big Circus*. Reading through his filmography is quite an experience for the noir enthusiast. Jack Okey, a minor art director, worked alongside D'Agostino through most of his career.

There are two stills that inform the noir style of *Out of the Past:* In the first one, it is night and Jeff has arrived at Kathy's rented cabin. The lighting in the house casts shadows outside, revealing Jeff's partner Fisher (Steve Brodie) holding on to the left staircase banister. Note that Jeff is wearing his wrinkled trenchcoat and Kathy is dressed in a light color garment while Fisher appears in a dark hat and suit.

In the second still, we are in Whit Sterling's home. Note the painting behind Jeff and Kathy as they stare downward over the couch that is supporting their hands. They are looking at Whit Sterling's body. "Can't make

Out of the Past (1947): Steve Brodie (left) surprises Jane Greer and Robert Mitchum in their sequestered San Francisco cabin.

Nine — RKO Radio Pictures and *Out of Past* (1947)

deals with a dead man," says Kathy. Note that she is dressed in a black coat and wearing a snood (fashionable for the period). Jeff realizes Kathy is running the show now. The source of the lighting is Sterling's fireplace or a lamp placed on the side of the living room. Jeff's trenchcoat seems old and used as Jeff realizes he must go with Kathy and face a life of doom hereafter.

Out of the Past (1947): **Robert Mitchum in rumpled raincoat and Jane Greer in snood and coat look down at Kirk Douglas' body off-camera.**

Out of the Past is quintessential film noir, stylish, brilliantly scripted, professionally photographed. It uses both city and country locations and contains some of the best dialogue written since Hammett's *The Maltese Falcon*. Mitchum is perfect as the ill-fated romantic detective, restrained, joyless with a look of doom on his mournful face. Greer is perfect as the lethal Kathie, erotic, sensual, enigmatic. When Kathy kills Fisher, Jeff sees her true nature revealed; it is one of the most exciting epiphanies ever seen in a noir film.

All the elements that define noir are here, including the main character's cynicism, isolation and pending sense of doom. *Out of the Past* is one of the greatest multi-layered film noirs of all time, especially because its moral ambiguous atmosphere is interwoven with a convoluted and sometimes confusing plot. But we must acknowledge the greatness of director Jacques Tourneur, able to combine his tragic sensibility with the talents of his superb cast and the shadowy lighting of his photographer Nicholas Musuraca to pull off this very complex film where a man actually embraces his fate and accepts it, succumbing to the femme fatale's betrayal. Good girls never win their men in film noirs. And the burden of the past always follows and traps the flawed protagonist, no matter how hard he or she tries to escape it.

RKO Studios made film noirs than any other studio — 52 to be exact. If I were to pick out my other five favorites, they are the following:

Murder, My Sweet (1944) Edward Dmytryk, director. Cast: Dick Powell, Claire Trevor, Ann Shirley, Otto Kruger. A judge's wife is pursued by an ex-con who knew her as a burlesque queen. He hires detective Philip Marlowe to track her down. The film contains many surreal drug-dream sequences but Marlowe rises above it all and romances the judge's daughter.

Notorious (1946) Alfred Hitchcock, director. Cast: Ingrid Bergman, Cary Grant, Claude Rains. In Brazil, secret agent Bergman must find the source of uranium even if it means marrying Claude Rains, a German agent while she really loves Cary Grant. Sophisticated espionage shot in noir style.

The Locket (1947) John Brahm, director. Cast: Laraine Day, Robert Mitchum, Gene Raymond, Brian Aherne. In this tale told in multiple flashbacks, a kleptomaniac steals jewels and marries multiple times until her conscience catches up with her at the conclusion.

Crossfire (1947) Edward Dmytryk, director. Cast: Robert Ryan, Robert Mitchum, Robert Young, Gloria Grahame, Sam Levene, Jacqueline White. A Jew is murdered and three soldiers are the suspects. A story of anti–Semitism shot in noir style.

Angel Face (1953) Otto Preminger, director. Cast: Jean Simmons, Robert Mitchum, Herbert Marshall, Barbara O'Neil. A young woman detests her father's second wife and plans her death in a car accident. The problem is that father dies too so she decides to kill herself and her lover-chauffeur. Outrageous, nightmarish cinema, but memorable.

If I were to pick a runner-up, it would be *Born to Kill* (1947). Robert Wise, director. Cast: Claire Trevor, Lawrence Tierney, Walter Slezak, Elisha Cook, Jr., Audrey Long.

CHAPTER TEN

20th Century–Fox and *Laura* (1944)

The Fox Film Corporation was founded by William Fox in 1915. He was forced out of his own company in 1930. It became 20th Century–Fox with Joseph Schenck as president and Darryl F. Zanuck as vice-president in charge of production and William Goetz as executive vice-president in 1935. The Zanuck reign finally ended in 1971, when Darryl resigned as president. Fox exists now as a series of corporate conglomerates and currently releases many independent productions under its own banner.

During the thirties and forties, Fox was known for its bright musicals starring Alice Faye, Betty Grable and Carmen Miranda among other women and Tyrone Power, Cornel Wilde, and Dick Haymes among the male stars. It was second to RKO in its output of film noir and produced more classics than any other studio between 1941 and 1953, including some "color noirs" such as *Leave Her to Heaven* (1945) directed by John Stahl and starring Gene Tierney in one of her best shrewish roles. Another was *Niagara* (1953), directed by Henry Hathaway and starring the young, nubile Marilyn Monroe. But the studio's major noir films were in black and white and during the forties had a pseudo-documentary style because of producer Louis de Rochemont and his *House on 92nd Street* (1945), also directed by Henry Hathaway. In that film, and others that followed, an unidentified narrator described the "true" events that took place on screen. Director Samuel Fuller used a similar docu-noir style in his film *Pickup on South Street* (1953), one of the last noir films made by the studio in black and white. The best film noirs of 20th Century–Fox were made during the 1940s and *Laura* and *Leave Her to Heaven*, both starring Gene Tierney, were its most luxurious, richly decorated and romantic noirs.

Ten — 20th Century–Fox and *Laura* (1944)

Laura is one of the best thrillers ever made in black and white. Otto Preminger served as both producer and director after Rouben Mamoulian stepped out of the production at the behest of studio head Darryl F. Zanuck when the film was five weeks in production. Although his *City Streets* (1931) for Paramount with Gary Cooper and Sylvia Sydney showed Mamoulian's propensity for noir style, he was easily replaced by Preminger who become an A producer and director at Fox with this film.

After we see the Fox logo and hear Alfred Newman's score behind it, we hear David Raksin's wonderful score for *Laura*. Behind all the white titles of stars, producer, writer and director we see in the background a still life of lovely Gene Tierney, supposedly an oil painting but actually a photograph made to look like a painting, staring out from the screen with a mesmerizing quality. After the producer and director credits vanish, we hear this narration so typical of noir style: "I shall never forget the weekend Laura died..." We are in New York City, in the ornate bathroom of art collector–columnist Waldo Lydecker (dazzlingly played by Clifton Webb). "I was the only one who knew her," he says to Detective Mark McPherson (played by Dana Andrews) as he rises from his lavish marble bathtub. The detective notes a hall clock in Lydecker's apartment exactly like one in Laura Hunt's apartment, where she was murdered. McPherson is invited into Waldo's bathroom, while the latter types away at some article he is writing. Waldo is thin, affected, perhaps homosexual as he stands up (out of our view) while McPherson throws him his robe. He questions Waldo about another murdered woman, killed with a dual blast from a shotgun at close range, the way in which Laura supposedly died. Waldo answers: "Murder is my favorite crime." He gets dressed and accompanies the detective to Laura's apartment. Even though Waldo is the "wisest and wittiest" character in the film, he is still a suspect. When asked, "Were you in love with Laura?" Waldo does not answer.

The next scene takes place in Ann Treadwell's (Judith Anderson) Park Avenue apartment. Ann is Laura's wealthy aunt and McPherson knows that Laura was about to marry the Southern fortune hunter Shelby Carpenter. McPherson asks, "Did you approve of her marriage to Carpenter?" to which Treadwell replies simply, "Yes, I had no motive for killing Shelby's fiancée" (her niece). Carpenter (played with a Southern accent by Vincent Price) is present in Treadwell's apartment when the latter announces that Laura was going to her country house in Connecticut to think about their impending marriage.

The three go to Laura's apartment building by car. There are crowds of people, plus police and reporters, in front of the entrance. As Waldo enters the apartment, he asks the detective, "Is this the house of a dame?" McPherson notes the painting over the fireplace and remarks, "Not bad." Waldo tells him that Jacoby, the painter, was in love with Laura, another suitor in her life. McPherson traps Carpenter in a lie when the latter said he spent the evening Laura was murdered at a concert where they played Beethoven. McPherson says they played Sibelius all evening, and Carpenter counters with the excuse that he "fell asleep" which the detective seems to accept. While searching for a key to Laura's apartment, Carpenter finds one in the bottom drawer of Laura's dresser. McPherson accuses Carpenter of putting it there, which is true, but he had "private reasons" for lying about it that don't concern Waldo Lydecker. Waldo and Shelby begin to fight and McPherson breaks it up

The camera cuts to a scene in a nicely styled restaurant where Waldo is having a bottle of wine with the detective. "It was our favorite restaurant, Laura's and mine," he says. He took her there to celebrate her 25th birthday. Within this scene, we have a flashback to some years before where Laura enters the dining room of the Algonquin Hotel and intrudes on Waldo's lunch while trying to get his signature for an advertising agency, Bullock & Co., which will pay him $5000 for his endorsement of a pen. Waldo is so upset that Laura is disregarding his lunch, that she calls him "selfish," adding, "You must be a very poor man, and lonely, too." In his flashback narration of the scene, Waldo remarks to McPherson, "There was something about that girl ... I had to see her again."

Still in flashback, Waldo enters Bullock's Agency, apologizes to Laura, and signs her contract for the pen endorsement. Since she is delighted, he says he will call for her at six that evening for dinner. Then, in the flashback narration, Waldo recalls how his help gave her start in the advertising world. "On Tuesdays and Fridays, we stayed home — we dined together." But when Laura didn't show up on these evenings, he was upset. The camera cuts to a snowy street outside of Laura's apartment building. He saw the shadows of Jacoby and Laura through her window. Angrily, Waldo went home and wrote columns about Jacoby's poor artistic talent, destroying his reputation.

In the kitchen of Ann Treadwell's apartment, Laura meets Shelby Carpenter for the first time: tall, wealthy, Southern, handsome. They share a cigarette on the balcony and Laura offers Shelby a job at Bullock & Co.

Ten — 20th Century–Fox and *Laura* (1944)

Waldo tells us in a voiceover that he hides his discontent. In the flashback, Shelby shows Laura he does have a talent for advertising and shows Laura an ad for a bathing suit he designed with Diane Redfern, a model Laura hired the week before. We never meet Diane but see her photo. Waldo continues to spy on Shelby but Laura defends him to the police. Waldo had detectives follow Shelby, who gave Diane Redfern an expensive cigarette case, (Laura originally gave it to Shelby as a gift). Apparently Redfern pawned it and it winds up in Waldo's possession. Laura cannot believe all this chicanery going on and Waldo suggests they visit Ann's apartment where Shelby and Ann are having an intimate supper. They surprise Ann and Shelby, and Laura just hands over the cigarette case to Shelby and leaves with Waldo without saying a word. Waldo's words end the flashback; he says he blames himself for Laura's involvement with Shelby.

Back in present time, McPherson always notices Laura's portrait. He finds a bottle of Black Pony Scotch and asks Bessie, her maid, if Laura bought the bottle. "She's a real lady," she answers. Someone else must have brought it to the apartment. Treadwell, Carpenter and Lydecker enter the apartment. They mention Lancaster Cory, an art dealer who could easily dispose of the contents of Laura's apartment. But Waldo wants to reclaim certain items of furniture that he gave to Laura on loan — a fire screen, a vase and a full standing hall clock which he means to have back. He starts to take the vase but McPherson stops him.

The next scene is one of the most memorable in the film. McPherson returns to Laura's apartment that rainy evening. Taking off his raincoat and lighting up a cigarette, he stares at Laura's painting, goes through letters in her desk, her diary, her lingerie, her perfume, her clothes closet, and then pours himself a drink. He calls downstairs to the basement to the detectives who are wiretapping Laura's phone and they report there has been no activity. Waldo shows up and finds out that McPherson put a bid in with Lancaster Corey for Laura's painting and adds: "A doctor never had a patient who fell in love with a corpse." Waldo leaves and then McPherson begins to doze in an armchair facing Laura's portrait. We do not know how much time passes but we hear a key in the door.

Laura enters the apartment and puts on the lights, which awaken the detective. Laura asks for his identity and tells him she was in the country. She did not read any newspapers and knew nothing about a shotgun murder in her apartment. Also, the radio was broken. Laura investigates her clothes closet and finds a dress that belongs to Diane Redfern. Although police went to her Connecticut house on Saturday, Laura was out walking in the forest for most of the day. She saw nobody, picked up her car from a private garage and worked in her garden. McPherson asks her the essential question: "You went up there to decide whether you would marry Shelby Carpenter?" Laura says, "No, I decided not to…" After Mark leaves the apartment, he stops in the cellar and overhears (via the wiretap) Laura's phone call to Shelby Carpenter. The two of them meet in Shelby's car, talk a few minutes and Laura departs, returning to her apartment while Mark follows Shelby's to Laura's Connecticut house. It is a very rainy night and as Mark enters, he finds Shelby taking Laura's shotgun off hooks from over the mantelpiece. Mark concludes that Shelby knew it was Diane Redfern who was dead. He had borrowed a duplicate key to Laura's apartment from her office desk drawer. When the bell to Laura's apartment rang, he sent Diane to answer and heard the shot. He didn't want the blame to fall on Laura and so came up to the country house to reclaim the shotgun, thinking that Laura killed Redfern.

The next scene takes place the following morning in Laura's kitchen. Mark has brought a bag of groceries, eggs and coffee from the local supermarket. The back door to the kitchen opens and it is Bessie, Laura's maid, who enters and screams. She is shocked that Laura is alive and the latter says: "Have you ever had a ghost ask for scrambled eggs?" Bessie returns to her kitchen duties as Mark and Laura discuss the phone call of last evening. Shelby enters, bringing Laura a small bouquet of gardenias. "So it's on again," McPherson declares. The doorbell rings again. Bessie opens it and Waldo collapses to his knees when he sees Laura alive and well. Carpenter and McPherson carry him into a bedroom where Waldo swallows a pill he carries for attacks such as these and is left alone to rest. Back in the living room, Laura asks Shelby why he went to her cottage last night. Shelby thought that Laura killed Diane Redfern with the shotgun he had given her. Laura is revolted and hurries to her dressing table. Ann Treadwell enters and says, "She can afford Shelby — they're both weak and can't help it." Meanwhile, Waldo had telephoned his butler to invite everyone to Laura's apartment since she has been restored to life and so every one of her friends could see her. McPherson receives a telephone call from police headquarters and announces in a loud voice that he is going to make an arrest now. He glides by Ann, Shelby and Waldo and finally says to Laura, "Let's go!" Bessie screams out, "No, no!" and is the only one to defend her. Waldo tells Laura, "We will fight them [the police]" and Shelby tries to stop McPherson but receives a punch in the stomach and collapses into the arms of Ann Treadwell, seeing solace. "Too bad you didn't open that door," is McPherson's parting comment to Carpenter.

The next scene takes place at the local police station. Two bright lights are turned on in a darkened room as Laura is grilled by McPherson. "No, I didn't kill Diane ... and I asked a local handyman to fix my radio before I left the house." McPherson then asks Laura, "Did you really decide to call it off with Carpenter or did you tell me that because you knew I wanted to hear it? Are you still in love with Carpenter?" Laura answers: "I don't see how I ever could have been!" Mark says he needed official surroundings to hear Laura's answer — he was 99 percent sure she didn't kill Redfern but had to make sure of that last one percent. "Then it was worth it, Mark," Laura answers.

McPherson enters Waldo's apartment and notices the exact hall clock with its secret compartment in the bottom. Mark kicks it in and finds it empty. He quickly goes back to Laura's apartment. She is there arguing with Waldo about his jealousy of McPherson: "A strong body in a muscular sort of way is the measure of a man for you, Laura." Waldo wants to get back with Laura again, knowing about her split with Shelby. "You're the one that follows the same obvious pattern — first it was Jacoby, then Shelby, now McPherson." Laura asks Waldo to leave. McPherson and Laura examine Waldo's gift of the clock. Together they find the spring that opens the door and inside, the shotgun. "I wouldn't let myself believe it. Waldo, a killer."

For the first time, Laura and Mark kiss as he leaves the apartment. He's off to arrest Waldo. But Waldo re-entered Laura's apartment through the back door of the kitchen, slips into the living room, opens the clock and re-loads the shotgun with shells from his pocket. Laura is combing her hair at her dressing table in front of a mirror. She gets up to put on the radio and hears Waldo's voice by "electronic transcription." McPherson, downstairs, learns that Waldo never came out of the apartment. The police scurry to Laura's apartment, banging down the front and kitchen doors.

Seated again at the dressing table, Waldo surprises Laura: "Do you think I'd give up the best part of myself to anyone?" as he points the rifle down at her. "They'll find us together!" Laura gets up and runs, pushing Waldo's gun out of the way upwards, fiercely running into Mark's arms. The police shoot Waldo and we hear his last words: "Goodbye, Laura, goodbye, my love." The camera glides from his body past Laura and Mark, who move forward, and the camera rests on the destroyed clock face. The end titles are in white letters against the background of that iconic painting of Laura as the David Raksin music fades into its final, mysterious atonal chords.

Laura was certainly ahead of its time, casting Clifton Webb as the effete, homosexual writer. He was obviously gay and not only wanted to make-over Laura, her hair styles, her clothes, her choice of furniture and especially her choice of men. Unlike Pygmalion and Galatea, he didn't want her sexually but probably wanted to *be* Laura herself. Or, like Petrarch's creation of his ideal woman, Laura is his dream girl, unable to live up to his expectations and delusions of perfection. He doesn't want to see her in the arms of any other man — and so he kills her (or thinks he has killed her) until Laura mysteriously returns. Director Otto Preminger used Gene Tierney, one of the most beautiful and enigmatic actresses of her day, to make *Laura* as a love poem to her and her public.

Born in Brooklyn to an Irish socialite family, Tierney spent her first acting years as a teenager on Broadway before signing a film contract with 20th Century–Fox in 1940. She then spent much of her life making films at that studio. After she appeared in an early noir, Josef von Sternberg's *The Shanghai Gesture* (1941), and a few Fox films, *Laura* made her a true star. As writer Michael L. Stephen says, "As the object of romantic obsession, Tierney is the very image of ethereal beauty in early *film noir*."

Her next role for Fox was as Ellen Berent, a jealous, raging villainess who lets nothing stop her from possessing Cornel Wilde's love, even to the extent of letting his brother drown in a lake and aborting her own child to preserve their marriage. Based on Ben Ames William's novel *Leave Her to Heaven*, this first "color" noir film appeared in 1945 and cemented Tierney's stardom with an Academy Award nomination for Best Actress. She worked in several other noirs for Fox, *Night and the City* (1950) for director Jules Dassin and *Where the Sidewalk Ends* (1950) for her favorite director, Preminger. Failed romances, marriages and institutional stays prevented her from working for several years. She died in 1992 at age 72.

Her co-star Dana Andrews spent more than 40 years in the movie industry making some 80-plus films, co-starring with Tierney once again in *Where the Sidewalk Ends*, where he reprises the role of Detective Mark

McPherson. Andrews worked for Preminger again in the much underrated *Fallen Angel* (1945) with Alice Faye, who was trying to get away from musical roles. Other noir films for Andrews were *Beyond a Reasonable Doubt* (1956), directed by Fritz Lang, in which he plays a murderer (against his heroic type), and *While the City Sleeps* (1956), again directed by Lang; this time, Andrews plays a reporter in search of a teenage serial killer (John Barrymore, Jr.).

No matter how good Andrews was in noir films, his best role for me was as the veteran soldier returning from World War II after training as a bombardier in Sam Goldwyn's *The Best Years of Our Lives* (1946). Although Andrews looked the part of a noir detective with his trenchcoat and half-cocked fedora, his sensitivity as an actor made him the great success he was in films for over 40 years. He was tall, handsome and reflected a kind of immobile stoicism that made him perfect for these roles.

Clifton Webb spent many years on Broadway before he hit his stride in Preminger's *Laura*, which thrust him into stardom. Playing the homosexual Waldo Lydecker was not really a stretch for him since he reprised the type as Hardy Cathcart, an art dealer, this time married unbelievably to actress Cathy Downs, in Henry Hathaway's 1946 Fox production *The Dark Corner* which also starred Lucille Ball (in one of her first non-musical-comedic roles) and Mark Stevens as Det. Bradford Galt. He played the same corner in a "love triangle" as in *Laura*, with practically no alteration in character. The rest of his Fox years were mostly spent playing in Mr. Belvedere comedies, usually as a fusspot curmudgeonly old babysitter. He should have stuck to roles in noir films.

Vincent Price was a tall actor with a deep voice, perfect for noir films, especially *Laura*, where he plays Gene Tierney's masculine but weak-kneed suitor Shelby Carpenter who is dependent on other women for love, sex and money, the perfect cad. He is also in *Leave Her to Heaven*, again opposite Gene Tierney, as her jilted lover Russell Quintin, a D.A. who almost convicts her innocent sister and husband (Jeanne Crain and Cornel Wilde) of poisoning her with arsenic. Price made one more noir for Fox, the underrated 1946 *Shock* with Lynn Bari, directed by Alfred Werker, where he plays a mad psychiatrist who kills his wife and lover and had been spotted in the act by actress Anabel Shaw. His last "gothic noir" for Fox was *Dragonwyck* (1946), set in New York's upper Hudson valley, in which he played a demented drug addict, Nicholas Van Rijn. He killed his first wife to marry, once again, Gene Tierney as Miranda, a beautiful, religious girl who, after a miscarriage, escapes the estate called Dragonwyck and finds love with a young doctor from Greenwich, Connecticut (Glenn Langan in one of his earliest roles). Price appeared in three other noirs, *The Bribe* (1949) for MGM with Ava Gardner, *His Kind of Woman* (1951) for RKO with Jane Russell and *While the City Sleeps* (1956), again for RKO with Ida Lupino, but he never regained his noir hero-villain status after he left Fox. Instead he started a new career in films for Roger Corman based upon stories of Edgar Allan Poe. But many film fans remember his early noir days and his successes in those roles besides the popular Poe films.

Judith Anderson, who played Ann Treadwell, was of Australian origin and starred on stage there and on Broadway before coming to Hollywood. She appeared as Mrs. Danvers in Alfred Hitchcock's great "gothic noir" *Rebecca* (1940), based on the Daphne du Maurier novel, a role for which she will best be remembered. Although she worked in films and on the stage sporadically, she was no stranger to film noirs and appeared in Lewis Milestone's *The Strange Love of Martha Ivers* (1946), playing Martha's strict grandmother. She was also Edward G. Robinson's sister in Delmer Daves' *The Red House* (1947) and the wife of Dean Jagger in Raoul Walsh's over-the-top Western noir *Pursued* (1947) which starred Robert Mitchum and Teresa Wright. In another western noir, Anthony Mann's *The Furies*, she is married to Walter Huston, who has her eye gouged out by a jealous daughter (Barbara Stanwyck). Although never receiving top billing in films, she was a dependable supporting player and had a forty-year career.

Viennese producer-director Otto Preminger came to Fox when Hitler was on the rise in Europe in the 1930s and made two B films before hitting his stride with *Laura*, a true film noir because the detective falls in love with a painting of the presumed-dead Laura Hunt which is disquieting in itself; when he finds her alive, the obsessive quality of his investigation of her lends the film its true noir quality. Preminger's gliding camera and long takes endow the black and white film with a kind of obsessive romantic drama that had never before seen on the screen. *Laura* is probably Preminger's best noir although a string of others made for Fox have interesting noir premises. His *Fallen Angel* starred Alice Faye, who is taken advantage of by Dana Andrews, marrying for her money while carrying on with femme fatale Linda Darnell, who is ultimately murdered by Charles Bickford as a police detective because of her "infidelity." *Where the Sidewalk Ends* united Tierney and Andrews, again playing Mark McPherson. The time Tierney is married to Craig Stevens, a veteran with a plate in his head from World War II. In a fight, Andrews accidentally kills Stevens and hides his body, letting the blame fall on Tierney's father (Tom Tully). It is only because of the latter circumstance that Andrews admits the crime; Tierney, who has fallen for Andrews, agrees to wait for him. In 1949, he made Fox's *Whirlpool* which starred Tierney as a kleptomaniac who is induced to commit murder under hypnosis by Jose Ferrer until her psychiatrist-husband Richard Conte discovers the truth and Tierney is exonerated by Ferrer's confession and death. In 1951, Preminger remade Clouzot's French classic *Le corbeau* (*The Raven*) as. *The 13th Letter,* about the ravages in relationships and murders caused by a series of poison pen letters in a small Canadian town. It starred Charles Boyer, Michael Rennie, Constance Smith and Linda Darnell in a familiar femme fatale role It had a distinct "Preminger expressionist style" that could be traced as far back as *Laura*. His last real noir was *Angel Face* (1953) which starred Jean Simmons as a dangerous femme fatale who had no scruples about killing her stepmother (Barbara O'Neil) or ultimately her lover (Robert Mitchum) in a perverse auto accident, sending them both over a cliff in a tampered-with car, driving in reverse to their deaths. Once again, Preminger delivered a thriller in a perverse, Expressionist style.

Preminger was an iconoclast producer-director, testing the Production Code by using the word "pregnant" in his 1953 film *The Moon Is Blue* which was released without a Production Seal of Approval but gained popularity with audiences. *The Man with the Golden Arm* (1955) starring Frank Sinatra as a jazzed-up drug addict with a great score by Elmer Bernstein also did not receive a seal of approval because its subject matter was narcotics, and it was a financial success. Preminger continued to direct epic films: *Exodus* (1960), *Advise & Consent* (1962) and *The Cardinal* (1963), all based on best-selling novels. The films brought him further creative and financial success but his most extraordinary notoriety came when he made *Carmen Jones* (1954) and had a sexual affair with its star, Dorothy Dandridge. His best and most interesting credits are the film noirs, which show decadent, depraved and perverse characters, people of flesh and blood, not the epics which may have crowned his career in the late seventies and eighties. He died in New York City in 1986.

Preminger was fortunate to have screenwriter-novelist Jay Dratler as the principal co-writer for *Laura*. There is not a wasted line in the film said by any character; the dialogue is strong, the plot is concise and the noirish ambiguities invest the film with class. (He also wrote *The Dark Corner* for Fox which starred Clifton Webb in another Waldo Lydecker-type role.) The source novel by Vera Caspary was serialized in *Colliers Magazine* under the title "Ring Twice for Laura" before Caspary's publisher shortened the title. Dratler wrote two other film noirs, both for United Artists. *Pitfall* (1948) starred Dick Powell as an insurance investigator bedazzled by femme fatale model Lizabeth Scott, risking his marriage to Jane Wyatt while being pursued by villain Raymond Burr. *Impact* (1949) starred Brian Donlevy as the wealthy industrialist and loving husband of femme fatale Helen Walker, and he stands between her and her lover. On a road trip the lover tries to kill Donlevy with a tire iron. He is not quite dead but wanders into a gas station where Ella Raines, the good girl, gives him a job until Donlevy regains his memory and sends his wife and her lover to prison for attempted murder.

Laura cameraman Joseph LaShelle worked on a series of Fox films before *Laura* elevated him to the top-ranking cinematographer. He made some 70 films but his noir style was most interesting when his camera photographed night scenes of streets swept by the rain, fog and shadows. He worked particular well with Preminger; besides *Laura*, he also photographed *Fallen Angel, Where the Sidewalk Ends* and *The 13th Letter* for him. He also worked well with other directors such as Jean Negulesco on Fox's *Road House* (1948) with Ida Lupino as the femme fatale caught between right guy Cornel Wilde and psychotic killer Richard Widmark. Two other noirs he did were for United Artists: *Storm Fear* (1956) was directed by Cornel Wilde and starred his wife Jean Wallace and Dan Duryea as the villain; *Crime of Passion* (1957), directed by Gerd Oswald, starred Barbara Stanwyck as the social-climbing wife of cop Sterling Hayden; she has an affair with his boss (Raymond Burr) that leads to murder. LaShelle's photography transformed these routine plots into archetypal film noir.

David Raksin once told an audience at the Museum of Modern Art that he had three days to come up with the music from *Laura,* and he managed to write the score within this time limit. Of course, the popular song (never sung in the film) followed the opening with lyrics by Johnny Mercer, who had never seen the film. All he had to work with were the opening bars of Raksin's score; his "Laura" became a wildly popular hit in 1944–45. When asked by the composer which was my favorite Raksin score, I replied, "*Forever Amber*," the 1947 film adaptation of a scandalous

Ten — 20th Century–Fox and *Laura* (1944)

novel of the mid–forties by Kathleen Windsor. Raksin worked on other noir films: *Fallen Angel, Force of Evil* (1948), *A Lady Without a Passport* (1950), *Suddenly* (1954) and *The Big Combo* (1955). Of all of these, my favorite was the score and script for *Force of Evil* starring John Garfield, Thomas Gomez and Beatrice Pearson. Raksin used so many atonal shadings that added to the photographic genius of George Barnes that our journey from Wall Street to Hell (the stony banks of the Hudson River under the George Washington Bridge where Garfield discovers the body of his brother [Gomez] dead, tossed on the rocks like a piece of garbage) seem particularly nightmarish. Raksin's score for this film, spoken in blank verse, is the epitome of greatness.

Art and set director Lyle Wheeler worked on over 300 films in his lifetime, entering films in the mid–thirties. After his experience on *Gone with the Wind* (1939) and Hitchcock's *Rebecca*, he joined 20th Century–Fox in 1940 and stayed with this company for the rest of his career. Beginning with *Laura*, he worked on all the important film noirs produced by

Laura (1944): Dana Andrews gazes up at the portrait of Gene Tierney.

Laura (1944): Dana Andrews grills Gene Tierney at police headquarters while a policeman (actor unidentified) looks on.

the studio through 1955, about 25 films. His sets were always in good taste and matched the noir style perfectly. He worked well with all the cinematographers at Fox and elsewhere because of his background as an industrial designer and magazine illustrator.

Laura is one of the best film noirs about obsession. Tierney's Laura is the apex of a triangle: On the one side there is the hero MacPherson, and on the other side, the villainous art critic Waldo Lydecker. It seems everyone she knows has a reason to murder her in this '40s stylish world of Manhattan advertising and cultural decadence. But there are two Lauras, the dream and the real woman. Laura *is* a real woman, alive and ready for love. The audience wants her to fall in love with the detective to the detriment of the art critic who can love her only symbolically. At least, we have a film noir with "almost" a happy ending. Tierney is wonderful as Laura Hunt, beautiful, secretive, enigmatic, perhaps unattainable. She is not a femme fatale but subtle, mysterious, desirable. The film is an excellent, classy entertainment, a tribute to Otto Preminger's direction, its actors and crew.

The first truly noir still shows the portrait of Gene Tierney and Dana Andrews, in a wet raincoat, staring up at it, thinking, "This is not just a dame who was murdered in this Park Avenue apartment." He later falls asleep looking up at the portrait when Tierney awakens him from out of a dream. The second, more noirish still takes place down at the local police station.

20th Century–Fox filmed the second highest number of film noir after RKO: 32. Among them, here are my five favorites:

The Dark Corner (1946) Henry Hathaway, director. Cast: Mark Stevens, Lucille Ball, Clifton Webb, Cathy Downs, William Bendix, Kurt Kreuger. An art dealer frames a detective for murdering his young wife's lover. Fascinating New York locales.

The Brasher Doubloon (1947), John Brahm, director. Cast: George Montgomery, Nancy Guild, Conrad Janis, Franz Kortner. Favorite '40s detective Philip Marlowe finds himself looking for the elusive coin of the title and involved in several murders.

Nightmare Alley (1947) Edmund Goulding, director. Cast: Tyrone Power, Coleen Gray, Joan Blondell, Helen Walker. An itinerant carnival hand becomes a wealthy spiritualist in nightclubs, but loses everything and becomes "a geek."

Kiss of Death (1947) Henry Hathaway, director. Cast: Victor Mature, Brian Donlevy, Coleen Gray, Richard Widmark. An ex-con turns state's evidence on local gangster and his family goes through a nightmare of threats. Widmark debuts as Tommy Udo, a sadistic gangster who pushes a crippled Mildred Dunnock in a wheelchair down a staircase to her death. Scary and memorable.

Night and the City (1950) Jules Dassin, director. Cast: Richard Widmark, Gene Tierney, Googie Withers, Frances L. Sullivan, Hugh Marlowe, Herbert Lom. Widmark steers tourists to a nightclub where girlfriend Gene Tierney works; not satisfied, he becomes a con artist and promoter for a gangster's father who believes in classical Greek wrestling. Fascinating locales and noirish settings.

If I were to pick a runner-up to *Laura*, it would be *Pick-up on South Street* (1953).

CHAPTER ELEVEN

United Artists and *Too Late for Tears* (1949)

United Artists was created in 1919 by a group of wealthy actors and directors (Charles Chaplin, Douglas Fairbanks, D.W. Griffith and Mary Pickford) to make films of their own and distribute them as well. They also distributed other producers' movies. Arthur Krim took over the studio in 1951. Chaplin and Pickford sold their shares in UA in the mid–1950s and then the company went public in 1957. So United Artists did not have a real production company with its own producers, writers, directors, composers, designers and photographers but was its own entity, financing independent producers and then releasing their films.

Readers may wonder why this author has picked Byron Haskin's 1949 film noir production *Too Late for Tears* as a seminal noir produced and released by United Artists when there are so many great UA directors like Josef von Sternberg, Fritz Lang, Andre de Toth, Joseph H. Lewis, Stanley Kubrick and so many others, who produced A products like *The Shanghai Gesture* (1941), *Pitfall* (1948) and *The Big Combo* (1955), among others. *Too Late for Tears* is a relatively "unknown and unseen" noir and deserves this recognition, especially for its storyline, acting and the incredible performance of Lizabeth Scott in the femme fatale role.

The film begins showing off the Los Angeles skyline at night as the white titles roll. This film is perhaps the darkest noir I have seen in this series of films, both photographically and emotionally. Alan Palmer (played engagingly by Arthur Kennedy) and his wife Jane (the screen's most sadistic femme fatale, played by Lizabeth Scott) are arguing in the front seat of their convertible at night, high in the hills on a virtually untraveled road

Eleven — United Artists and *Too Late for Tears* (1949)

above the L.A. skyline. Jane does not want to go to a party the couple has been invited to because "she cannot keep up with the Joneses" and that as a guest she will feel uncomfortable because she has no diamonds to show off and a rather unfashionable dress. While asking her husband to turn the car around, she fools with the dashboard, causing the headlights to flicker twice. Another car approaches and drops a leather bag into their back seat and speeds away. They stop their car and Jane asks Alan to open the bag, which contains $100,000 in small unmarked bills. Another car, signaling with its headlights, suddenly comes upon them and Jane takes the wheel, driving off furiously, finally losing the car following them closely in L.A. city traffic. Jane says, "The money was literally thrown in our laps ... no one knows we have it." Followed by a motorcycle cop, Jane takes Alan's revolver out of the glove compartment and places it under her bag. Alan had gone through a red light on a fast turn and Jane lies to the cop that they are hurrying to get married in Las Vegas. The cop lets them go and they arrive at their fashionable apartment house with a private garage in the basement. Pete, a black man who washes cars and takes care of the garage, questions Alan about the bag. "Just some storage," quips Jane and they go up to their fifth floor apartment. Locking the door behind them and putting on just a few lights, Alan opens the bag again and throws the contents on the bed. He believes they should return the money to the police, saying, "It's a blind alley, with a big barred gate at the end, if we keep the money." Jane says that all she has to look forward to is debts and installments, as if Alan is not a good provider. "We have no right to this money," Alan declares. Persuaded by Jane, he decides to keep it for a week.

There is a knock on the door. Alan hides the money as Jane answers the knock. It is Kathy (played by Kristine Miller), Alan's sister, who lives right across the hall. After Kathy leaves after a few minutes of conversation, Alan is determined to go to the district attorney with the money but once again, Jane convinces Alan to check the bag with only $60,000 in it at Union Station and keep it for a week. Alan places the claim check into his overcoat pocket, which has a hole in it, and the ticket falls into the lining of the coat. They drive back to their apartment and the next day (one of the few daylight scenes in the film), Jane begins buying presents for herself, among them a fur wrap. Another knock at the door, but his time it is Detective Danny Fuller of the Fuller Detective Bureau (played by that wonderful sleazy actor Dan Duryea). Jane lets Danny in "without a search warrant," and after going through several rooms he discovers the presents in Jane's lower kitchen closet. "So you started to spend it already!"

Jane denies having any money and Danny begins to slap her in the face. She then lies that they handed the money over to the police and there should be a newspaper story about it in tomorrow's papers. Danny leaves and says he'll return if there is no story. Alan comes home early from work because a bank employee called him about a large number of checks that have come through their joint account. Jane lies to Alan that she bought a few things she needed. He mentions her last husband, Blanchard, who lost all his money and committed suicide because of it. Jane is horrified at Alan bringing up the past but Alan still does not want to keep the bag. They compromise: They will check the bag at Union Station and at the end of the week, if nobody claims it, they'll keep it.

The next morning, Danny returns to the apartment and wants his cash. She tries to seduce him with a drink but he refuses. She is so possessed with the thought of losing that money that "it makes her deathly sick inside when she thinks about it." She asks Danny to meet her at West Lake Park by the big palm tree on the lake at 9 P.M. and she will signal him with a flashlight. Of course her husband is unaware of Danny's existence and the 9 P.M. meeting. At his suggestion, they have a reprise of their first date: dinner at Romoli's and a boat ride on the lake afterwards. Jane has taken Alan's gun from his dresser drawer for protection, supposedly from Danny. At the lake, the couple rents a motorboat for four but Jane changes her mind and wants to return to shore. The scene is very darkly lighted. Jane declares she does not want to keep the money and, while looking for cigarettes in Jane's purse, Alan finds his gun. They struggle over it and Alan is shot once and dies. She signals Danny and they sink Alan's body. Danny wears Alan's hat and overcoat when they return the boat to the landing and she pays as Danny runs ahead. Jane now says the money is buried in Coldwater Canyon, but first Danny must take the car back to their apartment garage so Pete, the garage man, will think he returned with her. Then Danny goes off with the car, supposedly to buy some alcohol and cigarettes.

Jane, returning to her apartment, asks Kathy in for a night cap. Apparently Alan has not shown up at the local liquor store or drugstore after a few hours and Jane calls the police. Jane and Danny drive to retrieve the money at Coldwater Canyon. Danny realizes Jane is going to kill him. ("I didn't know they made them that way anymore — beautiful as you and

Eleven — United Artists and *Too Late for Tears* (1949)

as hard!") Jane drives the car a bit further down the road and leaves it with the keys inside. Two vagabonds pick up the car and drive it to the Mexican border.

The following day, Jane visits Danny's apartment after finding out where he lives. He treats her badly because she is there for only one purpose — to retrieve Alan's coat and hat without telling him why. So Danny looks through the hatband and the pockets of the coat but comes up only with a blank ticket in the lining. Jane faints and the scene shifts to Jane's apartment while she is out. Kathy has a pass key, looks in the drawer where Alan keeps his gun, but it is not there. However, under the wrapping for his gun, she finds a claim check for Union Station. Don Blake arrives at Jane's door just as Kathy is leaving and she pushes him into her apartment upon hearing the sound of the elevator, presumably because Jane is returning. Jane visits Kathy that evening, after lying about going to the Dept. of Missing Persons and invites her into her apartment. Jane accuses Alan of lying about his "supposed" affair and Kathy believes if Alan was going to leave, he would take his favorite war possession with him — his gun. Jane opens the drawer to Kathy and she is surprised it is there! Now Kathy knows for certain Jane is lying about the entire situation.

The doorbell rings again and it is Lt. Breach (played by Barry Kelley) from the Bureau of Missing Persons. He asks Jane to describe the "other woman" in front of Kathy and the latter realizes it's almost a description of Jane herself. Jane has lied again and the police notify Jane her car was found near San Diego on the Mexican border. Kathy wastes no time in telling Jane there was no "other woman" in Alan's life. Then Jane invites Don Blake in for a drink and questions him about his military service with Alan in Ipswich, England during World War II. Don feels there is a "third degree" quality to her questions, but tells Jane there is a guy in a plaid suit hanging around her apartment. Of course, it is Danny, who enters Jane's apartment as Don leaves it, but waits to follow him home, taking his license number. Don returns to Kathy's apartment, tells Don about the claim ticket and gives it to him just as they head out for dinner. Kathy has to trust someone with her discovery but Jane interrupts their evening out, inviting Don to meet Judd Sharber, supposedly a fellow flyer who cannot identify Don as a member of the same air squadron. In the interim, Jane sees Danny a few hours earlier, asking him to buy some poison for she knows too much and wants her dead. Don meets Kathy in her apartment and they decide to go sleuthing in Westlake Park. They question the boat operator (played by child actor Billy Halop) who remembers that the woman paid for the ride and the man hurried off the boat quickly. While investigating this incident, Don and Kathy fall in love. After three kisses in Don's car, she goes up to her apartment. Meanwhile, Danny also secures the best poison and returns with it to Jane's apartment. The man he bought it from says Danny doesn't look like a killer, but wonders what he would have said if Jane had bought the bottle.

The next scene takes place in Kathy's apartment. Kathy takes the Claim Check and gives it to Don. Jane meets them in the hall, and after Sharber had exposed Don's identity as a charlatan, not knowing Alan or flying with him, Sharber leaves Jane's apartment and Kathy asks Don for the little "something" she gave him. Don appeals to Kathy to trust him but Jane pulls out Alan's gun, guesses it is the claim ticket while Kathy runs out to call the police and Jane knocks Don unconscious. With the help of a doctor who lives in the apartment building, Kathy helps Don to revive. Don reveals his name is Don "Blanchard," the brother of Jane's first husband who never believed his brother committed suicide unless Jane drove him to it.

The scene changes to Union Station where Jane lies to a handsome grifter she'll pay him $5 if he goes to the claims area and secures her bag. Sexually attracted to Jane, he claims the bag and reads the note attached to it: "If a woman tries to claim this bag, call the police at once!" Hurriedly, he asks her for the $5 and takes off. Jane reads the note and since the police could not go to Union Station on a wild tip, Don steers them to Danny's apartment where Jane has some unfinished business. Jane arrives with the bag of money and Danny reveals to her how he blackmailed an insurance agent who sold false policies and was collecting the premiums for years. The money is in small, unmarked bills and could be spent anywhere. After Danny reveals this information, now Jane knows everything she wanted about the "drop-off" and the racket itself, so no one will come after them. Danny says to Jane: "Don't ever change. I don't think I'd like you with a heart." They decide to drink a toast to their success at retrieving the money and their future in Mexico. Jane prepares the drinks. They toast, she swallows hers first and then Danny takes his in one long gulp. Jane steps back and Danny suddenly realizes he has been poisoned. He steps towards her and falls to the floor. Jane starts to cry a little but its "too late for 'real' tears."

In the next scene, the police arrive at Danny's apartment and realize it's too late for him. The darkness of the scene is oppressive. Don asks the Police Lieutenant to have the lake dragged for Alan's body which would cost about $4000. Meanwhile, a female floozie and friend of Danny's stops by the apartment; she thought he killed himself because this big deal he had going didn't work out.

The next scene cuts to bright daylight and the highway from California to Mexico. Jane has stopped her car to re-arrange her luggage, stuffs the stolen money into an elegant suitcase and some in back of the trunk. A Western stranger stops behind her on the road, and picks up a $100 bill. The police drive up behind the two stopped cars and the officer asks if the Westerner is bothering her. Jane says no curtly and drives off. She passes through the Mexican border and drives straight to the capitol, Mexico City. Registering at one of the most elegant hotels and taking a penthouse, Jane signs the register with her maiden name "Petrie." Coming out of the dining room with an elegant mustachioed Mexican on her arm, she is wearing a beautiful evening gown, a fur stole and a diamond bracelet. "Carlos" asks her out to see the jai'alai games but Jane says, "Mañana," and returns to her elegant penthouse suite. There is a knock at the door and thinking it is Carlos, opens it willingly, but it is Don Blake. "Widows don't need divorces, do they?" he asks.

As Don questions Jane about Danny Fuller, she denies knowing him or having $60,000. Then Don says "he'll drop Alan's body back in the lake where he found it unless she gives him half of the money." Don is counting on this lie to secure $4000 to drag the lake in Los Angeles. Jane then offers to give him $30,000, having tricked Jane into her admission of guilt. But Jane keeps on lying, saying the money is in the hotel safe, then later brings out a suitcase filled with money. Don just takes $4000 to have the lake dragged, then phones Lieut. Rivera in the lobby to arrest Jane. Rivera arrives with another cop armed with a pistol and Jane backs away from them towards the French windows of the suite. Don then tells her his real name is "Blanchard" as Jane grabs handfuls of the blackmail money and backs out through the doors of the balcony, tumbling over the guard rail to her death twenty floors below. We do not see her bloodied body, only her hand with the diamond bracelet grasping the blackmail money for which she killed two men. Don comes down to the lobby and Kathy was waiting there for him. "Short honeymoon," he tells her as he grasps her arm. "Jane?" she says, aware of the commotion outside of the hotel and Jane's accidental fall. The honeymooners go off on arm and arm together. The End title is seen against dark clouds on a grayish background that says in black letters "An Astor Films Release."

Lizabeth Scott made only about 20 films in her entire career. She had a very sultry, deep voice, blonde hair and blue eyes and was originally hired by Paramount Pictures for color films. Her only color noir *Desert Fury* (1947) had John Hodiak playing a gangster hiding out in a small town. But Scott's career really began in 1946, when she played the girlfriend of Van Heflin in Lewis Milestone's *The Strange Love of Martha Ivers*. Director John Cromwell thought she could play a femme fatale opposite Humphrey Bogart in Columbia's *Dead Reckoning* (1947). Returning to Paramount, she played Burt Lancaster's girlfriend in Byron Haskin's only other film noir *I Walk Alone* (1948). At United Artists, she played a model engaged in chicanery with Dick Powell in Andre de Toth's *Pitfall* (1948) before making *Too Late for Tears* that same year. In 1950, she played the girlfriend of gambler Charlton Heston in William Dieterle's *Dark City* for Paramount. Then she was the nice girlfriend of reporter Robert Hutton in *The Racket* (1951) with Robert Mitchum and Robert Ryan. Her noir roles ended with this film although she continued to work in 1972.

Don Defore played in scores of motion pictures as a second or third lead with his name usually below the title. He appeared in several film noirs beginning with *Too Late for Tears* and *Southside 1-1000* (1950) but his best role in noir was as Charlton Heston's gambling brother in *Dark City*. Tall and handsome, Defore appeared in many westerns and was considered a reliable leading man, but not especially heroic.

Dan Duryea was another actor who was no stranger to film noir. He never signed a contract with any studio, but worked as an independent actor, especially in noir roles as the villain during the 1940s and 1950s. He was always the second or third lead actor in a drama, and always the most memorable in the cast. He began his noir career in the mid–1940s; his early genre credits include musical star Deanna Durbin's first film noir *Lady on a Train* (1945), directed by Charles David. He worked with directors Fritz Lang in *Ministry of Fear* (1944) and *Scarlet Street* (1945). His other memorable roles were in *Black Angel* (1946) as an amnesiac piano player, *Criss Cross* (1949) as the proprietor of a nightclub double-crossed by Burt Lancaster and Yvonne de Carlo, *Manhandled* (1949) as a thief trying to kill Dorothy Lamour, *One Way Street* (1950) as a gang leader who tries to reclaim his girlfriend and $200,000 of stolen money in Mexico,

Eleven — United Artists and *Too Late for Tears* (1949)

Storm Fear (1956) as a wounded bank robber and *The Burglar* (1957) in the title role.

Arthur Kennedy began his film career in the early forties, usually playing a good guy in the 100-plus films he made for various studios. A solid character actor, he starred in several film noirs. In his early career, he played a bank robber accomplice with Humphrey Bogart in Warner Bros.' *High Sierra* (1941) the brother of fighter Kirk Douglas in United Artists' *Champion* (1949), and a newspaper reporter in Paramount's *Chicago Deadline* (1949). Also in 1949, he starred in RKO's *The Window*, based on the Cornell Woolrich story "The Boy Cried Murder," as the father of a boy (Bobby Driscoll) who witnessed a murder while on a fire escape in Manhattan's tenement district. Kennedy's meanest role (and perhaps a bit unbelievable) was in Fox's *Peyton Place* (1957), when he played the rapist of virginal Hope Lange. Reliability was Kennedy's forte as a character actor and you could always count on him for an excellent performance, especially as the intimidated husband Alan Palmer in *Too Late for Tears,* where he easily succumbs to the charms (and lies) of Lizabeth Scott.

Kristine Miller had a very short Hollywood career, always playing the "good girl." Film noir–wise she was also in *Desert Fury*, *I Walk Alone* and *Shadow on the Wall* (1950). A very likable actress, she rarely saw her name above the title.

Barry Kelley appeared in several film noirs during the fifties, usually playing a tough Irish cop or gangster. His memorable roles are as a detective in MGM's *Force of Evil* (1948), a judge in Columbia's *Knock on Any Door* (1949), a corrupt detective in MGM's *The Asphalt Jungle* (1950), a gambler running a horse race betting operation in Columbia's *711 Ocean Drive* (1950) and a treasury agent in Columbia's *The Killer That Stalked New York* (1950).

Producer Hunt Stromberg worked for MGM before he started to independently produce his own films, released mostly through United Artists. Of the 31 independent films he made, he is best known for his last one, *Too Late for Tears*, *Lured* (1947), a film noir starring Lucille Ball and George Sanders, and *Between Midnight and Dawn* (1950) which starred Edmond O'Brien and Mark Stevens as good cops chasing gangster hoodlum Donald Buka.

Byron Haskin directed only two film noirs in a long career which spanned over 40 years as a director and a special effects professional. Directing films late in the forties, he made *I Walk Alone* for producer Hal Wallis at Paramount and then *Too Late for Tears* for United Artists, both starring Lizabeth Scott in good and bad girl roles respectively. Although many critics consider his noir films marginal, there is a kind of darkness that permeates them and a fatalism that he excels in creating despite low budgets.

Writer Roy Huggins will mostly be remembered for the creation of the long-running television series *The Fugitive*, writing 23 episodes starring David Janssen as the doctor looking for his wife's murderer, a one-armed assailant. He also wrote for the big screen in the fifties and sixties. He barely ventured into film noir, writing only two film scripts: *Too Late for Tears*, which was drawn from a series first published in *The Saturday Evening Post*, and *Pushover* (1954) starring Fred MacMurray, Kim Novak and Dorothy Malone. MacMurray played a "bad cop" seduced by Novak in the same style as Billy Wilder's *Double Indemnity* (1944). Huggins achieved most of his success from writing for the television series *Maverick, The Virginian, 77 Sunset Strip* and *Run for Your Life*. He died in 2002.

Cameraman William Mellor worked on 88 films during his career, most famously for director George Stevens' super-production *The Greatest Story Ever Told* (released in 1965, two years after the cinematographer's death in 1963). During the fifties, he worked on many CinemaScope and color productions for Fox. His only noirs were *Too Late for Tears*, photographed in a very dark style to match the "evilness" of the characters, and MGM's *The Unknown Man*, in which his noir style virtually disappeared: Most scenes were photographed in daylight, mostly in courtrooms, where an ethical lawyer (Walter Pidgeon) defended a murderer who was found innocent but proved to be guilty. Noir style was not Mellor's specialty, but it certainly worked in a B like *Too Late for Tears*.

R. Dale Butts was a composer, mostly for Republic Pictures. His *Too Late for Tears* music matches the dark moods of the film. At Republic he scored two more noirs, *The City That Never Sleeps* (1953) and *Hell's Half-Acre* (1954), the first about a Chicago police unit and the second with Wendell Corey trying to identify a soldier who went missing for several years only to turn up under a different name in Hawaii.

The first still shows avaricious Lizabeth Scott as Jane Palmer, after she has opened a bag full of money in the Palmer bedroom. Her lustrous smile indicates she wants to keep it but her husband Alan (Arthur Kennedy) looks at a group of bills dubiously.

Eleven — United Artists and *Too Late for Tears* (1949)

Too Late for Tears (1949): Lizabeth Scott looks at the money on the bed as Arthur Kennedy reproves her for her greed.

The second still shows Danny Fuller (Dan Duryea) drunk and holding a gun on Jane in his cheap apartment. Note the dark lighting in both stills. Jane's greed is the dark shadow that haunts us throughout this film.

Among United Artists' best noirs are the following:

Body and Soul (1947) Robert Rossen, director. Cast: John Garfield, Lilli Palmer, Hazel Brooks, Anne Revere, William Conrad. A boxer from a poor neighborhood becomes champion, loses love and regains it after he leaves gambling and the boxing ring. One of the great Garfield performances!

D.O.A. (1949) Rudolph Mate, director. Cast: Edmond O'Brien, Pamela Britton, Luther Adler. A CPA (Edmond O'Brien, brilliantly cast) goes on a pleasure trip to San Francisco and in the hotel bar drinks a beverage containing luminous poisoning. With only a few days, he wants to

Too Late for Tears (1949): Unshaven Dan Duryea and Lizbeth Scott have a face-off.

track down his murderer before he dies. Wonderful use of locales and a terrific Dimitri Tiomkin score.

Gun Crazy (1950) Joseph H. Lewis, director. Cast: John Dall, Peggy Cummins, Berry Kroeger. A Bonnie and Clyde story where lovers meet at a carnival, share a love for guns and ammunition and rob banks. Of course the law tracks them down with a surprise ending in a swamp. One of Dall's best roles; British actress Cummins was never better.

He Ran All the Way (1951) John Berry, director. Cast: John Garfield, Shelley Winters, Wallace Ford. A murderer holes up in the apartment of his girlfriend, who both intend to make a getaway. A hostage drama with an unhappy ending.

99 River Street (1953) Phil Karlson, director. Cast: John Payne, Evelyn Keyes, Brad Dexter, Peggie Castle. An ex-boxer drives a cab for a living; his dissatisfied wife falls for a gangster and regrets it. A particularly menacing noir.

Eleven — United Artists and *Too Late for Tears* (1949)

The Killing (1956) Stanley Kubrick, director. Cast: Sterling Hayden, Coleen Gray, Vince Edwards, Jay C. Flippen, Elisha Cook, Jr., Marie Windsor. Suspenseful tale of a racetrack robbery with betrayals galore; everything goes wrong. Great direction from Kubrick and his ensemble team of actors.

My favorite runner-up is *Kansas City Confidential* (1952).

Chapter Twelve

Universal Pictures and *The Killers* (1946)

Universal Pictures was founded by Carl Laemmle, Sr., in 1915. It's the oldest studio in Hollywood. Laemmle appointed Irving Thalberg his production chief in 1920. Thalberg moved over to MGM in 1924; Carl Laemmle, Jr., was appointed production chief in 1929. In 1936, Laemmle Sr. sold Universal.

Ten years later, Universal merged with William Goetz's International Pictures, founded in 1943. It was now Universal-International, with Goetz as production chief. All films made by Universal were released under their own original banner with that famous globe of the world turning, indicating the wide reach of "Universal."

The Killers (1946) was one of the first productions released under the Universal-International banner. After the U-I logo appears, one hears the first somber notes of a Miklos Rosza score, "dum, de, dum, dum," later to become the musical motif for a famously successful cops-and-robbers series, Jack Webb's *Dragnet*. In the opening shot, the camera is placed behind the front seats of a car speeding down a dark highway. Two men are talking, looking for a sign, Brentwood (New Jersey), as the credits of the film roll by in white letters against this shadowy background.

Two men, one heavy (Max, played by William Conrad), the other of average build (Al, played by Charles McGraw) leave their car and walk down a street, casting long, dark shadows behind them. First they look into the Tri-State Gas Station. They walk up the street to Henry's Diner from where all the light source, except for one lamp post, seems to be emanating from. Henry, the owner and only counterman (played by Harry Hayden), has just passed a bottle of ketchup over to Nick Adams (Phil

Brown), the only customer in the diner. There is much banter going on about the items on the dinner menu when the killers try to order and are told "Dinner will be ready at 6 o'clock" and it's only 5:50 P.M. and the dinners are not ready. So the pair settle for orders of ham and eggs and bacon and eggs. They then ask for "a real drink" but the diner does not serve hard liquor. The camera shows Nick eating his sandwich. The killers ask Nick to identify himself and call him "another bright boy." They order Nick to go around the counter, also ordering Sam (Bill Walker), the cook, to come out of the kitchen. "Anybody comes in, tell 'em the cook is off for the evening." Nick asks, "What's it all about?" McGraw pokes his gun through the kitchen service window and says, "We're here to kill 'The Swede.'" They ask, "Why are you killing him?" They answer, "For a friend." "What are you going to do with us afterwards?" asks the counterman. "That depends," says Max.

At that point, a train conductor comes in and asks for dinner. They tell him Sam is sick and so he'll have to have supper up the street. Another customer enters and is turned away by the owner. The owner goes into the kitchen immediately and unties Sam and Nick. After the killers leave, Nick says, "Why would anyone want to kill the Swede?" and runs out of the diner, down back alleys, jumps over fences and goes up to Swede's room. The door is unlocked. Swede (Burt Lancaster in his first screen role) is lying down in an athletic shirt and slacks, his face completely covered by shadow. Nick tells him the story about the killers coming for him. "There's nothing I can do about it. Thanks for coming," he answers. Nick asks Swede to go to the police, get out of town. "I'm through with all that running around." Nick asks, "Why do they want to kill you?" Swede replies, "I did something wrong, once! Thanks for coming." Nick leaves.

The camera stays trained on Swede, lying in bed. He is waiting for the killers. He hears the front door open and we watch the killers climb the stairs. Swede never gets out of bed; he looks towards the door. The killers take out their guns. The door opens and 11 shots are fired, the dark room filling with their deadly light. The camera cuts to Swede's right hand gripping the bedpost, sliding down into a deathly repose. We hear the killers running down the stairs and out the front door. (The aforementioned is literally a description of the original 11-page story by Ernest Hemingway with one exception: Nick returns to the diner and is told by the cook and the counterman to forget about the whole incident. The director and writer chose not to put this scene into the film.)

The next scene takes place in the Brentwood Police Station. Riordan, an insurance investigator (played by Edmond O'Brien), is looking through Swede's papers. He finds a life insurance policy leaving $2500 to a Mary Ellen "Queenie" Dougherty (Queenie Smith), a maid who worked in an Atlantic City hotel. He also finds a green silk scarf in another envelope — "Could be a souvenir," Riordan remarks. At the morgue, the mortician describes the eleven bullets "that nearly tore him in half." Riordan repeats Swede's last words, "Once I did something wrong."

Nick tells Riordan that he remembers a "big guy" driving into the gas station in a large black four-door Cadillac. In a flashback, we see the big guy (Colfax, played by Albert Dekker) recognize Swede and ask him to check the oil, then clean the windshield outside and inside the car. They don't say a word to each other but after the car leaves the station, Swede says he doesn't feel very well — he knew his number was up! Nick feels he can identify the heavyset man with the Cadillac. He also realizes that Swede must have been a fighter from the latter's broken knuckles he noticed in the morgue.

The film cuts to a new location, Atlantic City. Riordan visits the hotel where Queenie works as a maid. She doesn't know anyone by the name of "Swede" or Pete Lund but upon seeing a photograph, she recognizes "Mr. Nielsen," a guest back in 1940. Queenie says he stayed a few days with a woman and when she entered the room to clean it, the room was a wreck and Nielsen tried to throw himself out the window. He shouted, "She's gone! She's gone!" Queenie stopped him from committing suicide. Nielsen also said, "Charleston was right!"

The next scene takes place at the Atlantic Insurance Company. Riordan's boss Kenyon (Donald MacBride) wants Riordan off the case but the latter asks for one more day. Meanwhile, Kenyon's secretary finds out the identity of Swede: Ole Anderson, born 1908 in Philadelphia, weight 173, arrested for robbery and served three years, and was caught by Detective Sam Lubinsky (played by Sam Levene) in Philadelphia.

On the rooftop of Lubinsky's apartment building, Riordan finds out the detective and Ole were childhood friends; Lubinsky joined the P.D. and Ole became a professional fighter. Riordan asks, "Why did you pinch him?" In another flashback, we watch Ole and Tiger Lewis boxing in a crowded arena. Ole is getting murdered and refuses to throw his right fist at his opponent. His girlfriend, Lilly (Virginia Christine), is watching the massacre. Ole is knocked out. In the next scene, we are in Ole's dressing room. "Doc" looks at Ole's right hand and tells him he'll never fight again. His manager complains he lost a $10,000 investment in sponsoring Ole. "No next time for you, Ole. The bones are all broken in your right hand." Lilly is waiting outside the dressing room and she goes home with him, accompanied by Lubinsky. Ole wouldn't think of joining the police force for a mere $2200 a year and so Lilly married Lubinsky!

There is another flashback that supports Lilly's choice of a mate. Apparently Lilly had a date with Ole to go to the movies, but instead they went to a party given by Jake the rake (John Miljan), a rather nefarious type associated with gangsters, and Big Jim Colfax, who owns the apartment and apparently is serving out a prison sentence. Lilly does not like the atmosphere or people at the party but enters the room anyway. The hostess Kitty Collins, sings "The More I Know of Love." All Kitty says to Ole is "Hello" and the latter is completely attracted to her. Ole walks over to the piano. Kitty is wearing a black evening gown with a strap over one shoulder. Ole says to Lilly, "She's beautiful," and Ole is a goner. Lilly realizes she's lost Ole forever. As Kitty (played by 21-year-old Ava Gardner) sings and hums the song "The More I Know of Love," Gardner, all dimpled and sexy, is just gorgeous and irresistible. We believe Kitty has some relationship to Big Jim Colfax or Jake but don't know exactly what it is. "The boat had sailed," remembers Lilly and so she went home alone.

Returning to the Lubinskys' rooftop, Riordan asks about Colfax and Lubinsky replies, "A thief with a touch of class. But he went straight as soon as he got out of jail." In another flashback, Lubinsky takes us into Lou Tingle's Café. He tells Riordan he was given a tip about some "hot" jewelry. Upon seeing Kitty at a table smoking and talking with some friends, Lubinsky notices she is wearing a diamond brooch. Kitty is now Ole's girl. Kitty tries to hide the brooch and puts it in a bowl of soup, but Lubinsky finds it. Kitty lies about wearing the brooch and then Ole enters the scene. Looking prosperous and wearing a beautiful camel coat, Ole is now working in the numbers racket. Lubinsky accuses Kitty of shoplifting the brooch but Ole takes the blame for it as Kitty sobs. He clouts Lubinsky in the face and dares him to catch him. Three days later Ole is picked up by the police and serves a three-year term for Kitty.

The camera cuts from Lubinsky's flashback to the present, Ole's burial scene, where he identifies Charleston, Ole's prison-mate for three years. The two of them are talking in a bar where Charleston (played by Vince

Barnett) reveals that you can't help knowing a man for three years when you spend that time together locked up in a cell only eight feet apart. It seems Ole had a green silk scarf with harps and was always twirling it in his hands, thinking of Kitty in prison. He asks Charleston to look Kitty up when he gets out. In the bar, he tells of his experiences with Ole in flashback, trying to interest him in astronomy, but Ole is only interested in the green silk scarf. In the bar, once again, Charleston admits he never found Kitty but he did see Swede again. In yet another flashback, we witness a meeting arranged by Colfax with Kitty, Charleston, Dum Dum Clarke (played by Jack Lambert) and Blinky Franklin (played by Jeff Corey)—in short, the entire gang is waiting for Swede to talk about a future caper. Swede enters the room and is surprised to find Kitty there, sitting sexily on a bed. Apparently, the "heist" will be a $250,000 payroll job, with Colfax taking $100,000, the largest slice since he designed the caper. Charleston is out, he says, since he doesn't want to spend any more time in prison. Charleston leaves willingly, thinking Swede will come out after him, but he never sees Swede exit the hotel room.

The next scene takes place in Riordan's office. After scanning many newspapers, he finds out that a quarter of a million dollars was stolen from the Prentiss Hat factory in Hackensack, New Jersey. In another flashback, we cut to the robbery scene. Four men from the gang are lined up with a group of workers at the entrance to the factory, waiting to punch in time cards; these four enter the paymaster's office on the second floor. With guns drawn, they hold up the office and make their escape, walking parallel to a truck that proceeds through an open gate. As they run towards two different cars to make their getaway, a policeman is shot and one gang member is shot. Another is described as wearing a green silk handkerchief over his face. This event took place on July 26, 1940, according to the newspapers.

We cut back to the present and find Riordan in Kenyon's office, the latter pleading with him to drop the case. The claims were already paid out but Riordan wants to retrieve the quarter million dollars and find the robbers. Just then, Lubinsky telephones the office.

The camera cuts to a hospital and Blinky's death bed. He was caught in the local shootout and is rambling about the hat factory robbery. We listen to Blinky's ramblings and flashback to the half-way house. Colfax is reviewing the plans for the robbery and wants to make sure everything goes as scheduled. Colfax is also threatened by Swede for trying to slap

Kitty because she is paying attention to the ex-boxer. Kitty says she can take care of herself, but during a card game, Swede knocks over Colfax and threatens to beat him. But Swede was wrong to do it since Colfax had the winning hand and both agree to settle their personal business later. The scene cuts back from the flashback to Blinky's hospital bed and Blinky's death. But Riordan realizes that Blinky left a clue about Swede "running away with the hold-up money."

In another flashback, everyone involved in the robbery arrives at the "farm," not the half-way house. We watch Swede, armed with a gun, enter the farmhouse through the second floor and get the drop on the gang counting the money. He retrieves all the cash, runs out, fires bullets into the tires of the parked cars of the gang and takes off. It seems the group forgot to tell him that the half-way house burned down and they were supposed to meet elsewhere. But Kitty went to Swede's hotel room and told him of Colfax's change of plan, infuriating him more by calling Swede dirty names and telling him of the new rendezvous.

The scene changes to Swede's room in Brentwood. Riordan is there in an adjoining room, waiting for some gang members to show up since Swede took their money. Only Dum Dum arrives and Riordan gets the drop on him. Dum Dum admits to shooting Blinky under Colfax's orders but a fight ensues and Dum Dum gains control over Riordan, taking his gun. Now he says that Swede and Kitty spent some time together in an Atlantic City hotel and they had the money. Dum Dum knocks Riordan out and escapes from Swede's old room, also eluding the police in Brentwood.

The next scene takes place on a train to Pittsburgh as Riordan and Lubinsky discuss the fact that Big Jim Colfax has become a successful contractor there and built a new firm called Colfax & Ward. Riordan interviews Colfax, who says he knows nothing about Ole Anderson or the robbery. Riordan accuses Colfax of heading the gang and is also interested in the whereabouts of Kitty Collins.

Colfax denies knowing Kitty's whereabouts but hates "a double-crossing dame." You might say Kitty signed Ole's death warrant after hearing Riordan's story. But through Colfax, Riordan sends out word to the gang that Kitty better show up by 10 P.M. tonight to contact Riordan about her role in the robbery. Colfax claims he wants to have a word with her himself: "We've got some unfinished business." Riordan claims that the maid in the Atlantic City hotel can recognize her and she risks a prison term if she doesn't show up to clarify what happened to Swede and to the stolen money.

The film cuts to Riordan's hotel room where he and Lubinsky are waiting by the telephone. "She'll call," says Riordan, and the phone rings. It is Kitty and they arrange to meet in front of the Adelphi Movie Theatre in 20 minutes. Riordan will send a man wearing a blue suit and a bow tie. (It's really Riordan himself!) Kitty shows up at the rendezvous and is followed in a car by an elderly man with a cane. In another car, the killers, Al and Max, follow them too.

We are now in New York City. Kitty and Riordan enter the Green Cat Club on Sullivan Street in Greenwich Village, sit at a corner table across from the bar and order. Riordan asks, "Where is the money?" He has Blinky's deathbed statement that she was in on the caper and the chambermaid's testimony identifying her as the woman who accompanied Swede in Atlantic City. Kitty says she is now married and has a whole new life built up over the last six years and would fight to keep her husband, home and everything she has. Riordan suggests they need a fall guy: Colfax. Kitty replies: "Even the old Kitty Collins never sang!" Riordan threatens to call the police and give her over to them. Then Kitty begins to fill him in on the details of what happened and how Colfax planned the robbery.

In flashback narrated by Kitty, she tells of going to Swede's place to tell him about the fire at the half-way house and the new meeting place at the farmer's house at 2 A.M. "They are going to double-cross you!" She plays up the "hate" angle of all the men. Swede says he won't give her away for telling him and they kiss passionately.

Back in the Green Cat Club, Kitty becomes nervous. She suggests leaving and goes to the powder room. The signature music sounds, "Dum de dum dum, dum de dum dum," and the killers enter the bar. They spot Riordan at a rear table alone, begin approaching him and start shooting. Riordan protects himself, using the overturned table as a shield while firing back at the men. What the men do not know is Detective Lubinsky is standing at the bar and shoots both Al and Max. Riordan goes directly to the powder room but Kitty has made her escape through a window. Obviously, Kitty had set Riordan up to be murdered.

The camera cuts to a long inside view of Colfax's house. We view the interior from the top of a grand carpeted staircase that leads to the front door. Shots are heard and Dum Dum falls dead, rolling to the bottom of the staircase. Riordan and Lubinsky, together with the police force, climb

Twelve — Universal Pictures and *The Killers* (1946)

the staircase after going through the front door; they find Colfax on an upper stairwell, mortally wounded. Colfax admits he was married to Kitty ("a wife cannot testify against her husband") but Riordan chose to make himself a target to bring her out into the open and get something on her that would send her to prison. Colfax asks for a last cigarette. He says that he couldn't let Swede live because other gang members would find him and Kitty. At this point, Kitty asks her husband to tell the police she did not know the killers were coming to the Green Cat to dispose of Riordan (but she did know) and she breaks down tearfully as Colfax dies on the stairs as she is handcuffed by the police. And the Swede never knew Kitty went back to Colfax which the rest of the gang knew — and that Kitty was Colfax's wife and went straight back to him with all the money. "A double-cross to end all double-crosses," says Lubinsky. None of this would have ever come to light if Riordan didn't investigate a $2500 payment on an insurance policy to a maid in Atlantic City.

Riordan returns to his office and is congratulated by his boss, Mr. Kenyon, for such fine work and he tells him somewhat amusingly, "This is Friday. Take the weekend off."

And we listen to the only comical musical bars from Miklos Rosza as the end titles come up. An extraordinary film noir, with a convoluted plot, but a satisfying ending and terrific performances by all actors.

Burt Lancaster made his film debut in *The Killers* after a single success acting on the Broadway stage. He was recommended for the part of Swede by Hal Wallis, who tested him for a color noir, *Desert Fury* (1947) but producer Mark Hellinger decided to use him while Lancaster waited for his Paramount contract to begin. Lancaster's early successes were in the following film noirs: *Brute Force* (1947), *I Walk Alone* and *Desert Fury* (1947), *Kiss the Blood Off My Hands* (1948), *Sorry, Wrong Number* (1948), *Criss Cross* (1949) and, for his own production company Hecht-Hill & Lancaster, *Sweet Smell of Success* (1957). Although he won the Academy Award for *Elmer Gantry* (1960), his earliest roles as a film noir anti-hero, where he appeared both tough and vulnerable, were the best of his career. He teamed up with *Killers* director Robert Siodmak twice more, in *Criss Cross* and in the adventure *The Crimson Pirate* (1952), a total disaster of a film.

Ava Gardner made some 60 films but never achieved stardom until she appeared in *The Killers* on loanout from MGM. She appeared in another two noirs, *Whistle Stop* (1946) with George Raft and *The Bribe*

(1949) with Robert Taylor. Her role as Kitty Collins struck the right notes with director Robert Siodmak, who made her into a key femme fatale, without using much makeup. Gardner was one of the most sensual and erotic actresses to appear on the screen in the forties and fifties and although she had achieved Hollywood stardom with MGM, her career never reached the heights of true art, perhaps because of her extraordinary lifestyle and multiple marriages.

Edmond O'Brien became a romantic leading man in the late thirties, but in costume dramas, especially RKO's version of *The Hunchback of Notre Dame,* not noir roles. His first and most important noir role was as insurance investigator Jim Riordan in *The Killers.* He never achieved real status in his noir roles although he gave convincing performances. His most memorable performance was in the noir thriller *D.O.A.* (1950) in which he plays a man who has been poisoned and has to find his killer, seeking revenge until he expires. His ten other noir films contain capable performances but are not extremely memorable, except for *The Hitch-Hiker* (1953), where he and co-star Frank Lovejoy are on a fishing trip in Northern Mexico and pick up William Talman, a psychotic hitchhiker who wants to murder them. Directed by Ida Lupino, this is the one film that scared me the most as a filmgoer. His noir titles are *The Web* (1947), *White Heat* (1949), *Backfire* (1950), *Between Midnight and Dawn* (1950), *711 Ocean Drive* (1950), *The Turning Point* (1952) and *Shield for Murder* (1954), which he also co-directed. O'Brien was good at playing men who were slightly corrupt and usually was never got the money or the dame.

Albert Dekker appeared in over 100 Hollywood films and is considered one of the industry's great villains, especially in *Among the Living* (1941) in which he played the dual role of twins, one of them a psychotic murderer, *Suspense* (1946) as a foil to gangster Barry Sullivan, *Destination Murder* (1950) and his best role as Dr. Soberin in Mickey Spillane's apocalyptic noir *Kiss Me Deadly* (1955). During the 1930s he was noted for his stage acting on Broadway but was more popular as a minor film noir icon.

Also coming from the Broadway stage was Sam Levene who frequently used his Jewish background to play a variety of roles in film noirs. He will always be remembered for his Detective Lubinsky in *The Killers.* He also appeared in other noirs: Elia Kazan's *Boomerang!* (1947), Jules Dassin's *Brute Force* (1947), and Dore Schary's *Crossfire* (1947).

Virginia Christine appeared in scores of films and only three film noirs, usually as the "good woman," not the femme fatale. Blonde, beautiful but lacking that necessary sexiness to be a star, she supported Burt Lancaster in *The Killers*, John Ireland in *The Gangster* (1947) and Joseph Cotten in *The Killer Is Loose* (1956). No stranger to television, she performed on many sitcoms and did commercials.

Jack Lambert has a face that is known to every film noir devotee. He appeared in all types of Hollywood films, especially film noirs where he usually played a hired killer or the henchman for some particular star actor. As Dum Dum, he participated in the heist in *The Killers*; as Press, a trucker and murderer, he was the dupe of Claude Rains in Michael Curtiz's *The Unsuspected* (1947). He also appeared in *Border Incident* (1949), *The Enforcer* (1951), *99 River Street* (1953) and *Kiss Me Deadly* (1955), but his presence in these noirs was not particularly distinguished nor emotionally frightening as he was in *The Unsuspected*. Lambert appeared in over 100 Hollywood films, many of them uncredited, in a variety of roles. He had a particularly malleable personae suited to all genres of films.

Just like Lambert, Charles McGraw played both good and bad guys during the forties and fifties and made some 140 appearances as both in Hollywood films. In addition to *The Killers*, he also appeared in the noirs *Brute Force* (1947), *The Gangster* (1947), *T-Men* (1947), *Berlin Express* (1948), *Reign of Terror* (1949), *Border Incident* (1950), *Side Street* (1950), *Armored Car Robbery* (1950), and *Roadblock* (1951). His most famous role was in Richard Fleischer's *The Narrow Margin* (1952), a glorious B film where he plays a police detective protecting a mobster's wife (Marie Windsor) on a train ride westward to California. What he does not know is that the woman is actually a cop who sacrifices her life to protect Jacqueline White, the real quarry. The film was made as a second feature although McGraw stood out magnificently in his role as cop and protector.

William Conrad began his career on films in *The Killers* as Max. The heavyset actor appeared in other film noirs with John Garfield (*Body and Soul*, 1947), Burt Lancaster (*Sorry, Wrong Number*, 1948), James Mason (*One Way Street*, 1950), Richard Basehart (*Tension*, 1950), Marshall Thompson (*Dial 1119*, 1950), Dick Powell (*Cry Danger*, 1951), and Robert Mitchum (*The Racket*, 1951). After his movie career fizzled, he made a success as a television detective, first in the series, *Cannon* in the 1970s, then *Nero Wolfe* in the 1980s. He also produced and directed.

It was producer Mark Hellinger's idea to take the 11-page Hemingway story and make it into a film by drafting writers Anthony Veiller do the screenplay. Hellinger, a newspaper columnist for the *New York Daily News*, brought together actors, writers and directors for the movies he produced: Besides *The Killers*, there were *They Drive by Night* (1940), *High Sierra* (1941), *Moontide* (1942), *The Two Mrs. Carrolls* (1947), *Brute Force* (1947) and *The Naked City* (1948). His films assure Hellinger (who died at age 44) a well-earned place in the noir canon of great films and producers.

Director Robert Siodmak is probably the most proflic noir director noted in this book. Deborah Alpi in her great book *Robert Siodmak* outlines Siodmak's complete career, from his Expressionist days in Germany, to his career in France and then finally his move to Hollywood, working in B films before hitting his stride in the film noirs *Christmas Holiday* (1944) with Deanna Durbin, *Phantom Lady* (1944) with Ella Raines, *Uncle Harry* (1945) with Geraldine Fitzgerald, *The Dark Mirror* (1945) with Olivia de Havilland playing twins, *The Spiral Staircase* (1946) with Dorothy McGuire as a mute, *Cry of the City* (1948) with Richard Conte, *Criss Cross* (1949) with Burt Lancaster and *The File on Thelma Jordon* (1950) with Barbara Stanwyck. These films represent his glory years. Siodmak's reputation rests upon the fact that he could create superior, entertaining thrillers. In collaboration with cameraman Woody Bredell and brilliant composer Miklos Rosza, he achieved the ultimate film noir style in sound and lighting and was gifted enough to extract the best performances from his stable of noir stars. He returned to Europe in 1955 and died there at age 73.

Screenwriter Anthony Veiller wrote about 40 screenplays in his entire career but is best known for his work on *The Killers,* taking the author's story and expanding into a cops-and-robbers detective story. It is rumored that John Huston helped with the dialogue but was under contract to another studio so took no screen credit. (Richard Brooks, a publicist, was largely responsible for the plot construction.) But it was the Hellinger-Siodmak team that created the master noir work that *The Killers* proved to be. Apparently Hellinger knew the crime scene intimately in New York as a reporter and had a fascination for the underworld. Having established his own production company, Mark Hellinger Productions, at Universal, he secured the talents of the writers mentioned above to work with Siodmak and turn out a realistic screenplay. Veiller co-wrote another fascinating noir screenplay with Orson Welles: *The Stranger* (RKO, 1946). He also wrote some of the *Why We Fight* shorts that were made during World War II.

Cinematographer Woody Bredell worked almost exclusively for Uni-

Twelve — Universal Pictures and *The Killers* (1946)

The Killers **(1946): (From left to right) Jeff Corey, Burt Lancaster, Albert Dekker, and Ava Gardener discuss the heist.**

versal Pictures and collaborated with Siodmak on the look of most of his famous film noirs like *Christmas Holiday* (1944), *Phantom Lady* (1944), and *The Killers*. Woody (real name Elwood) Bredell, of English origin, made only 75 films in a career which ended in 1975. He was equally adept at photographing in color, including Doris Day's Warner Bros. musical *Romance on the High Seas* (1947). But his greatest contribution is those rain-soaked, shadowy streets and unique placement of lighting that were his and Siodmak's contribution to film noir style.

Miklos Rosza's talents as a film composer were adequately described in Chapters 4 and 6. Of Hungarian origin, he spent most of his 85 years working in the musical departments, mostly at Paramount and MGM. His film noir scores, about a dozen of them, were always brilliant. His classical piece "Violin Concerto #2," written in 1956 for Jascha Heifetz, puts him in the realm of one of the really great composer of our time, apart from his motion picture scores.

The Killers (1946): Albert Dekker lies dead at the bottom of the staircase as (from left to right) Sam Levene, Edmond O'Brien and an unidentified actor look on.

Art director Jack Otterson worked on nearly four hundred films. He entered the film world in the early thirties as an architect. He only worked on three film noirs for Universal: *Black Angel* (1946) starring Dan Duryea as an alcoholic pianist who murders his wife and cannot remember, *The Killers* and *The Web* (1947), the latter with Edmond O'Brien as a lawyer who becomes the patsy of a murderer. Otterson and frequent co-worker Martin Obzina brought their expertise in style and setting to the noir films they worked on.

The first still takes place in a hotel room in New Jersey. Sitting from left to right are Blinky (Jeff Corey) and Big Jim Colfax (Albert Dekker). Standing are Swede (Burt Lancaster) and Kitty (Ava Gardner). The scene is appropriately lit for a poker game with men drinking beer in a crummy hotel room.

The second still comes from *The Killers*' final reel denoument of film.

Twelve — Universal Pictures and *The Killers* (1946)

The only light source is from the room on the right. Note the rich, ornate details of the post on the staircase and the wood carvings. The staircase is carpeted and the wallpaper has an autumnal leaf pattern. You can only see a table and the reflection of a lamp in the room to the right and a coat rack to the left of the policeman standing on the right, exquisitely carved out of wood.

The Killers is a quintessential noir film whose viewers must unscramble the disconnected story as told through flashbacks. It's as if each person's memory (or testimony) is part of a large puzzle — and one must make sense of the 11 flashbacks that lead to the conclusion. The initial element, Swede's murder, occurs because of his sexual obsession with Kitty Collins. Her greed brings about his total downfall. Ole is putty in her hands and accepts his fate as a passive victim of an avaricious virago.

Woody Bredell's sensational camerawork recalls Edwin Hopper's lonely paintings — all-night diners, gas stations, nightclubs, bars. Some scenes conjure up memories of Wegee's photos of mid–forties New York, especially the scene showing Swede's death. Cinematically speaking, *The Killers* mesmerized audiences, displaying all of the stylistic elements of crime films we now call film noir.

Also, it is the puzzle element, the flashbacks, the disjointed time elements, sometimes one overlapping the other that creates a corrupt universe, a chaotic environment, hopeless situations for most of the characters. When the film was remade in 1964, color replaced black and white. John Cassavetes and Angie Dickinson (in the Swede and Kitty roles) were no longer convincing in this new era, especially Ronald Reagan as Colfax because the world had changed and audiences felt more secure in the new techniques of the film world. The noir cycle only existed in a certain limited world, in black and white, where a scheming female could bring a man to his doom. Perhaps the 1964 version was in anticipation of the neo-noir movement and falls out of the classic film noir category, usually bracketed between the years 1940 and 1959. But let us never forget: Stories about flawed men and women who carry the burden of the past with them is one of the major themes of film noir and there is no easy exit for a noir protagonist. Their past usually catches up with them and there are no happy endings.

Universal made 24 film noirs during the heyday of this style. Some of the best are the following:

Shadow of a Doubt (1943) Alfred Hitchcock, director. Cast: Joseph Cotten, Teresa Wright, Macdonald Carey, Patricia Collinge, Hume Cronyn, Henry Travers. Charlie comes to visit his sister in the small town of Santa Rosa, California. His niece comes to believe he is the "Merry Widow Murderer" eluding capture by detectives. Terrific, unexpected ending.

Scarlet Street (1945) Fritz Lang, director. Cast: Edward G. Robinson, Joan Bennett, Dan Duryea. Based upon the French novel *La chienne* (*The Bitch*). A retired bank cashier meets and falls for a much younger woman whose pimp pushes her to inveigle a new apartment and sign his paintings as her own. The woman and the pimp meet tragic ends and the cashier is left quite alone.

Black Angel (1946) Roy William Neill, director. Cast: Dan Duryea, June Vincent, Peter Lorre, Broderick Crawford, Constance Dowling. An alcoholic composer murders his two-timing wife in a rage. Twisty noir film.

The Naked City (1948) Jules Dassin, director. Cast: Barry Fitzgerald, Don Taylor, Howard Duff, Ted de Corsia, Dorothy Hart. In New York, a jewel thief drowns a woman in a bathtub and another killer tries to outrun the law. Fascinating use of street locales, especially Ted de Corsia's entrapment by police on top of the Williamsburg Bridge. This film spawned a successful television series.

Touch of Evil (1958) Orson Welles, director. Cast: Welles, Charlton Heston, Janet Leigh, Akim Tamiroff, Joseph Calleia. A corrupt cop investigates the bombing of a rich couple's car and casts the blame on a Mexican teenager. But stateside detective Heston smells a frame-up. The camerawork by Russell Metty is extraordinary. Marlene Dietrich has a small part as fortune teller-prostitute.

The runner-up for Universal is Robert Siodmak's *Criss Cross* (1949).

CHAPTER THIRTEEN

Warner Bros. and *Possessed* (1947)

Joan Crawford won the Academy Award for Best Actress starring in Warner Bros.' adaptation of James M. Cain novel *Mildred Pierce*. The 1945 movie was described as a "woman's picture noir" by many critics. I prefer another film made two years later, *Possessed* (1947), for which Crawford received an Academy Award nomination. Warner Bros. had certainly put its mark on the Hollywood film industry by 1947, creating many film noirs.

Jack L. Warner was the studio head and his brother Harry the president of the company. It was founded in 1923; in December of 1928, Darryl F. Zanuck became the production chief and Hal Wallis became production chief of First National, a satellite company responsible to the Warners and Zanuck. By November of 1930, the companies merged and Zanuck took over till 1933. Wallis became production chief till 1944 when he left for Paramount Pictures. Zanuck was responsible for the hard-hitting style of the 1930s productions *I Am a Fugitive from a Chain Gang* (1932) and *"G" Men* (1935), but it was Wallis who introduced the expressionist style to the company, hiring directors like Michael Curtiz, Raoul Walsh and Curtis Bernhardt and producing the films *The Letter* (1940), *The Maltese Falcon* and *High Sierra* (both 1941), *Conflict* and *Mildred Pierce* (both 1945), and *Possessed*, directed by Bernhardt. Warner Bros. continued to produce a stream of film noirs, even neo-noirs through *Body Heat* (1981). By 1956, Harry and Albert Warner had sold their shares in the company and only Jack stayed on to merge with Seven Arts in 1967. Then the original company was taken over by Kinney National Service.

Possessed (1947) was a mainstream noir and not as entertaining as *Mildred Pierce*, winning fewer awards. Nor was it a glamorous A+ production, having fewer name stars than its predecessor and a less convoluted plot. In fact, one may call it an "anti-star" film for Crawford, for she is mentally out of control throughout this film until the very last frame.

When the Warner Bros. logo first flashes on the screen, we do not hear the usual WB fanfare but Franz Waxman's orchestration of Robert Schumann's "Carnival," setting the dislocated mood of the film as the white titles come up against a dawning Los Angeles downtown cityscape. Crawford is wandering the city streets in the early A.M. A bus passes as she tries to cross, then she stops at some trolley tracks. A trolley appears and the camera's view is from inside the trolley. Crawford tells the conductor, "I'm looking for David," and the conductor realizes her confusion and closes the doors, saying, "There's no David here, lady," and moves on. Crawford looks awful, hair disheveled, wearing absolutely no makeup. She continues walking slowly up the street, asking two male parishioners leaving an early church service for David. Then she wanders into a local café–chili house. The counterman and other people seated at the café bar notice she is ill. A white Los Angeles Municipal Hospital ambulance pulls up to the café and Crawford is placed on a gurney.

At the hospital, she is wheeled into the Psychopathic Department where she is placed flat on a bed in a room with barred windows and stays there many hours, from dawn to evening, until two psychiatrists come to visit her. Dr. Willard, played authoritatively by Stanley Ridges, diagnoses her condition as a catatonic stupor. He says she is a beautiful woman, probably frustrated with problems, many of which she couldn't cope with, is in a state of extreme confusion and has had a complete nervous breakdown. Crawford has not given the doctors her name. The labels from her clothing say she bought her coat and dress in Washington, D.C. The only thing Crawford says is, "David, David." The psychiatrist is going to give her an injection of sodium pentothal, using narcosynthesis to get her to surrender her identity. Crawford is identified as Louise Howell. She's in L.A. to "get away from them." "Tell me about David," says the doctor. We hear notes from Schumann's "Carnival" and then, the first of several flashbacks begin.

Louise Howell and David Sutton (played by Van Heflin) have just come back from swimming in the lake. Louise tells David she has to go back to work. David is sitting at the piano, playing the Schumann piece for her. There were many, many women in David's life before Louise. Louise is a romantic woman. She asks him, "Do you love me?" He doesn't answer. They kiss. Obviously she loves him but he does not return her love. She says she just existed before meeting him. He doesn't like the trap of marriage and is not in love with her. He loves his work — mathematics and engineering. He is a World War II vet. Louise has no pride and wants nothing but him. He suggests they stop seeing each other for a while: "You're choking me to death! You hang on too hard." Louise gets up and demands that David take her home to another, more grandiose lakeside house. The music by Franz Waxman reflects the turmoil Louise feels inside her.

At home, Louise hears an argument between Dean Graham (Raymond Massey) and his wife Pauline, who we never really see in the film. Louise is a nurse and she works in the Graham home. Mrs. Graham has accused her husband of making her sick and depressed and of having affairs with his nurses. Louise wants to leave their employ, but Graham convinces her to stay on.

The next morning, David arrives and talks to Graham about "the Canadian deal." David is looking for a job and gets one with Graham's industrial company. Louise believes that David is angry with her. She couldn't sleep. David vows he does not want to be together with Louise. She threatens to follow him to Canada. "Don't leave me, David! Daaaavviiiid!" she screams as his boat pulls away from the dock.

Louise Howell suddenly awakens in her hospital bed. This is the end of the first flashback. She tells the doctor she thought "everyone knew of her affair with David Sutton." The doctor determines that her psychosis began at this point in her life. Louise has a great lack of emotional response — the seeds of her illness were already there. Louise looks at a water pitcher which reminds her of the black, cold waters of the lake.

The next flashback begins here. It is dark and police are dragging the lake for Mrs. Graham's body. Apparently she committed suicide on Louise's day off. The police find her body close to the dock near some large rocks. The chief investigator (played by John Ridgely) interrogates Graham. Louise blames herself for the "suicide" since she took the day off, but Graham says, "She did it deliberately! She was probably trapped by the weeds."

In the next scene, the inquest is taking place inside the Graham living room. The investigator says the police were called at 8:15 P.M.; they arrived at 9 P.M. and found Mrs. Graham's body at 2:15 A.M. Graham repeats his statement that it was not an accidental death. Dr. Sherman (played by Erskine Sanford) testifies about Mrs. Graham's depression. The Graham children, Carol, a pretty college girl (played by Geraldine Brooks), and her brother Wynn (played by Gerald Perreau), who is ten years younger, enter the room. Louise breaks down crying and goes upstairs to her room. She hears what she thinks is Mrs. Graham's voice — but it is Carol's. The latter expresses her intense dislike for Louise and says she knew about her father's attentions and attraction to her. After a short argument, they agree that Miss Howell should go from the house, but Mr. Graham wants Louise to stay and take care of his son Wynn. Facing Louise, Carol says, "She killed herself because of YOU!" Her father hears this accusation and demands Carol apologize to Louise. He slaps his daughter who replies, "She'll never take mother's place!" Louise vainly tries to straighten out the misunderstanding but Carol leaves and goes back to college at her father's suggestion.

After revealing this much of her past, we flash forward to the hospital and Louise is given another injection to continue her story. In another flashback, Louise tells us she was not really needed at the Graham home but started taking care of Wynn in hopes of seeing "David" again. And walking through the main entrance with Wynn after school, she finds David there, discussing business with Dean Graham in his study. Louise looks radiant upon David's return but while pouring drinks for the two men as they work, Louise appears to have a headache. The men drink a toast: "Here's to oil, damn atomic energy." Louise asks David, "Are you going to be here long?" Dean replies for him: "Only a day if I can help it." Dean leaves the study and Louise literally throws herself at David, saying, "Aren't you going to kiss me? You don't have to mean it." They kiss and David reiterates that they were through before he left for Canada. However Louise is in the attack mode. She was not waiting for him and then she slaps him hard in the face. But after doing this, she finds herself very, very unhappy. When Dean returns, David leaves and the former asks her to stay at his home, taking care of Wynn and proposes marriage. He repeats the proposal and Louise replies she does not love him, reminding him of Carol's opposition. But she says yes and Dean replies, "It isn't easy for me to kiss a woman with dignity…"

The camera cuts to "Pleasant View College for Women." Louise tells Carol of her plan to marry her father, but the latter is way ahead of her. Louise surprises us by saying if Carol doesn't approve, she'll go away. Carol realizes her father needs someone, but asks Louise that she not call her "mother." They embrace.

Thirteen — Warner Bros. and *Possessed* (1947)

The next scene is the wedding at the Graham home. David Sutton shows up late to the proceedings, missing the entire ceremony but is looking only for the food and drink. Apparently, he was not invited. But as David washes down some hors d'oevures behind a potted palm, he hears Carol crying. She realizes it is David Sutton who doesn't recognize her at first. Then he realizes it is Dean's daughter. Louise interrupts their meeting and privately warns David to stay away from her. David leaves abruptly since he was an uninvited guest anyway.

The camera cuts to an evening piano concert in an unnamed Washington, D.C. music hall. Louise is on her way to a private box seat with Carol, when the latter waves at David Sutton, almost taking his seat with friends in the orchestra. Carol invites him over but Louise tells her to "get rid of him ... because I asked you to do it!" But it's too late. As the lights go down the pianist begins playing Schumann, reviving the significant memories she shared with David. Louise is wearing a fashionable evening gown and a diamond necklace, signifying her rise in society. Nevertheless, she complains of a headache midway through the concert and David says he will see her to her car. She argues with David not to accompany her on this rainy night. When she arrives home, Louise is reminded by the Schumann music of her love for David and the time they spent together in his lake side cabin. But she is distraught. It is 11:25 P.M. and Louise can't get the Schumann melody out of her mind. Here the style of the film becomes particularly noirish. Her clock is ticking wildly; we hear the wind whistling loudly through the room as the strains of Schumann become louder; the rain keeps beating on the window sill of her bedroom. Louise shuts the window firmly and in the semi-darkness, we view Louise's tear streaked face through the rain. She is going mad. Out of that rain-streaked window she sees Carol come home in a car, accompanied by David. They enter the house and kiss in the doorway. Carol climbs the staircase and sees a troubled Louise in the hallway at the top of the stairs. They argue in Louise's room. Carol says about David "he doesn't hate you, but he doesn't love you either. But you killed my mother to get David back." Even though this is not true, Louise, in her confused state admits to killing Mrs. Graham and Carol intends to tell her father about it immediately. Louise runs after Carol in the hall and pushes her down the staircase. The image of her crumpled body soon disappears as we hear Carol entering the house again, just brought home by David. Louise still has a wild look about her as Carol tells her sweetly that she was worried about

Louise and her headaches. After their meeting in the hall, they each go into their separate bedrooms and Louise realizes she is hallucinating, perhaps going mad!

The next day the scene changes to a psychiatrist's office. Louise poses as "Mrs. Smith," even though she has the initials "LG" prominently displayed on her suit. The psychiatrist (played by Moroni Olsen) tests Louise's senses. At one point, when asked to hold a handkerchief, she says that one hand feels a handkerchief and the other feels sandpaper. She hears the pounding of her own heartbeat. "You are suffering from neurasthenia, where you cannot distinguish between reality and unreality. If you don't receive the proper treatment, this could lead to schizophrenia and possibly insanity." He suggests she put an end to what is troubling her and before recommending another psychiatrist, "Mrs. Smith" walks out the door.

Returning home, she goes up to her bedroom and cries the entire afternoon. When he returns from work her husband is told by the maid that his wife had been crying. Upon seeing Dean, Louise asks him for a divorce but she won't tell him what is troubling her. Finally, she says "It's Pauline" (Dean's dead wife). He insists on taking Louise to their lake side home and show her that Pauline is gone from their lives — "Let's face the problem!"

The caretaker of the lake house picks them up in a boat. Dean looks at some felled trees with the caretaker while Louise enters the house alone, first looking up at "Pauline's window" and noticing someone closing it. There are shadows around her everywhere until the lights are turned on. Louise is surprised by the caretaker's wife, Mrs. Norris, who goes off to make Mrs. Graham a cup of hot tea. Then, she hears the service bell and sees that it is Pauline, ringing. The Franz Waxman chords sound, underlining Louise' grip on reality. She climbs the shadowy staircase, enters Pauline's room and begins screaming, screaming, screaming. Dean runs into the house, up the stairs after Louise. Entering his ex-wife's room, Louise says, "She wants me to kill myself— now she's talking to me— drown yourself." Dean confronts Louise: "She's dead. There is no one over there." Louise answers: "She went back to the lake. She'll wait for me there." We realize Louise is incoherent, suffering from a bad dream and cannot tell what is real. She tells Dean she helped Pauline commit suicide but he says it is all in her imagination. "It's not true," says Dean. "You were nowhere near the house that night. It was your day off. I was with Pauline and went to get her a wrap. When I returned, I realized she killed herself. That's the truth! Pauline is gone and will never come back!" Finally, Louise feels relieved, even happy after Dean explains everything that happened that night to her.

Returning to Washington that evening, they decide to go out to celebrate — nightclubbing, dancing, champagne. The scene shifts from the Graham home to a nightclub, where David is sitting at the bar drinking heavily, and waiting for Carol. She arrives and he admits he is in love with her. They talk about engagement, marriage, the difference in their ages — he's 35, she's 20. Dean spots them at the bar and invites them to their table. Once there, Louise talks on and on about David's charms, going on erratically about her relationship with him, making a spectacle of herself. The scene ends, focusing on Louise's wild assertions.

The next scene takes place in Louise's bedroom. She calls Carol in to discuss their "love," but Louise says she dislikes David intensely. "He's after your money, Carol. David is in love with me and uses you as an excuse to see me!" She deliberately lies to Carol and this time, Carol says she'll tell her father all about this conversation.

At the Graham residence, David accuses Louise of telling lies to her husband but will tell him the truth about their former relationship. She admits to telling the lies. "Any jailbreak can be tough, but I can manage this one," David says. As for Carol's money, it won't be an obstacle and we'll spend as much of it as possible."

The camera cuts to Louise's bedroom. She'd been crying all day again. She admits she doesn't feel well and Dean had already asked a "mental specialist" to come to the house for dinner. Louise's reaction: "You're trying to get rid of me, put me in an institution." Dean says he'll wait till she comes down for dinner. However, Louise has other plans. She dashes to her closet and puts on a fashionable black suit, coat and runs out of the house.

The next scene takes place in David Sutton's apartment. He wants to throw Louise out but she pushes her way inside. Telling David she is ill, she admits to doing some terrible things. "All I did was fall out of love with you," David answers. He acknowledges her husband's love, but Louise tells him Dean thinks she's insane. "He wouldn't do anything to hurt you," David replies. Louise answers: "You're all against me! David is packing a suitcase, telling Louise that he and Carol are going to marry tonight. At that point Louise pulls out a revolver from her coat (which we had never seen before in the film anywhere in her possession). "Let's be honest about it, Louise. As for killing me, I don't think you're that good a shot." David moves across the room to the right and makes a lunge for the gun. He falls and lies on his right side, mortally wounded and expires. Louise fires her gun five times and realizes she has killed him.

End of flashbacks. The camera cuts to the hospital. Louise shouts, "David, David" and now realizes she has killed him, revealing her crime through narcosynthesis. Her husband, Dean Graham comes to her ward in the hospital. Dr. Willard tells him of her psychosis which caused her insanity — but with good care, she could be restored to good health. Lying in her hospital bed, Louise looks almost peaceful now, almost happy that she could tell her story and come back to reality. (Joan Crawford is wearing a bit of make-up in this final scene.) After all, she did kill David Sutton, the homme fatal. One cannot predict what the verdict of a court will be for she did not act responsibly because of her mental illness, if a jury would even believe Louise's story. But Dean says he'll be there for her whatever it takes. The doctor closes the door behind him and walks to his office.

The End title comes up in white as well as the Cast of Players.

Joan Crawford made over 100 films in her 50-plus years as an actress and was no stranger to the film noir style. Although *A Woman's Face* (1941), directed by George Cukor, is not considered noir in any sense, it was a great rehearsal for Joan. *Mildred Pierce*, her first film at Warner Bros., began the renewal of her career under producer Jerry Wald. Although she usually played femmes fatales in the thirties, her noir roles in the forties were of a more heroic type, competing with men. She was tough, business-like — the type usually played by a Cagney or Bogart but from the feminine point of view. Although *Mildred Pierce* was her great success commercially and artistically, I believe it was this role that propelled her through even greater noir roles in her career, such as Louise Howell in *Possessed* and the strong heroines of other noirs: Ethel Whitehead, David Brian's moll in *The Damned Don't Cry* (Warner Bros., 1950), Myra Hudson, the intended murder victim of her husband Jack Palance in *Sudden Fear* (RKO, 1952) and finally, Lynn Markham, a socialite seduced by murderous Jeff Chandler in *Female on the Beach* (Universal, 1955). Some other Crawford films have noir qualities: Felix Feist's *This Woman Is Dangerous* (Warner Bros., 1952) where a tough female criminal falls in love with her doctor attempting to save her eyesight, and Nicholas Ray's operatic noir western *Johnny Guitar* (Republic, 1954) where she plays a barkeep vying for the love of Sterling Hayden while battling with Merecedes McCambridge for her land and her lover. Crawford's roles displayed her as a strong, cynical woman, the equal or better of most men. That is why *Possessed* is so out-of-character for her, acting a role where she is hardly dominant or clever, so against her type.

Van Heflin was a leading man during most of the forties but not a strong character type or hero, rather playing nebulous personalities. His film noirs were not particular outstanding. He first played opposite Robert Taylor and Lana Turner in *Johnny Eager* (MGM, 1941) as the alcoholic friend of the hero and won a Best Supporting Oscar. He seemed to aspire to stardom, playing the childhood friend and lover of Barbara Stanwyck in *The Strange Love of Martha Ivers* (Paramount, 1946), then the "homme fatal" David Sutton in *Possessed*. He hit his stride in Fred Zinnemann's MGM film *Act of Violence* (1949), in which he played a coward who revealed plans of several soldiers to escape from the Nazi concentration camp during World War II and is relentlessly pursued by Robert Ryan postwar. But his most amazing role was in Joseph Losey's *The Prowler* (United Artists, 1951) in which he plays an unscrupulous cop, who seduces the wife (Evelyn Keyes) of a wealthy man, making his murder look like an accident and then marrying her for her wealth. Spencer Selby says *The Prowler* "is a first rate-thriller with [a] noir protagonist corrupted by American materialist values." It was Heflin's best role to date.

Raymond Massey was a stranger to film noir roles. He played a district attorney in Fritz Lang's *Woman in the Window* (RKO, 1944) and Dean Howell in Curtis Bernhardt's *Possessed*. A Canadian, he entered Hollywood films in the 1930s and never had any starring parts with his name above the title but had a long career in movies and television till the mid–seventies. He is best remembered as the title character actor in John Cromwell's *Abe Lincoln in Illinois* (RKO, 1940). I liked him better as Gale Wynard, the publisher in King Vidor's *The Fountainhead* (Warner Bros., 1949), based upon the Ayn Rand novel; he displays his ruthlessness both in business and love, taking Patricia Neal away from Gary Cooper. Now that is a feat for any actor of "nobility," the singular quality that comes through in all of his performances.

Geraldine Brooks made her movie debut at Warner Bros. in 1946, co-starring with Errol Flynn and Barbara Stanwyck in a gothic noir directed by Peter Godfrey, *Cry Wolf*. Her next two noir films were *Possessed* and Max Ophuls' *The Reckless Moment* (Columbia, 1949), with James Mason and Joan Bennett, playing the "reckless" daughter of Bennett having an affair with an older married man (Shepperd Strudwick). Other than these features, she made few films and spent most of her career working in television. TV was better suited to her talents for as a Warner Bros. hopeful, she really never lived up to her star status.

When Jerry Wald became a producer at Warner Bros. in the 1940s, he worked on many film noirs. His noirs with Joan Crawford were *Mildred Pierce, Humoresque, Flamingo Road* and *The Damned Don't Cry*. Wald first came to Hollywood and spent time scriptwriting until he took the place of Hal Wallis as Warner Bros.' production chief while the latter moved on to Paramount Pictures. Wald always had a good sense for melodramas and he continued the tradition of the Warner Bros. hard-boiled action school of realism, especially in his noirs like *Dark Passage* (1947) and *Key Largo* (1948), both starring Humphrey Bogart and Lauren Bacall, *The Breaking Point* (1950) with John Garfield and *Caged* (1950), a woman's prison film starring Eleanor Parker. In the '50s he moved on to other studios like Columbia and Fox where he produced more conventional films based on colorful novels like *Peyton Place* (1957) and *The Best of Everything* (1959), both in CinemaScope and Deluxe Color; the latter featured Crawford in a minor role as a frustrated book editor. Wald always moved forward with the new technologies of the motion picture industry and produced 70 films that were all fascinating entertainments.

Curtis Bernhardt, like so many Hollywood directors of the thirties and forties, emigrated from Germany to the United States where he used the pseudo-expressionist techniques at Warner Bros. that defined their "studio style" during the forties and fifties, especially noted in their film noirs. Bernhardt made 43 films and directed three film noirs: *Possessed*, *Conflict* (1945) with Humphrey Bogart, about a crazed man who murders his wife (Rose Hobart) and tries to romance and marry her beautiful sister (Alexis Smith); and *The High Wall* (1947) with Robert Taylor, where a World War II vet is accused of murdering his wife (Dorothy Patrick) and is sent to an asylum because of "memory blackouts." Bernhardt made films until 1964, but in his subsequent assignments after leaving Warner Bros. for MGM, he could never recapture that old "expressionist frisson" of his strongest noir period.

Ranald MacDougall co-wrote the screenplay of *Possessed* with Sylvia Richards, based on the novella *One Man's Secret* by Rita Weiman. Mac-

Thirteen — Warner Bros. and *Possessed* (1947)

Dougall wrote some thirty scripts for various studios, his most famous being *Mildred Pierce*. He was a cracker-jack writer of dialogue, used flashbacks and had psychological insights into his characters. Note the framing devices of *Mildred Pierce,* which is an essentially a woman's melodrama made into a film noir. In *Possessed,* he pulled out all the stops, literally, letting Bernhardt's expressionist style take over the nearly mute Crawford until she "talks" in her flashback scenes. MacDougall scripted two other noirs for Warner Bros.: *The Unsuspected* (1947), where Claude Rains, a radio personality, is trying to drive his ward (Joan Caulfield) mad to inherit her estate, and *The Breaking Point* (1950), an adaptation of Ernest Hemingway's *To Have and Have Not,* with John Garfield, Patricia Neal and Phyllis Thaxter, which was more faithful to the original story than the Bogart-Bacall version made a few years earlier. MacDougall also did some directing and he was responsible for Crawford's success in Columbia's 1955 *Queen Bee,* sometimes considered a "late noir" with Crawford as an evil, controlling bitch of a wife to Barry Sullivan. MacDougall worked on many projects through the late seventies.

Co-scenarist Sylvia Richards had a short career as a screenwriter, only ten films and *Possessed* being her first. Universal's *Secret Beyond the Door* (1948) starring Michael Redgrave and Joan Bennett, directed by Fritz Lang, was her second and last noir. She was married to A.I. Bezzerides, a noir specialist himself. She had difficulty finding work in the late forties because of the era of the "blacklist" initiated by Senator Joseph McCarthy. This might be a reason her career was so shortened in Hollywood.

Cinematographer Joseph A. Valentine died at age 49 but worked on 75 films in his career. He shot Alfred Hitchcock's *Saboteur* (Universal, 1942) and *Rope* (Warner Bros., 1948), the latter Hitchcock's first foray into color. Hitchcock's *Shadow of a Doubt* (Universal, 1943) starring Joseph Cotten as "The Merry Widow Murderer" put Valentine into noir territory. Valentine made his last noir for director Douglas Sirk, the 1948 United Artists release *Sleep, My Love* starring Don Ameche as a photographer who is trying to drive wife Claudette Colbert mad.

Franz Waxman, along with Miklos Rozsa, Max Steiner and Erich Wolfgang Korngold, are the most important of Hollywood's golden age of composers. Waxman composed music for nearly 170 films in all genres. A German émigré in Hollywood since the 1930s, he first worked for Universal where he specialized in horror scores, and then graduated to more lush romantic scores, including many of film noir's best scores of the era. They include *Rebecca* (United Artists, 1940), *Suspicion* (RKO, 1941), *Dark Passage, Nora Prentiss, Possessed, The Two Mrs. Carrolls* and *The Unsuspected* (all Warner Bros. films, 1947), *Sorry, Wrong Number* (Paramount, 1948), *Sunset Boulevard* (Paramount, 1950), *Night and the City* (Fox, 1950), *A Place in the Sun* (Paramount, 1951), *He Ran All the Way* (United Artists, 1951) and *I, the Jury* (United Artists,1953). Waxman won two Academy Awards for his work. There have been many recordings of Waxman's film scores. His son John is helping to keep his music alive and well known in the world of classic cinema.

Anton Grot was a Polish émigré who worked almost exclusively for Warner Bros. as art-set director. He was largely responsible for the hardboiled realism in films from *Little Caesar* (1930) to *Backfire* (1950). His stylistic use of German expressionism was used by all sorts of directors, from Michael Curtiz to Curtis Bernhardt. He was especially noted for his lighting schemes and influenced many cinematographers who worked on

Possessed (1947): Raymond Massey (left) and Van Heflin discuss job plans while Joan Crawford mixes drinks and pretends to have a headache.

Thirteen — Warner Bros. and *Possessed* (1947)

***Possessed* (1947):** Geraldine Brooks jokes with Van Heflin who stares at Joan Crawford, who does not want him in her private box at the concert.

film noirs with him in the classic era of the forties — all Warner Bros. films such as *Mildred Pierce, Deception* (with Bette Davis), *Nora Prentiss* (with Ann Sheridan), *Possessed, The Two Mrs. Carrolls, The Unsuspected* (all 1947) and *Backfire* (1950) with Virginia Mayo and Gordon MacRae, the popular singer. Grot's legacy is the gothic style he imparted as art director in the film noirs he made for Warner Bros.

During the 1940s, films about psychiatry and Freudian concepts were the rage as well as narratives told from the subjective viewpoint. Critics have called *Possessed* one of the best films "on the dark side," with Crawford probably giving her best performance. Van Heflin as the sought-after homme fatal leads her into a life of violence, confusion, and crime because he will not reciprocate her love; rather, he became her obsession. His murder precipitated her entire mental collapse.

The look of the film, the intense shadows and extreme lighting, reflect the mental states of the character. Louise is confused, mentally ill and unbalanced, all supporting the noir style by projecting a state of anxiety on to the audience. Even the city is a character in film noirs, where aberration is a form of the environment and Louise's mind is contained in a sad city of the imagination as we watch her wander aimlessly about in the opening scenes. Combined with the use of flashbacks, and the atmosphere created by the director and his photographer Joseph Valentine, this film becomes a prime example of "oneiric" tonality, the dreamlike tone so prevalent in the film noirs made in the 1940s. It is one of the best film noirs ever made. It did not attain the popularity of *Mildred Pierce*, but it did capture the entire mood of a woman going out of her mind.

Possessed is a film that never lets up, showing us the inner turmoil of its characters, through its music and its noir visuals. It is another example of a particular studio's quintessential noir.

I have used the word "quintessential" several times in the course of writing about the films under discussion. According to *Webster's Dictionary*, "quintessential' is an adjective derived from the noun "quintessence" which has two meanings: 1. The purest essence of something, and 2. the most typical example.

If I had to choose the most quintessential noir film cited in this book, it would be Billy Wilder's 1944 *Double Indemnity*, because it was the very first film where all the characteristics of film noir style came together cohesively and became the norm for all other film noirs made after 1944.

To sum up this critique on *Possessed,* American film critic James Agee said: "Miss Crawford performs with the passion and intelligence of an actress who is not content with just one Oscar." This film is one of the best examples of American film noir of the forties and according to London critic Richard Winnington, "[It offers] acting with bells on."

Warner Bros. made some 30 film noirs during the 1940s and also some pre-noirs like *I Was a Fugitive from a Chain Gang* (1932) and some neo-noirs like *Dirty Harry* (1971) and *Night Moves* (1975). Some of the best film noirs are the following:

The Letter (1940) William Wyler, director. Cast: Bette Davis, Herbert Marshall, Gale Sondergaard, James Stephenson. Murder and adultery on the Malayan rubber plantations, based upon a Somerset Maugham novel and play. A top performance from Davis.

The Maltese Falcon (1941) John Huston, director. Cast: Humphrey

Thirteen — Warner Bros. and *Possessed* (1947)

Bogart, Mary Astor, Peter Lorre, Sydney Greenstreet. Detective Sam Spade is in search of the elusive diamond-studded statue. Many murders are committed to own it. Mary Astor, in one of her finest roles, is the most deceptive villainess of them all.

Dark Passage (1947) Delmer Daves, director. Cast: Humphrey Bogart, Lauren Bacall, Agnes Moorehead. Bogart breaks out of prison, assumes a new identity through plastic surgery, takes revenge on Moorehead and falls in love with Bacall. Excellent San Francisco locales.

White Heat (1949) Raoul Walsh, director. Cast: James Cagney, Virginia Mayo, Edmond O'Brien, Margaret Wycherly, Steve Cochran. In Cagney's last gangster film he is caught by police, imprisoned and befriends undercover cop O'Brien while planning a prison break. When his mother (Wycherly) is murdered by a rival gangster (Cochran), Cagney has a complete breakdown in the prison cafeteria (one of Cagney's best scenes), then escapes and takes revenge. Trapped by police on top of a huge gas storage tank, Cagney fires his gun, setting the tank ablaze, and cries out, "Top of the world!" An excellent police procedural with top performances from everyone in the cast.

Strangers on a Train (1951) Alfred Hitchcock, director. Cast: Farley Granger, Robert Walker, Ruth Roman. Based upon a novel by Patricia Highsmith. Two strangers meet, discuss their problems and talk about switching murders: Walker will kill Granger's estranged wife and Granger will murder Walker's father. Granger does not take Walker seriously until his wife is choked to death in an amusement park and Walker wants Granger to live up to his part of their bargain. Terrific suspense with homoerotic frissons.

My runner-up to *Possessed* is *Mildred Pierce* (1945).

CHAPTER FOURTEEN

Independent Production Units

Independent companies and releasing units made and released many film noirs, often employing facilities and professional staff and studio facilities from other major production companies.

Avco-Embassy Films was a releasing corporation formed by Joseph E. Levine and distributed mainly B films of the Steve Reeves muscleman variety. Its only contribution to film noir was the 1975 version of Raymond Chandler's *Farewell, My Lovely*, made in London and in color by director Dick Richards, starring Robert Mitchum.

Diana Productions was a company formed by director Fritz Lang, actress Joan Bennett and her husband, producer Walter Wanger. Universal Pictures released their product. They made two sensational film noirs: The first was *Scarlet Street* (1945) with Bennett and Edward G. Robinson, a remake of an early thirties French classic, *La chienne* (*The Bitch*). The other was a psychological drama with Bennett and Michael Redgrave, *Secret Beyond the Door* (1948). Both were produced by Wanger and directed by Lang.

Enterprise Studios was a short-lived creation of actor John Garfield. Its first film noir *Body and Soul* (1947) starred Garfield, Lilli Palmer and Anne Revere. It was a tremendous success for a boxing film. Enterprise's next noir production was *Force of Evil* (1948), using much of the same personnel as *Body and Soul*. It starred Garfield and Thomas Gomez in a story about Wall Street corruption and the numbers racket. Released by MGM around Christmas, it did little at the box office but became a cult classic.

Film Classics, a very small production company, released two film noirs in the late forties: *Blonde Ice* (1948) was a relatively unknown B

Scarlet Street (1945): Joan Bennett is a prostitute indulging older man Edward G. Robinson.

classic starring Leslie Brooks as a femme fatale destroyer of men. *Guilty Bystander* (1950) starred Zachary Scott and Faye Emerson, actors who brought some class to the Film Classics Releasing Corporation. This company added little to the noir canon.

The Filmmakers were a group of actors, directors and writers who released their product through RKO. Their outstanding film noir was *The Hitch-Hiker* (1953), directed by actress Ida Lupino and written by her partner (and husband) Collier Young. Edmond O'Brien and Frank Lovejoy star as fishing buddies on a trip to Mexico who pick up psychotic William Talman; he wants to murder them and steal their car. This was the company's only noir production. The Filmmakers, a class act, disappeared too quickly from the noir and Hollywood scene.

Lippert Films' best noir was *Loan Shark* (1952) starring George Raft as an ex-convict trying to infiltrate the gang of loan sharks which killed

Sweet Smell of Success **(1957:) Barbara Nichols (left) is asked a sexual favor by Tony Curtis. Here, Curtis pimps Nichols out to a leering unidentified actor.**

his brother. Lippert Films was begun by Robert L. Lippert, a successful theater manager in California in the forties.

Of all the noir films from independent studios, I would like to comment on two. First, in *Scarlet Street* (1945), directed by Fritz Lang and starring Joan Bennet, Edward G. Robinson, and Dan Duryea a prostitute (Bennett) pretends to fall in love with an older man who is a cashier and amateur artist. Her pimp/boyfriend (Duryea) forces her to obtain a Greenwich Village apartment and falsify her name on Robinson's paintings.

In *Sweet Smell of Success* (1957), directed by Alexander Mackendrick and starring Burt Lancaster, Tony Curtis, Susan Harrison, Martin Milner, and Barbara Nichols, a powerful newspaper columnist (Lancaster) enlists a press agent (Curtis) to break up his sister's romance with a Jazz musician (Milner).

CHAPTER FIFTEEN

The Runners-Up

The runners-up or second-best film noirs are organized by studio. It is not necessary to say that each is a "great" example of the noir style, but each belongs in the noir canon for certain reasons. Approximately 315 films were shot in the noir style between 1940 and 1959.

Allied Artists produced eight. *The Big Combo* (1955) was ahead of its time with its lighting techniques, sadism and outrageous sexuality.

Dead Reckoning (1947) is one of 36 noirs produced by Columbia. Set after World War II, it features a murderess who double and triple crosses men. She meets her end literally and figuratively when she jumps in a parachute to her death.

Among Eagle-Lions' five noir releases is *He Walked By Night* (1949). Its main setting is the sewers of Los Angeles where police track down a thief and a murderer.

MGM filmed some 30 noirs, most of them "borderline" with more "white" than "black." The darkness is in the mind of a husband who believes his wife is having an affair with their doctor. The film shows how casual circumstances can make for disaster in marriage.

Monogram Pictures made only seven film noirs, among them *Decoy* (1946), about a woman who will go to any lengths to murder her lovers for a mythical treasure of bank notes buried in the California wilderness.

Sunset Boulevard (1951) is the second best after Billy Wilder's *Double Indemnity* (1944) among 34 other film noirs from Paramount. It is the story of a silent film star gone mad, wreaking havoc in the life of her chauffeur/husband, her lover and his girlfriend.

Republic Pictures produced four film noirs. Set in Chicago, *The City That Never Sleeps* is about a married cop who is attracted to a floozie cooch dancer working in a nightclub under an elevated train, where the villain, William Talman, falls to his death.

R.K.O. produced the most film noirs between 1940 and 1959, 52 to be exact. Its second best noir, *Born to Kill* (1947), has Lawrence Tierney as a psychopath who shows his murderous nature when he doesn't get his way.

Another studio big in the noir style was 20th Century–Fox, with 32. Samuel Fuller's *Pick-up on South Street* (1953) featured espionage and a love story.

United Artists made some 40 films in the noir style, among them *Kansas City Confidential* (1952). Set in Mexico, its star, John Payne, is hunted by police for a robbery he didn't commit.

Universal-International Pictures set the standard for noir crime films. After *The Killers* (1946) came the runner-up, Robert Siodmak's *Criss Cross* (1949), another heist classic, where a *ménage a trois* double crosses each other leading to a fatal end. Universal produced 24 film noirs.

And finally we arrive at Warner Bros., which produced 33 film noirs, among them *Mildred Pierce* (1945). Joan Crawford won an Academy Award for the title role.

The Film Noir Runners-Up by Studio

For Allied Artists, the second major film noir was *The Big Combo* (1955), directed by Joseph H. Lewis and starring Cornel Wilde, Jean Wallace and Richard Conte.

Principal photography was by John Alton (see Chapter 3). Some critics have called this film the best B movie of all time. I would hesitate a bit there but it is an extraordinary melodrama about a gangster, Mr. Brown (Richard Conte), in love with a mixed-up society girl, Susan Lowell (Jean Wallace), who is also loved by a detective, Leonard Diamond (played by Wallace's real-life husband Cornel Wilde).

One still is especially fascinating. It is the film's end shot where Susan Lowell, standing inside an airplane hangar, sees detective Leonard Diamond approaching to embrace her after killing Mr. Brown in the same scene. Note the noir lighting effects, a wheelbarrow on the left and two principal stars caught in shadow facing each other. Alton's use of lighting is superb because of the "striking contrasts he uses between light and dark which, at times, seems to isolate the characters in a dark insular universe of unspoken repression," says critic Michael Stephens in *Film Noir*. This is one of the most underrated noirs ever filmed and certainly Lewis' best.

Fifteen — The Runners-Up

The Big Combo (Allied Artists, 1955): Jean Wallace walks toward her lover Cornel Wilde in the ultimate noir still from the last scene of the film. Note the lighting by John Alton behind the actors, casting them in deep shadow.

Columbia Pictures released *Dead Reckoning* (1947), directed by John Cromwell starring Humphrey Bogart and Lizabeth Scott, a year after its stunning noir sensation *Gilda* starring Rita Hayworth and Glenn Ford. It's another film about a nightclub singer, Coral Chandler, married to the boss of the club (Morris Carnovsky as Martinelli), Imagine Lizabeth Scott center stage, in the spotlight in an American nightclub noir setting, dressed in black, seducing her audience with a love song, dressed very similarly to Rita Hayworth in her famous "Put the Blame on Mame" number, with gloves, too. She is holding a microphone near her mouth and there are guards posted at the French doors in the background. She may be singing to Humphrey Bogart sitting in a chair closest to her, partially seen in the spotlight. Apparently responsible for the murder of Johnny Drake (played by William Prince), she does her best to hide it until Bogart discovers her evil motives and she tries to shoot him coming out of a doorway.

She tries to convince Bogart that she's telling the truth, so she decides to shoot him as he drives through a terrific rainstorm and causes a huge auto accident. Bogart survives, but Scott dies. Leo Tover's camera is placed in the back seat of the car and the lighting is supposedly from oncoming cars. Bogart looks at her as if she really does not mean to shoot him, but Scott, wet and bedraggled and discovered to be a murderess, has no other choice. Tover filmed several noirs, three with Scott, *I Walk Alone* (Paramount, 1947), *Paid in Full* (Paramount, 1950) and this film. He also shot *The Secret Fury* (RKO, 1950) with Claudette Colbert, *Payment on Demand* (RKO, 1951) with Barry Sullivan, *A Blueprint for Murder* (Fox, 1953) with Jean Peters and *Man in the Attic* (Fox, 1953) with Jack Palance. Tover worked for Fox on a variety of films till his death in 1964.

He Walked by Night (1948) is an interesting noir produced by Eagle-Lion the same year as *Hollow Triumph* aka *The Scar*, beautifully photographed by John Alton, one of the consummate cinematographers of the '40s. It is a police procedural about an ex–Navy radio operator who is an electronics genius but steals his equipment for cash and other nefarious purposes. In one scene, Richard Basehart is showing his latest piece of electronic equipment to Whit Bissell in a pretty well-lighted laboratory office. Not much noir lighting here. But there is plenty of noir lighting as Basehart is escaping the L.A. police net through the sewer system of the city. The scenes in the tunnel, with flashlights blazing and running police covering hatches to sewers, preventing a possible escape are really quite inventive. But at the conclusion, Basehart is killed and the film returns to its "documentary style," explaining away another routine day in the life of the Los Angeles police force.

MGM released a relatively interesting noir, full of light with dark passions beneath the surface of the actors. *Cause for Alarm* (1951), directed by Tay Garnett, starred Loretta Young, Barry Sullivan and Bruce Cowling. Young is an abused housewife in a hopeless marriage to Sullivan; she is bedridden throughout most of the film. The plot turns on a letter he wrote to the local D.A., accusing his wife of having an affair with his doctor and then murdering him. No great noir stylistics here. The d.p. Joseph Ruttenberg did better earlier work for Anthony Mann in his 1950 film *Side Street* with Farley Granger, Cathy O'Donnell, Jean Hagen and James Craig, about a postal worker on the run after stealing money from a crooked lawyer and trying to return it. Still, nothing from MGM can compete with *The Asphalt Jungle* (1950). Ruttenberg spent most of his career at Metro but rarely did noir films. He did do some "women in distress" stories that had some noir overtones.

Monogram Studios' best release in 1946 was a noir called *Decoy*, directed by Jack Bernhard, starring Jean Gillie (an English actress), Edward Norris, Herbert Rudley, Robert Armstrong and Sheldon Leonard. Gillie is anxious to recover a buried box full of cash from her boyfriend who is about to be hanged at the local penitentiary. She has a doctor resurrect him after the hanging so he'll reveal the hiding place of the box. If anyone gets in her way, she murders them. She ends up dying from a bullet wound inflicted by the doctor. The box contains a single dollar bill and warns his cohorts against greed. It's a solid noir with some startling scientific ideas; the femme fatale uses her sexuality bluntly and dies at the end with no remorse.

Paramount Pictures had Billy Wilder, who made spectacular noir films. When he made *Sunset Blvd.* (1950) with Gloria Swanson as Norma Desmond, a former silent film star, he struck gold. William Holden plays Joe Gillis, a screenwriter down on his luck who accidentally turns into Swanson's driveway and develops a sexual and professional relationship with her. She buys him clothes and keeps him on a short leash, away from Nancy Olson, playing another screenwriter. Holden wants to leave after finishing a sound version of *Salome* but Desmond shoot him dead and Gillis winds up in her swimming pool as a dead man narrating the entire film in flashback. After the shooting, the newsreel cameras start rolling and Desmond descends the grand staircase of her home into madness. A terrific noir!

Producers Releasing Corporation, after *Detour* (1945), could only mildly capture the spirit of noir in a crime film, *Strange Illusion* (1945), also directed by Edgar G, Ulmer, about a lecherous cad (Warren William) who murders the husband of Sally Eilers for her wealth but makes no headway with her son, played by Jimmy Lydon. Critics have drawn parallels between *Hamlet* and this screenplay but for this observer, it's more of a low-budget noir helped along by good actors such as Regis Toomey who believes that Eilers' lover murdered her husband and helps Lydon prove it. There is also a claustrophobic scene in an asylum, where Lydon thinks he is going mad, but the truth is finally revealed and Lydon is freed to go home and the lover is jailed. It's a noir with a happy ending, but lots of "dark atmosphere" provided by the director and his acting ensemble.

The City That Never Sleeps (1953) is another police procedural released by Republic Pictures, directed by John H. Auer and starring Gig Young, Mala Powers, William Talman, Edward Arnold and Marie Windsor. Unlike the Jules Dassin film *The Naked City* (1948), this film is a lesser police procedural, taking place in Chicago. It's the love story of a cop and a stripper mixed in with gangsterism and a cold-blooded murderer (William Talman in his usual bad guy performance). There is one scene where the police are in pursuit of Talman on the elevated tracks of Chicago's Metro system where he is shot and falls to his death, duplicating Ted de Corsia's fall off the Williamsburg Bridge in *The Naked City*. The cop wins back the love of his wife (played by Paula Raymond) and the stripper leaves Chicago. It's a minor noir.

Out of the Past (1947) is one of the quintessential noirs, and Robert Wise's *Born to Kill* (RKO, 1947) comes closest to being second best from that studio that year. Lawrence Tierney as Sam Wild gives a terrific performance as a maniac who kills before he really thinks situations through. In one scene, smoking a cigarette, he sits on the bed of his best friend Marty (played by Elisha Cook, Jr.); perhaps the latter is telling him you cannot go around killing people any time you want to just to get them out of the way. The bars of the bed's backboard throw shadows on the wall in this very claustrophobic scene. Tierney is anxious to marry Audrey Long and become head of her publishing company. But he gives himself to Claire Trevor, playing divorcee Helen Trent, who is just as strong as he is but not as murderous. The lighting from above frames actress Long sitting in a high wing-backed armchair in the library of this wealthy home, hidden by its height while Sam makes love to Helen behind her. Robert de Grasse, not a very talented cinematographer, made five film noirs: *Crack-up* (1946), *Bodyguard* (1948), *A Dangerous Profession* (1949), *Follow Me Quietly* (1949) and *The Window* (1949). The latter is his best RKO noir from a story by Cornell Woolrich about a boy who sees a sailor murdered through a window in his apartment building; nobody, not even his parents will believe him. De Grasse worked in television till his death in 1971.

When I originally decided to do this book, my first choice was Samuel Fuller's *Pick-up on South Street* (1953) for 20th Century–Fox. But on reflection, I went with Preminger's *Laura* (1944) instead because it had all the sophisticated elements of noir I was looking for. Especially class! Fuller's tale is a rough-and-tumble story of a hooker named Candy (Jean Peters) who traces a pickpocket, Skip McCoy (Richard Widmark), to his hideout on a barge under the Brooklyn Bridge in search of a piece of microfilm he stole from her bag on the subway without her knowing the contents of the envelope. As photographed by Joe MacDonald, the film is a standard chase melodrama. But violence is the theme in this Fuller film noir. Peters is slapped around by her boyfriend Joey (played by Richard Kiley) who is angry at her for not obtaining the microfilm (with one frame missing) intended for the Communists but now in the hands of the grafter-pickpocket McCoy. MacDonald does his best in this violent scene, on an apartment set at Fox, but his best scenes are of Widmark and Kiley fighting in the New York subway. MacDonald is known principally for his noir films in collaboration with director Henry Hathaway. He made nine noir films for Fox including two color ones, *Niagara* (1952) with Marilyn Monroe and *House of Bamboo* (1955), a remake of *The Street with No Name* (1947). He spent most of his time at Fox studios as a staff cinematographer and died in 1968.

United Artists released many film noirs during the 1950s and the best was *Kansas City Confidential* (1952), directed by Phil Karlson and starring John Payne, Coleen Gray, Preston Foster, Jack Elam, Neville Brand, and Lee Van Cleef. A retired police officer (Foster) plans a payroll heist with four other men who wear masks whenever they meet. The robbery goes smoothly. A flower delivery truck is used for the getaway and John Payne, its driver, is blamed for the crime. There is insufficient evidence so he is released but makes contact with one of the robbers. They all plan to meet in Mexico in a small coastal town. Payne shows up with the rest of the criminals and we learn from the retired policeman that he had no intention of giving up the money but planned the heist so the police would recognize his talents and perhaps re-hire him. Nearly everyone gets killed and Payne falls in love with Preston Foster's daughter. A very well executed heist-noir film by Karlson.

If I did not choose *The Killers* (1946), directed by Robert Siodmak, for Universal's best noir entry, I would have used his film *Criss Cross* (1949), photographed by Franz Planer. A German refugee, he came to the U.S. in 1937, was familiar with the Expressionist film movement and applied it to at least six film noirs he made between 1946 and 1954. Critic Deborah L. Alpi calls this film "the best 'noir' Siodmak ever made."

In the parking lot still, one notices the darkness and the single source of light as Yvonne de Carlo and Burt Lancaster, once husband and wife, are now consorting to cheat her new husband Dan Duryea out of the proceeds of a planned heist in an armored car robbery. They both have a look of guilt on their faces as if someone has discovered them talking in the parking lot, holding a flashlight on their faces. In this still, notice how

Criss Cross (Universal, 1949): Yvonne de Carlo and Burt Lancaster rendezvous in a dark, crowded parking lot, renewing their affair and planning an armored car robbery.

compressed the pair is, squeezed by those older forties vehicles to add to the tension. The heist goes badly and at the conclusion we are at a beach house on the California coast. In the foreground, Dan Duryea (as Slim Dundee) is holding a gun on both Yvonne de Carlo (as Anna Dundee) and Burt Lancaster (as Steve Thompson). Thompson is wounded. He bribes a henchman in the employ of Dundee to bring him to the beach house where Anna and the money are waiting for him. But as fate has it, you cannot double-cross a double-crosser.

Ernest Haller was the chief cinematographer for *Mildred Pierce* (1945). He made another film noir for Warner Bros., *The Unfaithful* (1947) with Ann Sheridan, a remake of William Wyler's *The Letter* (1940), and he made *Plunder Road* (1957) starring Gene Raymond for Fox Studios. At the beginning of the film, Mildred (Joan Crawford) is contemplating suicide by jumping off the pier into the black waters below. A policeman comes towards her, banging his stick on the rail to stop her from climbing over.

Fifteen — The Runners-Up

What is she doing there? The next scene shows Jack Carson leaning over a dead man, Zachary Scott as Monte Beragon, who minutes before was shot six times by Mildred's daughter Veda (played by Ann Blyth). Scott utters the name "Mildred" before he expires. This scene occurs after Mildred with a promise of seduction, has let Carson into the house and locked him in so he can explain to the Police who will eventually visit the scene what he was doing there with a dead body in the house. Carson as Wally Fay, a former suitor of Mildred is holding an empty liquor bottle in each hand when he comes upon the overturned lamp and discovers Mildred Pierce's husband's body. The lighting picks up the texture of the rug and the shadows in the rest of the living room impart a dark feeling of murder and suspense in the eye and mind of the viewer.

After much investigation, most of the cast is finally gathered in the police captain's office. In this still, the captain (played by Moroni Olson) is standing at the left, showing a gun that was dropped at the previous

Mildred Pierce (Warner Bros., 1945): In a darkened office at police headquarters, Moroni Olson as the chief inspector explains a few things to Joan Crawford. Bruce Bennett, James Flavin and an unidentified actor are from left to right on the right. The actor in the back is unidentified.

Touch of Evil (Universal, 1958): Janet Leigh has been drugged by Akim Tamiroff (right). Orson Welles looks on.

scene, the gun of her former husband Bert Pierce (played by Bruce Bennett) standing to the right between two detectives. There are only two light sources in the room, the lamp light from the desk and another lamp behind the three men standing to the right and probably one light in the hall that shows letters that probably spell out "Dept. of Criminal Investigations" with an arrow indicating the proper entrance. Police stations, like bars and nightclubs are always excellent noir settings and Ernie Haller makes the most of his camera placement and the serious faces of the actors. Veda is caught at the local airport, arrested for Monte Beragon's murder and Mildred goes off with her first husband to the tinkle of Max Steiner's wedding bells. Perhaps Mildred will re-marry her first husband. A bit of "soap opera noir" but very entertaining. Crawford won the Best Actress Oscar for playing a working mother who would do anything for her daughter, except go to jail for her.

Conclusion

In writing this book, I have analyzed "film noir style" by taking examples of important noir films from eight major studios, five smaller studios and listing various independent studios who have contributed to the body of films known as "noir," films made between 1940 and 1960 and have left their distinct, indelible original studio imprint during the era of World War II — the period of noir style and studio production at its zenith.

It is no accident that the 13 films I have chosen from various studios are all noir films judging from their titles alone — titles like *Detour, Double Indemnity, Out of the Past,* and *Possessed.* All 13 films were created from scripts written by a multitude of writers, some adapted from novels and original stories by other authors. Thirteen different producers oversaw the development of these screenplays into motion pictures, working with 13 different directors and 13 cinematographers. These films employed many different actors under contract as part of the studio system and most of these films were scored by different composers, with one exception (Miklos Rosza). Finally, the films were released by eight major studios and five minor ones.

Film noir does express a certain realism of style, narrative of events and character sentiments. Film noir is a "group movement," according to a conversation I had with director Paul Schrader, that took place only in black and white films from 1942, beginning with John Huston's *The Maltese Falcon* (Warner Bros., 1941) and ending with Orson Welles' *Touch of Evil* (Universal, 1958). These parameters are generally accepted by most film critics. The film noir style entered various other genres and invaded their story lines and themes into westerns, horror films, psychological dramas, and even musicals. I have not examined these cross-genre mixtures, which would require another writer's research and another entire book. What I have done is examine this style by presenting the background of each studio and why it was accessible to make films in the noir style at its peak in the forties. I have also presented a detailed plot analysis and listed the personnel of each studio — producers, directors, stars, writers, cinematographers, art directors, and composers. I have also shown that noir was a spontaneous group movement where filmmakers shared the same political and/or aesthetic beliefs and therefore demonstrated a common stylistic approach during the forties. That commonality always caught the dark side of the American dream, expressing both the emotional and existential dysfunction of its protagonists. As the noir style continues to surface today — call it neo-noir, new noir or film après noir — there will always be a woman or femme fatale dragging a weak man down, using her sexuality as a weapon to make him commit criminal acts. He won't get the money or the dame, just punishment, legal or self-inflicted, for his stupidity. Film noir and its permutations will go on as long as long as there are men, women and conflicts over love, money and power.

Selected Bibliography

The works listed below are only those that had a great influence upon the text and this author. It is not meant to be all-inclusive but as up to date as possible.

Books

Alpi, Deborah L. *Robert Siodmak. A Biography with Critical Analyses of His Films Noirs and a Filmography of All His Works.* Jefferson, NC: McFarland, 1998.
Borde, Raymonde, and Etienne Chaumenton. *Panorama du Film Noir Américain (1941–1953).* Paris: Editions du Minuit, 1955.
Brion, Patrick. *Le Film Noir: L'Age d'or du film criminal américain d'Alfred Hitchcock à Nicholas Ray.* Paris: Editions Nathan, 1991.
Cameron, Ian, ed. *The Book of Film Noir.* New York: Continuum, 1993.
Christopher, Nicholas. *Somewhere in the Night: Film Noir and the American City.* New York: Free Press, 1997.
Derry, Charles. *The Suspense Thriller.* Jefferson, NC: McFarland, 1988.
Dumont, Hervé. *Robert Siodmak: le maître du film noir.* Lausanne: Editions l'Age d'Homme, 1981.
Hannsberry, Karen Burroughs. *Femme Noir: Bad Girls of Film.* Jefferson, NC: McFarland, 1998.
Hirsch, Foster. *The Dark Side of the Screen: Film Noir.* New York: A.S. Barnes, 1981.
_____. *Detours and Lost Highways: A Map of Neo-Noir.* New York: Limelight, 2004.
Keaney, Michael F. *Film Noir Guide.* Jefferson, NC: McFarland, 2003.
Muller, Eddie. *Dark City: The Lost World of Film Noir.* New York: St. Martin's Griffin, 1998.
Palmer, R. Barton. *Hollywood's Dark Cinema: The American Film Noir.* New York: Twayne, 1994.
Phillips, Gene D. *Creatures of Darkness: Raymond Chandler, Detective Fiction and Film Noir.* Lexington: University Press of Kentucky, 2000.
Robson, Eddie. *Film Noir.* London: Virgin, 2005.
Schwartz, Ronald. *Neo-Noir: The New Film Noir Style from Psycho to Collateral.* Lanham, MD: Scarecrow Press, 2005.
_____. *Noir, Now and Then: Film Noir Originals and Remakes, 1944–1999.* Westport, CT: Greenwood Press, 2001.
Selby, Spencer. *Dark City: The Film Noir.* Jefferson, NC: McFarland, 1984.

Silver, Alain, James Ursini, Elizabeth Ward, and Robert Porfirio, eds. *Film Noir: The Encyclopedia*. New York: Overlook Duckworth, Peter Meyer, 2010.
_____. *Film Noir*. Cologne: Taschen Gmbh Books, 2001.
_____. *Film Noir: The Directors*. Milwaukee: Limelight Press, 2012.
Spicer, Andrew. *Film Noir*. New York: Longman, 2002.
Stephens, Michael L. *Film Noir: A Comprehensive, Illustrated Reference to Movies, Terms and Persons*. Jefferson, NC: McFarland, 1995.
Tuska, Jon. *Dark Cinema: American Film Noir in Cultural Perspective*. Westport, CT: Greenwood Press, 1984.

Electronic and DVD Sources

Alpha Video. www.oldies.com
Amazon. DVD's, etc. www.amazon.com
Barnes & Noble. www.bn.com
Darker Images Video. www.darkerimagesvideo.com
DVD Savant. www.dvdsavant.com
Evergreen Video. www.evergreenvideo.com
Facets Video. www.facetsvideo.com
Internet Movie Database. www.imdb.com
Kims Video. www.kimsvideo.com
Kino Video. www.kinovideo.com
Movies Unlimited. www.moviesunlimited.com
New York Times. www.nytimes.com/search
Sinister Cinema. www.sinistercinema.com
Turner Classic Movies. www.tcm.com
TLA Video. www.tlavideo.com
Turner Classics. www.tcm.com/database and www.tcm.com/index
Variety. www.variety.com/archives

Films

The Asphalt Jungle: MGM, DVD, (2004); VHS, 1993.
Detour: DVD-Wade Williams, 2000; VHS, 1996.
Double Indemnity: Universal Legacy Series, DVD, 2006; VHS, 1992.
The Gangster: DVD, Warner Bros. Archive, Collection, 2010; VHS, Fox, 1993.
Gilda: DVD, Columbia Pictures Classics, 2000; VHS, 1994.
Hollow Triumph aka. *The Scar*: DVD, Alpha Video, 1995; VHS, 1998.
House By the River: Kino Video, DVD and VHS, 2005.
I Wouldn't Be in Your Shoes: Monogram 16mm transfer, DVD-R, Video 2000.
The Killers: DVD Criterion Collection, 2003; VHS, 1998.
Laura: DVD Film Noir Series-2009; VHS, 1995.
Out of the Past: RKO DVD-2004; VHS, 1990.
Possessed: Warner Bros., DVD, 2005;VHS, 1998.
Too Late for Tears aka. *Killer Bait*: United Artists Enhanced DVD, 2009, Dark City DVD, 2003; VHS, 1991.

Index

Numbers in **_bold italics_** indicate pages with photographs.

À Bout de souffle (Breathless) 55
The Accused 50
Ace in the Hole (aka The Big Carnival) 74, 79, 108
Act of Violence 54
Adler, Luther 139
Advise & Consent 125
Affair in Trinidad 26, 27
Against All Odds 107
Aherne, Brian 114
All the King's Men 16
Allied Artists 9, 11–14, 17, 19, 39, 55, 86, 175, 177
Alton, John 21, 38, **_40_**, 41, 99, 100, 176, **_177_**, 178
Ameche, Don 167
Among the Living 150
Anderson, Judith 117, 124
Anderson, Maxwell 73
Andrews, Dana 110, 117, 122, 123, 124, **_127_**, **_128_**, 129
Andrews, Edward 21
Angel Face 107, 114, 115, 125
Antheil, George 96
Apology for Murder 80, 85
Appointment with Danger 15, 16
Armored Car Robbery 151
Armstrong, Robert 63, 179
Arnold, Edward 54, 99, 179
Arnt, Charles 34
The Asphalt Jungle 42, 50, 51, 53, 76, 137, 178
Astaire, Fred 29, 100
Astor, Mary 171
Auer, John H. 179

Autry, Gene 90
Avco-Embassy Films 107, 172

Baby Face Nelson 110
Bacall, Lauren 166, 167, 171
Backfire 150, 168, 169
The Bad & the Beautiful 108
Balaban, Barney 64
Ball, Lucille 123, 129, 137
Bari, Lynn 123
Barnett, Vince 145–146
Barr, Byron 68
Barrymore, Ethel 99
Barrymore, John, Jr. 109, 123
Basehart, Richard 4, 151, 166, 168, 178
Baxter, Anne 111
Beast of the City 51, 54
Beaumont, Hugh 80, 89
Behind Locked Doors 40
Belita 10, 11, 17, 55, 63
Bendix, William 129
Ben-Hur 75
Bennett, Bruce 84, 140, 153, 183, 184
Bennett, Joan 31, 36, 39, **_40_**, 156, 166, 167, 172, **_173_**, 174
Bergen, Polly 107
Bergman, Ingrid 114
Berlin Express 109, 151
Berman, Pandro S. 100
Bernhard, Jack 179
Bernhardt, Curtis 157, 165
Bernstein, Elmer 125
Berry, John 140
The Best of Everything 166
The Best Years of Our Lives 123

189

INDEX

Betrayed (aka *When Strangers Marry*) 17, 19, 55, 60, 62, 106
Between Midnight & Dawn 137, 150
Beware, My Lovely 96
Beyond a Reasonable Doubt 123
Bezzerides, A.I. 167
Bickford, Charles 124
The Big Carnival 74, 79, 108
The Big Circus 112
The Big Clock 16, 27, 75, 78, 109
The Big Combo 9, 21, 127, 130, 175–177
The Big Heat 24, 27
The Big Sleep (1946) 3, 17, 54, 75
The Big Sleep (1975) 107
The Big Steal 110, 107
Bissell, Whit 178
The Black Angel 18, 136, 154, 156
The Black Arrow 95
Black Book (aka *The Reign of Terror*) 39, 151
Black Gold 59
Black Tuesday 73
Blind Alley 29
Blonde Ice 37, 172
Blondell, Joan 129
The Blue Dahlia 75
The Blue Gardenia 111
A Blueprint for Murder 178
Blyth, Ann 183
Body & Soul 139, 151, 172
Body Heat 157
Bodyguard 180
Boetticher, Oscar (Bud) 40, 108
Bogart, Humphrey 31, 36, 51, 72, 73, 127, 166, 167, 170, 171, 177–178
Bolte, Raymond, Jr. 60
Bonanova, Fortunio 17
Bonnie & Clyde 17
Boomerang! 50, 95, 150
Borde, Raymond 3
Border Incident 151
Born to Kill 114, 176, 180
Borzage, Frank 90, 99
Bowman, Lee 91, 94, 95
"The Boy Who Cried Murder" 137
Boyer, Charles 125
Brackett, Charles 74
Brady, Scott 41, 44
Braham, John 110, 114, 129
Brand, Neville 151
The Brasher Doubloon 75, 129

The Breaking Point 166, 167
Bredell, Woody 152, 155
Bremer, Lucille 40
Brent, George 108–110
The Bribe 76, 124, 149
Britton, Pamela 139
Brodie, Steve 102, ***112***
Brooks, Geraldine 31, 160, 165, ***169***
Brooks, Hazel 139
Brooks, Leslie 37, 173
Brooks, Richard 152
The Brothers Rico 22
Brown, Phil 142–143
Brute Force 17, 51, 76, 149–152
"Build My Gallows High" 101, 110
Buka, Donald 137
A Bullet for Joey 110
The Burglar 137
Burnett, W.R. 42, 51
Burr, Raymond 111, 126
Butts, R. Dale 138

Caged 166
Cagney, James 171
Cahiers du cinéma 90
Cain, James M. 64, 65, 157
Calhern, Louis 49
Calleia, Joseph 24, 27, 150, 156
Cannon (TV) 151
Canon City 47
Canyon Passage 110
Cape Fear (1962) 107
Captain Pirate 95
The Cardinal 125
Carey, Macdonald 156
Carlson, Richard 40
Carmen Jones 126
"Carnival" 158
Carnovsky, Morris 177
Carson, John 183
Caruso, Anthony 50, 52, ***53***
Caspary, Vera 126
Cassavetes, John 155
Castle, Don 56, 59, 60, ***61***, ***64***
Castle, Peggie 140
Cat People 100, 110
Caulfield, Joan 167
Cause for Alarm 96, 178
Celli, Teresa 46
Champion 108, 137
Chandler, Jeff 164

190

Index

Chandler, Raymond 4, 17, 65, 74, 172
Chaplin, Charles 130
Charisse, Cyd 54
Chesterfield Pictures 90
Chicago Deadline 137
La Chienne 156, 172
Chopin, Frédéric 56, 58, 60
Christine, Virginia 66, 144, 160
Christmas Holiday 151, 152, 153
Citizen Kane 100
City Streets 117
The City That Never Sleeps 60, 90, 99, 138, 175, 179
Clark, Dane 99
Clash by Night 111
Clurman, Howard 110
Cochran, Steve 171
Cohen, Harry 22
Colbert, Claudette 167
Collinge, Patricia 156
Columbia Pictures 22, 109, 136, 137, 175, 177
Conflict 157, 166
Conrad, William 16, 139, 142, 151
Conte, Richard 21, 111, 125, 152, 176
Conway, Tim 110
Cook, Elisha, Jr. 12, 14, 61, 80, 115, 141
Cooper, Gary 117, 165
Le Corbeau 125
Corey, Jeff 146, 153
Corey, Wendell 108, 138
Corman, Roger 124
Corrigan, Crash 80
Cotten, Joseph 108, 151, 155
Cover Girl 95
Cowling, Bruce 178
Crabbe, Buster 80
Crack-up 180
Craig, Catherine 99
Craig, James 178
Crain, Jeanne 123
Crawford, Broderick 156
Crawford, Joan 96, 109, 157, 158, 163–166, 167, 168, 169, 176, 183
Crime of Passion 126
Crime Wave 48
The Crimson Pirate 149
Criss Cross 76, 96, 136, 149, 151, 152, 156, 176, 181, 182
Cromwell, John 136, 177
Cronin, Hume 156

Cronjager, Edward 96
Crossfire 107, 115, 150
Cry Danger 108, 151
Cry of the City 152, 156
Cry Vengeance 9, 20
Cukor, George 164
Cummins, Peggy 140
Curtis, Tony 174
Curtiz, Michael 157, 168

D'Agostino, Albert 111
Dahl, Arlene 109
Dail, John 140
The Damned Don't Cry 164, 166
Dandridge, Dorothy 125
A Dangerous Profession 180
Dante, Michael 21
Dark City 16, 126, 136
The Dark Corner 123, 126, 129
The Dark Mirror 152
Dark Passage 166, 168, 171
The Dark Past 29
Darnell, Linda 124, 125
Darrow, Frankie 55
Da Silva, Howard 54
Dassin, Jules 42, 53, 122, 129, 150, 156
Daves, Delmer 124
David, Charles 136
Davis, Bette 36, 169, 170
Day, Doris 15
Day, Laraine 107, 110
Day of the Triffids 37
Dead Men Wear No Plaid 76
Dead Reckoning 22, 29, 31, 60, 136, 177
Deadline at Dawn 60, 110
de Carlo, Yvonne 136, 181, **182**
Deception 36, 169
de Corsia, Ted 156, 180
Decoy 17, 63, 175, 178
Dee, Frances 110
Defoe, Don 17, 136
de Grasse, Robert 180
de Havilland, Olivia 152
Dekker, Albert 17, 63, 99, 144, 150, **153**, **154**
Desert Fury 96, 136, 137, 149
The Desperate Hours 76
DeSylva, Buddy 74
Detective Story 27, 76, 108
De Toth, Andre 95, 130
Detour (1945) 61, 80–85, **88**, 179, 185
Detour (2003) 85

191

Dexter, Brad 45, 50, 140
Dial 1119 51
Diana Productions 172
Dickinson, Angie 155
Dietrich, Marlene 154
Dillinger 9, 50, 55
Dinelli, Mel 95, 99
Dirty Harry 170
Dmytryk, Edward 5, 100, 115
D.O.A. (1949) 29, 139, 150
Domergue, Faith 107, 111
Donlevy, Brian 126
Doran, Ann 78
Double Indemnity 1, 20, 31, 33, 51, 64, 80, 81, 85, 101, 138, 170, 175, 185
A Double Life 75
Douglas, Don 25
Douglas, Kirk 71, 74, 78, 79, 101, 108, 113, 137
Douglas, Michael 108
Douglas, Paul 111
Dowling, Constance 156
Downs, Cathy 123, 129
Dragnet (TV) 16, 33, 37, 142
Dragonwyck 123
Drake, Charles 98
Drake, Claudia 81, 85, **88**
Dratler, Jay 125, 126
Dreier, Hans 76
Driscoll, Bobby 137
Duff, Howard 156
Du Maurier, Daphne 124
Dunnock, Mildred 129
Durbin, Deanna 136, 152
Durlaf, Frank 39
Duryea, Dan 126, 131, 136, 139, **140**, 154, 156, 174, 181, 182
Duvall, Robert 107
Duvivier, Julian 36
Dwan, Allan 109

Eager, Johnny 54
Eagle-Lion Films 32, 39, 80, 175, 178
Edwards, Vince 141
Eilers, Sally 87, 179
Eisinger, Jo 29
Eisley, Anthony 21
Elam, Jack 181
Ellington, E.A. 29
Elmer Gantry 149
Emerson, Faye 173

Enterprise Studios 19, 172
Erdody, Leo 86
Erickson, Leif 11
Exodus 125
Experiment Perilous 109

Fairbanks, Douglas, Jr. 150
Fall Guy 55
Fallen Angel 124, 126, 127
Farewell, My Lovely (1975) 16, 107, 172
Farmer, Frances 111
Farrow, John 16, 29, 73, 78, 109
Father Knows Best (TV) 95
Faye, Alice 116, 123, 124
Fear in the Night 60, 77
Feist, Felix 164
Fellia, Arthur *see* Wegee
Female on the Beach 164
Ferrer, Jose 125
The File on Thelma Jordon 71, 152
Film Classics Releasing Corporation 77, 172
The Filmmakers 111, 173
"The First Time I Saw You" (song) 111
Fisher, Steve 60
Fitzgerald, Barry 156
Fitzgerald, Geraldine 152
Flamingo Road 166
Flavin, James 183
Fleischer, Richard 151
Fleming, Rhonda 104, 108, 109
Flippen, Jay C. 141
Flynn, Errol 115
Foch, Nina 27
Follow Me Quietly 95, 180
"For Whom the Bells Toll" 16
Force of Evil 127, 137, 172
Ford, Glenn 22, 26, **30**, 31, 177
Ford, John 37, 90
Ford, Wallace 41, 140
Foster, Preston 16, 55, 181
The Fountainhead 165
Fowley, Douglas 43
Fox, William 116
Fox Film Corporation 116
Framed 15, 26, 51
Frank, Nino 3
Franz, Eduard 33, 36
Fregonese, Hugo 73
Fuchs, Daniel 10, 17, 37
The Fugitive (TV) 138

Index

Fuller, Samuel 21, 116, 176, 180
The Furies 124

G-Men 157
Gabin, Jean 4, 36
Gable, Clark 51
Gaines, Richard 69
The Gangster 9–20, 37, 151
Gardner, Ava 124, 145, 149, 153
Garfield, John 51, 127, 139, 140, 151, 166, 167, 172
Garnett, Tay 3, 54, 178
Gaslight 51
The General Died at Dawn 16
Geray, Steven 23, 27
Gibbons, Cedric 51, 52
Gilda 11, 22–28, 177
Gillie, Jean 55, 63, 179
The Girl from Avenue A 59
Gish, Lillian 107
The Glass Key 27
Godard, Jean-Luc 55
Godfrey, Peter 165
Goetz, William 116, 142
Goldwyn, Sam 52, 76
Gomez, Thomas 172
Gone with the Wind (1939) 127
Goodis, David 4
Goosoon, Stephen 29
Grable, Betty 116
Grahame, Gloria
Granger, Farley 171, 178
Grant, Cary 114
Granville, Bonita 55, 63
The Grapes of Wrath 37
Gray, Coleen 129, 141, 181
The Greatest Story Ever Told 138
Greenstreet, Sydney 171
Griffith, D.W. 3
Grot, Anton 168
Gruenberg, Louis 10
The Guilty 55, 59, 60, 63
Guilty Bystander 173
Gulf & Western Corporation 64
Gun Crazy 17, 140
Gunga Din 50
Gwynne, Ann 62, 63

Hagen, Jean 48, 178
Hall, Porter 69
Haller, Ernie 182, 184

Hamlet 86, 87
Hammett, Dashiell 4, 51, 114
Harrison, Joan 27, 174
Hart, Dorothy 156
Haskins, Byron 130, 137
Hathaway, Henry 116, 123, 129, 181
Hawks, Howard 3
Hayden, Sterling 43, 53, 126, 141, 165
Haymes, Dick 116
Hayward, Louis 94, 96, **97**, **98**
Hayward, Susan 110
Hayworth, Rita 11, 22, 31, 177
He Ran All the Way 140, 168
He Walked by Night 39, 41, 175, 178
Heather, Jean 67
Hecht, Ted 15
Hecht-Hill & Lancaster 149
Heflin, Van 54, 136, 158, 165, **168**, **169**
Heifitz, Jascha 153
Hellinger, Mark 149, 151, 152
Hell's Half-acre 138
Hemingway, Ernest 143, 152, 167
Henried, Paul 32, **38**, 39, **40**
Heston, Charlton 136, 156
High Sierra 51, 152, 157
The High Wall 166
The High Window 75
Highsmith, Patricia 177
His Kind of Woman 16, 107, 124
Hitchcock, Alfred 1, 65, 69, 76, 91, 100, 108, 111, 124, 155, 167, 171
The Hitch-hiker 110, 111, 150, 173
Hobart, Rose 166
Hodiak, John 96, 136
Holden, William 74, 78, 179
Hollow Triumph (aka *The Scar*) 18, 32, 178
Homeier, Skip 21
Homes, Geoffery (pseudonym for Daniel Mainwaring) 101
Hopper, Edwin 155
Hornblower, Arthur, Jr. 51
Horror Noir 180
House by the River 90–99
House of Bamboo 181
House of Strangers 75
The House on 92nd Street 111
Huggins, Roy 138
Hughes, Howard 111
The Human Jungle 37
Humoresque 166
The Hunchback of Notre-Dame 150

INDEX

The Hunted 16
Hunter, Kim 17, 55, 62, 106
Huston, John 3, 42, 43, 124, 152, 170, 185
Huston, Virginia 101, 109
Huston, Walter 51
Hutton, Robert 136
Hyer, Martha 21

I Am a Fugitive from a Chain Gang 157, 170
I Married a Communist (aka *The Woman on Pier 13*) 111
I, the Jury 168
I Wake Up Screaming! 17, 60, 62
I Walk Alone 50, 108, 136, 137, 138, 148, 178
I Walked with a Zombie 100, 110
I Wouldn't Be in Your Shoes 55, 59
Ilou, Edward 39
Impact 126
In a Lonely Place 22, 31
Independent Production Units 178
Ingster, Boris 3, 100, 110
International Pictures 142
Invasion of the Body Snatchers 110
Invincible Pictures 90
Invisible Wall 59
Ireland, John 11, 19, 89, 151
Irish, William *see* Woolrich, Cornell
It Happened One Night 22
It's All in the Family 108
Ivano, Paul 11, 18

Jaffee, Sam 43, **53**
Jagger, Dean 17, 62, 106, 124
Janis, Conrad 121
The Jazz Singer 100
Jean-Louis 29
Jeopardy 96
Jewell, Edward C. 86
Joe Palooka 59
Johnny Angel 60
Johnny Eager 22, 29, 165
Johnny Guitar 90, 164
Johnson, Rita 78
The Jolson Story 22
Jourdan, Louis 16
Journey Into Fear 100
Julie 15

Kansas City Confidential 39, 42, 141, 176, 181
Kaplan, Sol 39
Karlson, Phil 19, 21, 42, 73, 140, 181

Kay, Edward J. 60
Kazan, Elia 95, 150
Keith-Albee-Orpheum (K.A.O.) 100
Kelley, Barry 43, 52, 132, 137
Kelley, DeForest 41
Kelley, Gene 27
Kelly, Paul 78
Kennedy, Arthur 130, 137, 138, 139
Kennedy, Joseph 100
Key Largo 51, 73, 166
Keyes, Evelyn 19, 140, 165
Kiley, Richard 21, 181
The Killer Is Loose 108, 151
The Killer That Stalked New York 137
The Killers (1946) 16, 17, 43, 51, 76, 142, 149, 151–155, 176, 181
The Killers (1964) 155
The Killing 17, 42, 48, 53, 141
King, Andrea 17
King Brothers (Frank & Maurice) 9, 15, 17
Kingsley, Sidney 108
Kinney National Service 151
Kiss Me Deadly 150, 151
Kiss of Death 129
Kiss the Blood Off My Hands 51, 149
Kline, Benjamin H. 86
Knock on Any Door 27, 96
Knox, Elyse 55, 56, 61, 62
Korngold, Erich Wolfgang 167
Kortner, Franz 129
Kramer, Stanley 108
Krim, Arthur 130
Kroeger, Barry 140
Kruger, Otto 114
Kubrick, Stanley 17, 42, 48, 53, 130, 141

Lady from Shanghai 22, 26, 29, 31
Lady in the Lake 60, 75
Lady on a Train 136
Lady Without a Passport 127
Laemmle, Carl, Jr. 142
Laemmle, Carl, Sr. 142
Lamarr, Hedy 109
Lambert, Jack 146, 151
Lamour, Dorothy 136
Lancaster, Burt 18, 71, 96, 108, 136, 143, 149, 151, 152, 153, 144, 181, 182
Landis, Carole 17
Lang, Fritz 27, 29, 36, 76, 90, 94, 95, 96, 98, 100, 109, 111, 130, 136, 156, 165, 167, 172, 174

194

Index

Langan, Glenn 124
Langton, Paul 21
LaShelle, Joseph 126
Lasky, Jesse 64
Laughton, Charles 27, 78
Laura 116, 117, 126, 180
The Lawless 110
Lawrence, Mark 43, 50, 52
Leave Her to Heaven 116, 122
Le Baron, William 111
Leigh, Janet 54, 156, 184
Leonard, Sheldon 12, 16, 63, 179
The Letter 157, 170, 180, 182
Leven, Boris 96
Levene, Sam 115, 144, 150, 154
Levine, Joseph H. 172
Lewis, Joseph H. 21, 130, 140, 176
Lewton, Val 100, 110, 116
Liberty Films 90
Lippert, Robert I. 174
Lippert Films 173, 174
Little Caesar 51, 64, 73, 168
Loan Shark 173
The Locket 107, 110, 114
Lockhart, June 41
Lom, Herbert 129
London, Julie 37
Long, Audrey 115
The Long Goodbye 48
Loophole 21
Lorre, Peter 110, 156, 171
Lorring, Joan 10, 15, 16
Losey, Joseph 5, 96, 165
The Lost Moment 16
The Lost Weekend 51
Love Finds Andy Hardy 59
Love Me or Leave Me 37
Lovejoy, Frank 31, 111, 150, 173
"Low Company" (novel) 10
Lubitsch, Ernst 76
Lukas, Paul 109
Lupino, Ida 67, 111, 114, 150, 173
Lured 137
Lydon, James 86, 87, 179

Macao 107
Macbeth 90
MacBride, Donald 144
MacDonald, Joe 180, 181
MacKendrick, Alexander 174
MacMurray, Fred 20, 31, 55, 77, 138

MacRae, Gordon 169
Macready, George 11, 23, 26, 27, 30, 79
Maddow, Ben 51
Madigan 50
Mainwaring, Daniel *see* Homes, Geoffery
Malone, Dorothy 31
The Maltese Falcon 3, 17, 51, 114, 157, 170, 171, 185
Mamoulian, Reuben 117
Man Hunt 36
The Man in the Iron Mask 95
The Man with the Golden Arm 125
Manhandled 136
Mankiewicz, Joseph 73
Mann, Anthony 41, 54, 80, 89, 124, 178
Mannix (TV) 110
Marin, Edward L 109
Marlowe 54
Marlowe, Hugh 129
Marshall, Herbert 115, 170
Mascot Pictures 90
Mason, James 31, 151, 165
Massey, Raymond 158, 165, **168**
Maté, Rudolph 139
Mature, Victor 129
Maverick (TV) 138
Mayer, Louis B. 42
McCambridge, Mercedes 165
McCarthy, Joseph S. 5, 78
McCoy, Tim 80
McDonald, Edmund 85, 86
McDougall, Ranald 167
McGraw, Charles 15, 16, 111, 142, 143
McGuire, Dorothy 152
McIntire, John 21, 43, 50
Mellor, William 138
Mercer, Johnny 121
Meredith, Burgess 16, 107
Metty, Russell 156
M-G-M (Metro-Goldwyn-Mayer) 15, 38, 42, 64, 100, 108, 137, 138, 142, 149, 153, 165, 172, 175, 178
Mildred Pierce 152, 164, 166–168, 170, 176, **182**
Milestone, Lewis 90, 124
Miljan, John 145
Milland, Ray 78
Miller, Kristine 131
Milner, Martin 157, 174
Milton, David 60
Ministry of Fear 76, 136

195

Index

Minnelli, Vincente 108
Miranda, Carmen 116
Mirisch, Walter 59
Mr. Arkadin 16
Mr. Smith Goes to Washington 22
Mitchum, Robert 16, 17, 55, 62, 106, 107, 109, 111, ***112***, ***113***, 114, 124, 125, 136, 151, 172
Mohr, Gerald 24, 27
Monogram Pictures 7, 17, 55, 90, 109, 175, 178
Monroe, Marilyn 39, 45, 50, 116, 181
Montalban, Ricardo 54
Montgomery, George 75, 129
Montgomery, Robert 75
The Moon Is Blue 125
Moonfleet 90
Moonrise 16, 99
Moontide 152
Moore, Dickie 101
Moorehead, Agnes 171
"The More I Know of Love" (song) 145
Morgan, Henry 10
Muni, Paul 16
Murder Is My Beat 21, 86
Murder, My Sweet 3, 75, 100, 101, 114
Murphy, George 54
Mursuraca, Nicholas 100, 110, 111, 114

The Naked City (film) 76, 152, 156, 177, 180
Naked City (TV) 50
The Naked Kiss 21
The Narrow Margin 16, 151
National Television Associates (N.T.A.) 90
Neal, Patricia 165, 167
Neal, Tom 81, ***84***, ***85***, ***88***, ***89***
Neal, Tom, Jr. 85
Negulesco, Jean 16, 126
Neill, Roy William 156
neo-noir 6, 18, 51, 186
Nero Wolfe (TV) 151
Newfield, Sam 80
Newman, Alfred 117
Niagara 39, 50, 116, 181
Nichols, Barbara ***174***
Nigh, William 59
Night & the City 29, 122, 129, 168
The Night Has a Thousand Eyes 60, 73, 75
Night of the Hunter 52, 107
Nightfall 109

Nightmare 60
Nightmare Alley 129
Niles, Ken 104
99 River Street 19, 50, 140, 151
Nobody Lives Forever 51
Noir, Now & Then ***100***
Nora Prentiss 168, 169
Norris, Edward 179
Notorious 111, 114
Novak, Kim 31, 73, 138

Oberon, Merle 109
O'Brien, Edmond 29, 111, 137, 139, 144, 150, ***154***, 173
Obzina, Martin 154
Odds Against Tomorrow 4
O'Donnell, Cathy 178
O'Keefe, Dennis 41
Olson, Nancy 74, 162, ***183***
On the Town 51
"One Man's Secret" (short story) 167
One Way Street 136
O'Neill, Barbara 115, 125
Ophuls, Max 31, 165
O'Sullivan, Maureen 78
Oswald, Gerd 126
Otterson, Jack 154
Out of the Past 100, 101, 107, 109, 111–112, 117, 118, 180, 185
The Outfit 54, 107

Paid in Full 178
Painting with Light (book) 38
Palance, Jack 164
Palmer, Lili 139, 172
Panic in the Streets 37
Panorama du film noir américain (book) 3
Paramount Pictures 64, 109, 117, 137, 138, 149, 153, 157, 165, 175, 177–179
Parker, Eleanor 78, 108
Parrish, Robert 108
Parsonnet, Marion 29
Patrick, Dorothy 91, 95, 97, 161
Payne, John 19, 109, 140, 176, 181
Payton, Barbara 21, 85
Penn, Leo 55
People on Sunday 86
Pepe Le Moko 36
Pereira, Hal 76
Perreau, Gerald 160
Peters, Jean 178, 180

196

Index

Peyton Place 137, 166
Phantom Lady 17, 152, 153
The Phenix City Story 9, 20, 50, 110
Pickford, Mary 130
Pick-up on South Street 66, 129, 176, 180
Pidgeon, Walter 138
Pitfall 95, 126, 130, 136
A Place in the Sun 168
Planer, Franz 181
Plunder Road 182
Poe, Edgar Allan 124
Point Blank 54
Polonsky, Abraham 5
Port of New York 39
Possessed 157, 164, 165, **168**, **169**, 185
The Postman Always Rings Twice (1946) 2, 34, 64
Poverty Row Studios (definition) 90
Powell, Dick 114, 126, 136, 151
Power, Tyrone 116, 129
Powers, Mala 9, 179
Powers, Tom 68
Preminger, Otto 114, 117, 122, 124, 125, 129, 180
The Pretender 90, 199
Price, Vincent 117, 123
Prince, William 31, 177
Producers Releasing Corporation (P.R.C.) 16, 32, 80, 81, 179
The Prowler 96, 165
Psycho 91
Pursued 124
Pushover 31, 77, 138
"Put the Blame on Mame" (song) 177
Pyle, Ernie 107

Qualen, John 33, 36
Queen Bee 167
Quicksand 96
The Quiet Man 90
Quine, Richard 31

Race Street 16
The Racket 51, 107, 109, 136, 151
Raft, George 64, 68, 109, 149, 173
Railroaded 16, 80, 87, 89
Raines, Ella 126, 152
Rains, Claude 111, 114, 167
Raksin, David 117, 122, 126
Ralston, Esther 81
Ralston, Vera Hruba 90

Rank, J. Arthur 32
Raw Deal 16, 32, 38, 16, 32, 38, 39, 41
Ray, Aldo 109
Ray, Nicholas 31, 54, 90, 164
Raymond, Gene 114, 182
Raymond, Paula 180
Reagan, Ronald 155
Rear Window 60, 76
Rebecca 124, 127
The Reckless Moment 31, 36, 165
The Red House 124
The Red Pony 90
Redgrave, Michael 167, 172
Reeves, Steve 172
Regeneration 3
The Reign of Terror (aka *Black Book*) 39, 151
Reinhardt, John 63
Rennie, Michael 125
Repeat Performance 86
Republic Pictures 90, 138, 175, 179
Revere, Anne 139, 172
Richards, Dick 16, 172
Richards, Sylvia 167
Ridgely, John 159
Ridges, Stanley 158
RINI 42, 53
R.K.O. Radio Pictures 100, 109, 116, 137, 150, 176, 180
Road House 126
Roadblock 60, 110, 111, 151
Rober, Richard 71
Robinson, Edward G. 64, 69, 73, 78, 124, 156, **173**, 174
Robson, Mark 100
Rochemont, Louis de 116
Rogers, Ginger 29, 73, 100
Rogue Cop 75
Roman, Ruth 171
Romance on the High Seas 153
Rope 167
Rossen, Harold 51
Rossen, Robert 100, 139
Rosza, Miklos 43, 51, 65, 75, 142, 152, 153, 167, 185
Roth, Lillian 95
Rudley, Herbert 39, 63, 179
Run for Your Life 138
Russell, Charles 44
Russell, Gail 99, 107
Russell, Jane 16, 124
Ruthless 95

Ruttenberg, Joseph 178
Ryan, Robert 54, 109, 111, 115, 136, 165
Ryan, Sheila 89, 107
Ryder, Alfred 41

Saboteur 167
Salt of the Earth 39
Sanders, George 72–73, 137
Sarnoff, David 100
Savage, Ann 80, 83, **84**, 85, **89**
Scandal Sheet 16, 36
The Scar (aka *Hollow Triumph*) 32, 38
Scarlet Street 73, 136, 156, 172, 174
Schary, Dore 150
Schenck, Joseph 116
Schrader, Paul 31, 185
Schumann, Robert 158, 161
Scott, Lizabeth 31, 96, 107, 108, 126, 130, 136, 137, 138, 139, 140, 177
Scott, Robert 24
Scott, Zachary 173, 177, 178, 183
Secret Beyond the Door 36, 76, 167, 172
The Secret Fury 178
Seitz, John 75
Sekely, Steve 32, 37
Selznick, David O. 108
Seven Arts Corporation 157
711 Ocean Drive 50, 95, 137, 150
77 Sunset Strip (TV) 138
Shadow of a Doubt 156
Shadow on the Wall 137
Shakespeare, William 86
Shane, Maxwell 78
The Shanghai Gesture 18, 22, 96, 122, 130
Shaw, Anabel 123
Shayne, Robert 29
Sheridan, Ann 169, 182
Shield for Murder 150
Shirley, Ann 114
Shock 123
Shoot to Kill 86
Side Street 151, 178
Silver, Alain 7
Simmons, Jean 107, 124, 125
Simon, Simone 110
Singin' in the Rain 49
Siodmak, Robert 1, 18, 43, 86, 99, 108, 110, 149, 150, 152, 176, 181
Sirk, Douglas 167
Sistrom, Joseph 74
Sleep, My Love 167

Slezak, Walter 115
Slightly Scarlet 109
Sloane, Everett 31
The Smash-up Story of a Woman 95
Smith, Alexis 72, 166
Smith, Constance 125
Smith, Kent 110
The Sniper 91
So Dark the Night 27
Soderbergh, Steven 38
Somewhere in the Night 16, 17
Sondergard, Gale 170
SONY Corporation 42
Sorry, Wrong Number 72, 149, 151, 168
Southside 1–1000, 17, 21, 136
Spellbound 51, 75, 108
Spillane, Mickey 150
The Spiral Staircase 96, 99, 108, 110, 152
The Split 50
Spy Who Came In from the Cold 39
Stahl, John 116
Stanwyck, Barbara 20, 64, 71, 73, 77, 108, 111, 124, 126, 165
Steele, Bob 80
Steiner, Max 167, 184
Stengler, Mack 60
Stephenson, James 170
Sterling, Jan 75, 108
Stevens, Craig 125
Stevens, George 18
Stevens, Mark 26, 123, 129, 137
Storm, Gale 55
Storm Fear 126, 137
The Story of G.I. Joe 107
Strange Illusion 80, 86, 87, 89, 179
The Strange Love of Martha Ivers 71, 108, 124
The Strange Woman 95
The Stranger 73, 152
Stranger on the Prowl 16
Stranger on the Third Floor 3, 17, 100, 110
Strangers on a Train 75, 171
Strangler of the Swamp 81, 86
Street of Chance 16, 60
The Street with No Name 182
Stromberg, Hunt 137
Strudwick, Sheppard 166
Sudden Fear 96, 109, 164
Suddenly 48, 127
Sullivan, Barry 9, 15–16, 17, 19, 21, 55, 63, 150, 167, 178

Index

Sullivan, Francis L. 129
Sunset Boulevard 74, 76, 78, 168, 175, 179
Suspense 15, 16, 17, 55, 60, 63, 150
Suspicion 100, 168
Swanson, Gloria 74, 75, 78, 179
Sweet Smell of Success 149, 174
Sweetheart of Sigma Chi 59
Sydney, Silvia 117
Sylos, F. Paul 18

T-Men 32, 38, 151
Tales of Manhattan 39
The Tall Target 110
Talman, William 99, 111, 150, 173, 175, 180
Tamiroff, Akim 10, 16, 20, 156, 184
Tanks a Million 55, 59
Taxi Driver 31
Taylor, Don 156
Taylor, Robert 54, 150, 155, 156
Teal, Ray 60, **61**
Tension 151
Thalberg, Irving 42, 142
Thaxter, Phyllis 167
"There's a Girl in My Heart" (song) 52, 59
They Drive by Night (1940) 67, 152
They Made Me a Killer 86
They Won't Believe Me! 107
This Gun for Hire 51, 75
This Woman Is Dangerous 110
Thompson, Glenn 86
Thompson, Marshall 151
Tierney, Gene 116, 117, 119, 122, 123, 125, 127, 128, 129
Tierney, Lawrence 9, 55, 115, 176, 180
Tight Spot 73
Tiomkin, Dimitri 140
To Have and Have Not 167
Toast of New York 111
Toland, Gregg 100
Tomack, Sid 34
Tone, Franchot 85
Tonight and Every Night 95
Too Late for Tears 130, 136, 137, 138
Toomey, Regis 55, 56, 59, 63, 86, 87, 179
Touch of Evil 4, 16, 27, **156**, **184**, 185
Tourner, Jacques 100, 101, 107, 110
Tourner, Maurice 109
Towers, Constance 21
Toyer, Leo 177, 178
Travers, Henry 156

Trevor, Claire 73, 115, 180
Tully, Tom 125
Turner, Lana 54, 165
The Turning Point 150
Twentieth Century–Fox 176, 182
The Two Mrs. Carrolls 152, 168, 169

Ulmer, Edgar G. 26, 37, 80, 81, 86, 87, 95, 179
Uncle Harry 18, 152
The Undercover Man 49
The Underneath 18, 38
Underworld 3
The Unfaithful 182
Union Station 29
United Artists 9, 18, 38, 39, 78, 108, 110, 111, 130, 136, 137, 165, 167, 176, 181
Universal-International 142, 176
Universal Pictures 142, 164, 172, 182, 185
The Unknown Man 138
The Unsuspected 151, 167, 168, 169
Ursini, James 7

Valentine, Joseph A. 67, 170
Valentine, Paul 101
Van Cleef, Lee 181
Van Nest, Polgase 29
Van Upp, Virginia 27
Veiller, Anthony 151, 152
The Verdict 16
Vertigo 76
Vidor, Charles 23, 29
Vidor, King 165
The View from Pompey's Head 95
Vincent, June 156
Violent Saturday 95
"Violin Concerto #2" (Rosza) 153
The Virginian (TV) 138
Von Sternberg, Josef 3, 18, 23, 96, 122

Wake Island 59
Wald, Jerry 164, 166
Walker, Bill 143
Walker, Helen 126, 129
Walker, Robert 171
Wallace, Jean 21, 176, 177
Wallis, Hal B. 95, 108, 138, 157, 171
Walsh, Raoul 124, 157, 171
Wanger, Walter 16, 36, 172
Ward, Rachel 108
Warner, Albert 157

Index

Warner, Harry 157
Warner, Jack L. 157
Warner Bros. 100, 157, 167, 176, 182, 185
Waxman, Franz 158, 167
Waxman, John 168
The Web 154, 159
Webb, Clifton 117, 122, 126, 129
Webb, Jack 33, 37, 142
Webb, Richard 101, 109
Webb, Roy 102, 111
Wegee (pseudonym for Arthur Fellia) 155
Weiman, Rita 155
Welles, Orson 3, 26, 31, 73, 90, 100, 152, 156, **184**, 185
Werker, Alfred 41, 123
Wheeler, Lyle 127
When Strangers Marry (aka *Betrayed*) 17, 19, 55, 60, 62, 106
Where Danger Lives 107, 131
Where the Sidewalk Ends 122, 124, 126
While the City Sleeps 109, 123, 124
Whirlpool 125
White, Jacqueline 115, 151
White Heat 150, 171
Whitmore, James 43, 49, **53**
Who Killed Doc Robbin 59
Why We Fight! 152
Widmark, Richard 108, 129, 180, 181
Wilbur, Crane 41
Wilde, Cornel 21, 126, 176, **177**
Wilder, Billy 1, 20, 64, 71, 74, 78, 85, 90, 108, 138, 170, 175, 179
Wiles, Gordon 17
William, Warren 62, 86, 87, 179
Williams, Ben Ames 122

Williams, Wade 85
The Window 60, 96, 137, 180
Windsor, Kathleen 127
Windsor, Marie 11, 17, 141, 151, 179
Winters, Shelley 15, 92, 107, 140
Wisbar, Frank 80–81
Wise, Robert 100, 115
Withers, Googie 129
The Wizard of Oz 51
Woman in the Window 36, 73, 100, 165
Woman on Pier 13 (aka *I Married a Communist*) 111
Woman on the Run 96
A Woman's Face 164
Woods, James 108
Woolrich, Cornell (aka Irish, William) 17, 19, 60, 63, 73, 137, 180
World for Ransom 21
Wright, Teresa 124, 171
Wyatt, Jane 92–95, **98**, 126
Wycherly, Margaret 171
Wyler, William 76, 78, 79, 108, 170, 182

Yates, Herbert J. 90
Yellow Sky 51
Young, Collier 173
Young, Gig 99, 179
Young, Loretta 15, 54, 178
Young, Robert 107, 115

Zanuck, Darryl F. 116, 157
Zeisler, Alfred 62
Zinneman, Fred 54, 165
Zukor, Adolph 4

www.ingramcontent.com/pod-product-compliance
Ingram Content Group UK Ltd.
Pitfield, Milton Keynes, MK11 3LW, UK
UKHW042007140426
5217IPUK00015B/1025